"Pardue challenges us with the truth that sidering the authority of Scripture and tak.. he challenges our assumptions about and broadens our understanding of Scripture, its interpretation, and its application. This book is an encouragement to readers to embrace the concept of unity in diversity that is vividly illustrated in Revelation 7. Pardue has succeeded in inviting Majority World evangelical voices into the theological conversation that has, for too long, been dominated by the West."

—**Elizabeth Mburu**, Africa International University, Kenya; Langham Literature Regional Coordinator, Anglophone Africa

"For too long, fear of compromising the primacy of Scripture has led evangelicals to marginalize the role of the Christian tradition and local cultures. In this lucid and well-argued work, Pardue has shown that tradition and culture are in fact indispensable theological resources for developing a robust 'catholic contextual theology.' Here is a work in constructive theology that should set the direction for the global evangelical movement."

—**Simon Chan**, editor, Asia Journal of Theology

"At the very moment when evangelical theologians are struggling with cultural issues on the Western home front, Pardue calls them to look east and south, to learn from the global church how to engage one's local context while maintaining biblical authority and respecting the Christian tradition. This is a signal contribution to evangelical theology from one who identifies with and understands both it and the global church. Pardue here integrates canon, culture, and catholicity in five theses that have the potential to revitalize evangelical theology in the West and worldwide."

—**Kevin J. Vanhoozer**, Trinity Evangelical Divinity School

"Pardue offers an impressively informed argument for Western evangelicals to welcome theological contributions from around the world. He responds to misgivings about the impact of culture on the theological enterprise by drawing on basic evangelical commitments and constructive work by significant Majority World scholars. This is a broad vision that conceives of a church committed to Scripture, diverse yet seeking unity, relevant yet appreciative of the Great Tradition. The tone is gracious, but the call is timely and challenging!"

—**M. Daniel Carroll R. (Rodas)**, Wheaton College and Graduate School

"Affirming the diversity but unity of the church, Pardue calls for an evangelical theology that engages with world Christianity—both past and present. *Why Evangelical Theology Needs the Global Church* provides solid theological frameworks along with relevant case studies that support a vision of an evangelical theology enriched by contextual and historical expressions of the Christian faith. This book is a gem, a precious gift to the global church!"

—**Theresa R. Lua**, general secretary, Asia Theological Association; director, Global Theology, World Evangelical Alliance

"Pardue bravely takes on Western evangelical theologians' varied responses to broad theological issues pertaining to the phenomenon of the global church and the field of contextual theology. His engagement with these issues is refreshing, insightful, and constructive."

—**Victor I. Ezigbo**, Bethel University

"*Why Evangelical Theology Needs the Global Church* is at once a theology of culture, a theology of plurality, and even a theology of ethnicity and the nations (the Greek *ethnos*, in the New Testament, is often translated 'nations'), although it is *not* a theology of nationalism (in the West or anywhere!). Pardue writes out of a hermeneutic of charity that welcomes the many voices from the global church to engage with the biblical and historic theological traditions, and hence invites us all to consider our own posture toward others that we may before have held at arm's length."

—**Amos Yong**, Fuller Theological Seminary

"Pardue's book is a timely and unique contribution to evangelical theology. He takes seriously the reality that evangelicalism is a worldwide movement, burgeoning especially in non-Western contexts, and makes a compelling theological case for principled engagement with global theology. He critically and charitably interacts with past attempts at embracing 'contextual' theologies and presents a way forward rooted in the doctrine of the church. The book is also helpful in providing illustrative case studies. Pardue is an expert and wise guide through this increasingly important terrain. I hope this book becomes the standard reference point for future conversations regarding how Western theology engages with the contributions of the Majority World."

—**Uche Anizor**, Talbot School of Theology, Biola University

WHY
EVANGELICAL
THEOLOGY
NEEDS THE
GLOBAL CHURCH

WHY
EVANGELICAL
THEOLOGY
NEEDS THE
GLOBAL CHURCH

Stephen T. Pardue

Baker Academic

a division of Baker Publishing Group

Grand Rapids, Michigan

Published by Baker Academic
a division of Baker Publishing Group
Grand Rapids, Michigan
www.bakeracademic.com

Printed in the United States of America

Library of Congress Cataloging-in-Publication Control Number: 2023010262
ISBN 978-1-5409-6074-0 (paperback)

Baker Publishing Group publications use paper produced from sustainable forestry practices and post-consumer waste whenever possible.

23   24   25   26   27   28   29   7   6   5   4   3   2   1

To Dan Treier
faithful saint, wise mentor, trusted friend

Contents

Acknowledgments

It is a joy to be able to thank many of the people who have supported this work, though it would be impossible to thank all of them. My friendship and collaboration with colleagues in the Philippines and around Asia over the last decade have in many ways driven and sustained my thinking. Tim Gener was a crucial early conversation partner, and his work has inspired and shaped my efforts in many ways. Bea Ang assisted in the earliest stages of preparation of the manuscript and offered productive engagement along the way. My supervisors and coworkers in the Asia Theological Association—Theresa Lua, Rico Villanueva, Andrew Spurgeon, Matthias Gergan, Angelica de Vera, Alex Lactaw, and Bubbles Lactaoen—helped me become more aware of the good gospel work taking root in Asia and sharpened my thinking about theology and context. I am similarly in the debt of the amazing and diverse faculty, students, and alumni of the International Graduate School of Leadership (IGSL), the Asia Graduate School of Theology, and the Center for Biblical Studies in Antipolo, Philippines. I am especially grateful for the encouragement of IGSL's former President Tom Roxas and former head of academic programs Abraham Joseph. Craig Thompson was a faithful companion and kept me from giving up on the project many times.

In addition, my experiences co-chairing the Scripture and Theology in Global Context groups at the Evangelical Theological Society and the Institute for Biblical Research—alongside Gene Green and K. K. Yeo—have afforded me rare and valuable opportunities to see firsthand what contemporary catholic dialogue looks like. Uche Anizor, Michael Allen, Ron Barber, Dan Ebert, Tim Gener, Dan Treier, Kevin Vanhoozer, and Hank

Voss interacted with me as I conceived the proposal and planned the book; they generously offered helpful feedback on drafts of chapters along the way, which led to significant improvements in the final product. Cynthe Burbidge created the index with great competence and care. Of course, the remaining shortcomings of the book are my own and should not reflect upon any of these friends and encouragers.

The staff of the library at IGSL provided generous assistance as I wrote, and the staff of Buswell Library at Wheaton College graciously hosted me for two weeks of intensive work as I finished the manuscript. The Godoy family welcomed me warmly during that time, which was a critical accelerant for the completion of the project. Pastor Chad Williams and the saints at Union Church of Manila have shaped and inspired me, demonstrating concretely the glory of God's project of creating a people of every tribe, tongue, and nation. Our small group in Manila and the saints at Bethel Church of Houston and College Church in Wheaton prayed for and supported the book in too many ways to mention. I am grateful to the excellent team at Baker Academic, especially Bob Hosack, who was unfailingly patient and encouraging through a prolonged writing process.

Teri offered unflagging support on the yearslong journey, especially on the frustrating days, when it was most needed. Ava, Lucy, Simon, and Ivy offered ample levity and distraction when I needed it. It is a joy to see the gospel at work in them. Frank and Rosa Pardue and Bill and Darla Ebert have generously encouraged my work from the start and are living examples of the good fruit that emerges from humble and faithful cross-cultural cooperation in kingdom work. I pray that the Lord of the harvest will send more laborers like them.

Introduction

This book seeks to answer a question that is hardly new but that has yet to receive adequate attention: What difference does it make for the practice of evangelical theology that the church is no longer primarily rooted in North America and Europe but increasingly comprises people from an astonishing variety of cultures and nations?

Over the last several decades, historians and missiologists have generally succeeded in making the case for studying the phenomenon of world Christianity.[1] For historians of Christianity, this means seeking to understand the history, nature, and future of Christianity as a global faith. Many have rightly noted that Western Christians will increasingly need to reckon with the reality that the faith's demographic center has radically shifted away from them, creating long-term questions about who will lead the next generation of churches and what form such new churches will take.[2] Yet these books typically only graze the edge of theological questions, asking, for example, how North American mainline churches will reconcile their

1. For a helpful overview, see Jonathan Y. Tan and Anh Q. Tran, SJ, eds., *World Christianity: Perspectives and Insights; Essays in Honor of Peter C. Phan* (Maryknoll, NY: Orbis Books, 2016).

2. For several prominent examples, see Philip Jenkins, *The Next Christendom: The Coming of Global Christianity*, 3rd ed. (New York: Oxford University Press, 2011); Mark A. Noll, *The New Shape of World Christianity: How American Experience Reflects Global Faith* (Downers Grove, IL: IVP Academic, 2009); Mark A. Noll, *From Every Tribe and Nation: A Historian's Discovery of the Global Christian Story* (Grand Rapids: Baker Academic, 2014); Scott W. Sunquist, *The Unexpected Christian Century: The Reversal and Transformation of Global Christianity, 1900–2000* (Grand Rapids: Baker Academic, 2015).

1

progressive approach to sexual ethics with the conservative approaches of their African counterparts.[3]

Perhaps closer still to our task are the discussions missiologists have been having for decades. Since at least the 1980s, missiologists have been a voice in the wilderness, calling evangelicals to recognize the contextually situated nature of their theology.[4] In addition, they have often highlighted the new ways in which evangelical beliefs have been or might be contextualized in order to facilitate better communication between Christians and their host cultures around the globe.[5] In some cases, they have even begun the process on behalf of evangelical theologians, bringing key theological topics into dialogue with global missions and world religions, raising excellent questions and yielding helpful theological insights.[6]

But theologians have a different vocation than our counterparts in history and missiology. We are not primarily called to document the changes in the church's center of gravity or to offer strategies for evangelism and missions, though such discussions are often complementary to the theological task. Rather, the unique calling of the theologian is to consider God and all things in relation to him. Theology exists because God has spoken, revealing himself and his designs for his people in Holy Scripture. The theologian's prime directive, therefore, is to guide the church in the patient, disciplined work of hearing and obeying the God who has rescued them and seeks the reconciliation of all things by the blood of his cross (Col. 1:20; 2 Cor. 5:18–20). It is

---

3. For example, this disagreement comes up multiple times in Philip Jenkins, *The New Faces of Christianity: Believing the Bible in the Global South* (New York: Oxford University Press, 2006).

4. E.g., David J. Bosch, *Transforming Mission: Paradigm Shifts in Theology of Mission* (Maryknoll, NY: Orbis Books, 1991); A. Scott Moreau, *Contextualization in World Missions: Mapping and Assessing Evangelical Models* (Grand Rapids: Kregel, 2012); Hwa Yung, *Mangoes or Bananas? The Quest for an Authentic Asian Christian Theology*, 2nd ed. (Maryknoll, NY: Orbis Books, 2014); Allen Yeh and Tite Tiénou, eds., *Majority World Theologies: Theologizing from Africa, Asia, Latin America, and the Ends of the Earth* (Littleton, CO: William Carey, 2018).

5. E.g., Bruce J. Nicholls, *Contextualization: A Theology of Gospel and Culture* (Downers Grove, IL: InterVarsity, 1979); David J. Hesselgrave and Edward Rommen, *Contextualization: Meanings, Methods, and Models* (Grand Rapids: Baker, 1989); Dean Flemming, *Contextualization in the New Testament: Patterns for Theology and Mission* (Downers Grove, IL: InterVarsity, 2005); Moreau, *Contextualization in World Missions*.

6. See, e.g., Craig Ott and Harold A. Netland, eds., *Globalizing Theology: Belief and Practice in an Era of World Christianity* (Grand Rapids: Baker Academic, 2006); Timothy C. Tennent, *Theology in the Context of World Christianity: How the Global Church Is Influencing the Way We Think About and Discuss Theology* (Grand Rapids: Zondervan, 2007); Matthew Cook et al., eds., *Local Theology for the Global Church: Principles for an Evangelical Approach to Contextualization* (Pasadena, CA: World Evangelical Alliance Theological Commission, 2010).

characteristic of the evangelical accent that the theological task is carried out not only with a joyful confidence in Scripture's authority and relevance but also alongside an abiding conviction that the news of Christ's atoning work is so good that it requires sharing with others. Moreover, evangelical theologians call the church to a life in step with the Spirit, who quickens and enables his people to echo divine holiness and justice.[7]

It is heartening that in the past two decades many leaders have publicly expressed their conviction that evangelical theology must reckon with the theological expressions of Majority World churches (which now outnumber in membership the historically dominant churches of North America and Europe). More heartening still is the proliferation of insightful theological work emerging from evangelical scholars in the Majority World, and the promise of much more to come in the years ahead.

Yet several challenges threaten to stifle this progress. The first is simply a matter of accessibility and awareness. Too often, students and scholars seeking to learn from theologians in the Majority World struggle to find the best resources emerging from the wider church. Sometimes this is because resources are written in an inaccessible language or published only locally. While there is still a long way to go, good resources are increasingly becoming available globally through translators and publishers who recognize that these resources and the theologians behind them bring fresh insight on the Christian faith. Yet even so, readers new to these regional works often face a bewildering diversity of voices and lack the necessary context to appreciate the proposals they encounter.[8] While by no means offering a comprehensive guide, this book highlights theological works that are especially helpful for evangelical students and scholars new to this conversation. Along the way, I will also articulate categories and commendations that may help readers discern how to engage these works more productively.

---

7. This description of evangelical theology is designed to echo David Bebbington's observations about the characteristics common to evangelicals as a group: conversionism, activism, biblicism, and crucicentrism (D. W. Bebbington, *Evangelicalism in Modern Britain: A History from the 1730s to the 1980s* [Boston: Unwin Hyman, 1989], 4; Timothy Larsen, "Defining and Locating Evangelicalism," in *The Cambridge Companion to Evangelical Theology*, ed. Timothy Larsen and Daniel J. Treier [New York: Cambridge University Press, 2007], 1–14).

8. This is a challenge not only for readers in North America and Europe but also for students and scholars in the Majority World. My students in Southeast Asia often find it difficult to find productive dialogue partners from other regions in Asia, let alone from Africa or Latin America.

A second, and more substantive, challenge is that significant questions still swirl around this movement for evangelical students and scholars in both the West and the Majority World. For some, there is basic skepticism about giving culture a seat at the theological table and an expressed preference for theology that is strictly biblical or exegetical in its method. Others might be inclined to learn from their counterparts in the Majority World but struggle when pressed to explain the theological reasons for their confidence in this enterprise. They may sense that it is not enough to pay attention to the realities of world Christianity out of a sense of political correctness or a naive admiration of "diversity" or "multiculturalism." They may recognize the insufficiency of pursuing these efforts out of merely pragmatic considerations, even with a growing demand for literature and resources attuned to the needs of Christians living in the Majority World. This book argues that there are compelling reasons internal to the Christian faith—and connected to evangelical theological commitments in particular—that should lead us to attend to the Spirit's ongoing work in the global church. Indeed, I will argue that we ought to regard the theologies emerging in Asia, Africa, and Latin America as underutilized resources for twenty-first century saints.

This leads to a third concern that often stifles the movement to bring Majority World theology into greater dialogue with evangelical thinkers: the vision for "contextual theology" (a term that will need some clarification) that has emerged in the last forty years is often unnecessarily narrow and in tension with evangelical theological commitments. An example is instructive here. Years ago, Singaporean theologian Simon Chan noted that what counts as "Asian theology" in most Western textbooks is almost universally characterized by "uncritical assimilation of Enlightenment epistemology." In practice, this generally means a strong suspicion of Scripture and Christian tradition and a preference for views that minimize Christian particularity.[9] Ironically, these commitments mean that what is marketed as "Asian theology" aligns far more with the values and beliefs regnant in Western academia than with the actual faith lived out in the vibrant and rapidly expanding Asian church, which generally has a high view of Scripture, openness to Christian tradition, and a robust commitment to the unique power of Jesus. As a result, academic theological work in this area ignores

9. Simon Chan, *Grassroots Asian Theology: Thinking the Faith from the Ground Up* (Downers Grove, IL: IVP Academic, 2014), 24.

"vast swaths of Christian movements in Asia: the evangelical and Pentecostal movements in much of Asia and, more specifically, the indigenous Christian movements in India, Japan and China."[10]

Chan's critique applies far beyond the boundaries of Asia. Around the globe there is a palpable gap between the scholarly work prescribing fresh and innovative visions of Christian theology and the faith of the everyday Christians who make up the rapidly growing Majority World church. Liberation theology, probably the most widely recognized example of "contextual theology" in Latin America, is another case in point. At least in its original expression—a potent mixture of Marxist ideology and biblical prophetic critique of oppressive social structures that emerged in the 1960s and 1970s—it has largely been rejected or ignored by vast segments of the church. The poor in Latin America, with whom the movement sought solidarity and to whom it offered a word of hope, have generally adopted other forms of Christianity centered more on divine revelation, Scripture, and a powerful experience of God's Spirit. As one observer wryly put it, "While Liberation Theology opted for the poor, the poor opted for Pentecostalism."[11]

The point here is not that theology must conform to the will of the largest groups of people, as if theology should be a functionally democratic or populist enterprise. On the contrary, sometimes speaking of the triune God faithfully will mean being a lone voice in the wilderness. Nor is it the case that academic theology has nothing to offer the church if its value is not immediately recognizable by everyday Christians. Often, academic theology takes a crucial step toward casting a new vision, even if that vision requires translation and adjustment to take real hold in the wider church. For example, while the often-utopian vision of the first-generation theologies of liberation may have won few minds and hearts, the movement unquestionably led most Christians, including evangelicals, to grasp the gospel's profound implications for economics and social justice in a new way.[12]

Yet in general, the chasm between prominent accounts of Asian, African, and Latin American theology and the lived faith of everyday Christians

10. Chan, *Grassroots Asian Theology*, 24.
11. This comment is documented in Donald E. Miller and Tetsunao Yamamori, *Global Pentecostalism: The New Face of Christian Social Engagement* (Berkeley: University of California Press, 2007), 12.
12. In fact, the story of liberation theology and evangelical movements that developed alongside it in Latin America has important implications for how we should think about the deliverances of contextual theology, so we will give it closer consideration in chapter 2.

in these regions should be a cause for concern. It seems increasingly clear that the disparity is not so much the result of academic theologians being "ahead of their time" but is instead the result of an overly restrictive vision of what contextual theology must entail.[13] Since the push for "contextual theologies" started in the 1970s, most of the proposals that have received widespread attention (with some important exceptions) regarded local culture as the primary source and norm for theological reflection, either purposefully or unintentionally diminishing the roles of Scripture and Christian tradition in the theological process. For decades, it was presumed that this was simply the cost of bringing theology into a shape that would be genuinely new and fitting for the emerging churches of the Majority World. To bring the Christian faith into the twenty-first century, it was thought, the global church needed new wineskins crafted with a new theological method, marked especially by a focus on the Spirit's work outside the church—in local cultures and non-Christian religions. Meanwhile, theologians with a higher view of Scripture and Christian tradition generally rejected the work of contextual theology altogether, reckoning it to be an offshoot of the modern theological project incompatible with evangelical faith.

In recent years, however, the situation has begun to change. Evangelical scholars from the Majority World, as well as some from the West, have begun producing theology that takes local and global cultural elements more seriously without simultaneously demoting the authority of Scripture or the relevance of the Christian tradition. Slowly, evangelicals in the West have begun to recognize that their counterparts in the Majority World church have important perspectives on the good news that can enrich their own understandings of the faith. Evangelical leaders who affirm the supremacy of Scripture increasingly acknowledge that there is wisdom in a diversity and multitude of theological voices.[14] If these emerging efforts succeed, they will represent a substantial broadening of the vision for contextual theological engagement.

13. Indeed, rather than being "ahead of their time," contextual theologies often lag behind the church as a whole. For example, Simon Chan rightly notes that most textbook treatments of Asian theology make it appear as if the discipline was frozen in the 1970s and 1980s (Chan, *Grassroots Asian Theology*, 25).

14. For a brief summary of these trends, see Stephen T. Pardue, "What Hath Wheaton to Do with Nairobi? Toward Catholic and Evangelical Theology," *Journal of the Evangelical Theological Society* 58, no. 4 (2015): 757–70.

This book seeks to introduce readers to these promising new developments and to give them a nudge forward by clarifying where evangelical approaches to contextual theology are likely to be particularly helpful. I hope to demonstrate how evangelical "contextual theologies" promise not only to breathe new life into the evangelical theological project but also to inject new energy into the broader project of contextual theological reflection, which has found itself in some ruts and dead ends in recent years.

To sum up, this book seeks to articulate some of the ways that evangelical theology ought to be influenced by the changing realities of the global church. This will mean addressing prevalent doubts about the prudence of incorporating culture into the theological process as well as outlining a biblical and theological framework that warrants and supports such efforts. Along the way, I will introduce readers to some of the most productive voices in this emerging movement, highlighting the material benefits that may accrue to evangelical theology when it embraces the Spirit-filled witness of the Majority World church as a substantive source and dialogue partner.

Plan of the Book

The argument of the book unfolds in six chapters. The first chapter grapples with the reality that evangelical theologians have often neglected—or even rejected—calls to embrace the role of culture in theological reflection. Whereas Roman Catholic and mainline Protestant theologians long ago welcomed the development of contextual theologies, evangelicals have often been suspicious that such efforts will devolve into uncritical slavery to culture or that they are inevitably tied to a relativistic view of reality. While these objections often reflect mistaken assumptions about theological method and its relationship to culture, they nevertheless help clarify how an evangelical engagement with these issues will have a distinctive character, differing in key ways from alternative efforts arising from other parts of the church. So chapter 1 examines these objections and considers what we can learn from them.

Thankfully, this book does not have to sketch the evangelical approach to contextual theology *de novo*. Chapter 2 maps the various efforts already underway, delineating the many different tasks that are often grouped together under the category of "contextualization" or "contextual theology." After getting the lay of the land, we will sketch a path forward by articulating five basic theses that seek to characterize a vision of contextual theological reflection emerging from within the evangelical tradition. The first of these theses—that *evangelical contextual theologies must look to Scripture as their magisterial authority, even as they increase their appreciation for the crucial ministerial role of culture for the theological task*—is discussed in chapter 2.

Chapter 3 focuses on clarifying the role of culture by developing a second thesis: *evangelical contextual theologies must acknowledge culture as a material theological good, a gift from God designed for the benefit of the church.* An important but often neglected starting point here is to understand what it is that we mean by *culture* and how this concept fits into the biblical narrative and the doctrinal architecture of the Christian faith. To this end, chapter 3 briefly sums up several anthropological insights regarding the nature of culture as a concept before turning its focus to the argument that the Christian Scriptures authorize, and perhaps even mandate, a different understanding of culture and theology than evangelicals have generally taken for granted. By tracing the biblical authors' engagement with culture—from Babel to the vision of Revelation 7—and by considering the location of culture in the theological economy, this chapter makes the case that contextual theology is not merely a practical solution for the diversifying church but also a proper response to the redemptive activity of the triune God.

Any theology that takes culture seriously must grapple with the challenge of attending to locality and diversity while also focusing on what unifies Christian teaching. So after having established that culture is theologically important, chapter 4 wrestles with the question of how contextual theologies can remain sufficiently attentive to the "once-for-all" of the gospel while also taking advantage of the diverse cultural gifts God has given his people around the globe. In contrast to efforts to root contextual theology in either the phenomenon of globalization or the doctrines of the Trinity and incarnation, this chapter will point to the doctrine of the church. This is the third thesis of the book: *evangelical contextual theologies should look to the Christian doctrine of the church in order to coordinate the once-for-all of the gospel and the remarkably diverse expressions of the faith that emerge in the real world.* Crucially, this prevents the fracturing of theology into thousands of self-contained local theologies disengaged from Christian witness elsewhere.

Chapters 5 and 6 zero in on one attribute of the church that has special importance for making diversity an asset rather than a liability for contextual theologies: catholicity. From the earliest centuries, Christians confessed that all believers form a single, global household composed of citizens of every tribe, tongue, people, and nation. They certainly recognized the challenges of such an arrangement (look no further than the difficult arguments between leaders in Acts, which have been echoed throughout church history again and again), but they held fast to the notion that, in the church's cultural diversity, God was creating a people that could uncover and reflect the untold riches revealed in Christ. This concept is more important today than ever before, given that the church is more diverse and more interconnected than it has ever been. So chapter 5 articulates a fourth thesis: *evangelical contextual theologies should seek to discern the plenitude of the riches of Christ through the cultivation of authentic Christian witness in every culture while seeking the unity of the Spirit by rejecting local theologies that fail to engage the worldwide church.*

Yet ensuring that theology faithfully reflects the church's God-given character does not simply require attending to the fullness of diversity in the Christian witness *today*; it also requires an engagement with Christians who lived *long before us*. Only in this way can we preserve the unity of the Spirit across the ages. Chapter 6 thus articulates a fifth thesis: *evangelical contextual theologies should engage the Great Tradition of the church, finding there a partner that helps prevent slavish obedience to all things present and that tempers theological novelty in favor of considered overtures toward unity.* If we are to pursue genuine catholicity, then attention to the church's present diversity must be complemented by a deep appreciation for the contributions of our spiritual forebears, especially in the first few centuries of Christian theology. While catholic theology does not require facile subservience to whatever is old, it does require that we attend to the contextual theological judgments developed by our ancestors in the faith, which offer us gifts in both form (as models of theology designed to meet contextual needs) and substance (offering significant and permanent gains for the Christian church). At times, the content of contemporary contextual theologies will appear, at least *prima facie*, to be in conflict with the convictions of early Christians, and this chapter will suggest some guidelines for approaching such disputes.

Finally, a brief conclusion will assess the horizons for contextual theologies and offer some final recommendations for further work in this area.

For the sake of quick reference, the five theses are as follows:

- Thesis 1: *Evangelical contextual theologies must look to Scripture as their magisterial authority, even as they increase their appreciation for the crucial ministerial role of culture for the theological task.*

- Thesis 2: *Evangelical contextual theologies must acknowledge culture as a material theological good, a gift from God designed for the benefit of the church.*
- Thesis 3: *Evangelical contextual theologies should look to the Christian doctrine of the church in order to coordinate the once-for-all of the gospel and the remarkably diverse expressions of the faith that emerge in the real world.*
- Thesis 4: *Evangelical contextual theologies should seek to discern the plenitude of the riches of Christ through the cultivation of authentic Christian witness in every culture while seeking the unity of the Spirit by rejecting local theologies that fail to engage the worldwide church.*
- Thesis 5: *Evangelical contextual theologies should engage the Great Tradition of the church, finding there a partner that helps prevent slavish obedience to all things present and that tempers theological novelty in favor of considered overtures toward unity.*

As I noted above, this book seeks not only to articulate the theological rationale for engaging the Majority World church in theological dialogue but also to demonstrate what such a dialogue looks like. To this end, chapters 2–6 each conclude with a brief case study that highlights a concrete example of the thesis advanced in the chapter. In each case, my aim is to show that the benefits for evangelical theology are not merely theoretical but also include material gains that benefit both the local and the worldwide church. These are just a few concrete examples that I hope will spur further thinking for readers; of course, it is impossible for five case studies to fully represent the breadth and depth of the riches emerging in the work of Majority World theologians.[15]

At the same time, I hope these examples will help readers form realistic expectations about what theological engagement with the global church is like. For one, it is hard and complicated. It requires learning about cultures and contexts foreign and confusing to us, often resulting (at least initially) in confusion, conflict, and misunderstanding. The Majority World church, moreover, is hardly monolithic; as in North American and European churches, various groups within regions or nations often point in opposing

15. For more examples, a helpful resource is Gene L. Green, Stephen T. Pardue, and K. K. Yeo, eds., *Majority World Theology* (Downers Grove, IL: IVP Academic, 2020). The excellent catalog of work that has emerged from Langham Literature in recent years is also worthy of attention.

doctrinal directions, each claiming an important element of biblical truth and contextual suitability.

Those looking to this book for revolutionary revisions of the faith—a transformation of the classical understanding of the Trinity, for example—will be disappointed. But the theological task in every generation is one of incremental growth in our understanding of God and his works, and right now, for those with ears to hear, engagement with the catholic church (the worldwide household of God, past and present) offers a largely overlooked opportunity to know more deeply the person and works of the triune God.

Other Preliminaries

It is important to note that I do not in this book claim to offer an authoritative word on what any part of the Majority World church is saying. While my conversion, baptism, and discipleship all emerged in churches outside of the West (mostly in the southern Philippines), I was born into an American family and did my undergraduate and postgraduate work in the United States. While Filipino culture has genuinely shaped my thinking and character (I have lived about three-quarters of my life in the Philippines), I hope not to stake the legitimacy of this book on my experiences or cultural identity. I do not claim to speak for the Majority World church—or for the North American church! And, in a strange way, having lived most of my life as an alien (both in my passport country and in the Philippines, which I call home), I cannot fully claim "insider" status in any place or culture.

Rather than offering an authoritative word, this book attempts to draw readers into a realm of theological engagement that has shaped my own thinking and to offer some modest proposals that summarize what I have learned from my colleagues and students thus far. I hope that it invites readers to "taste and see" the goodness of engaging in theological dialogue with the worldwide church. It thus relies less on my cultural identity—though I will appeal at times to experiences I have had in flourishing evangelical churches in Asia—and more on the rich opportunities for friendship and dialogue that have shaped me. I hope I can impart to readers some of the joy and insight that I have gained on this journey of faith seeking contextual and catholic understanding.

1

On God and Gravity

Evangelical Objections to Contextual Theology

> Trust in the LORD forever,
> for the LORD God is an everlasting rock.
>
> —Isaiah 26:4

> . . . and the Rock was Christ.
>
> —1 Corinthians 10:4

Evangelicals have historically been skeptical about the degree to which the theological task is or should be subject to the influences of culture.[1] While mainline Protestant and Roman Catholic theologians have recognized and embraced the significance of culture in shaping the theological enterprise

---

1. Although we often use the word without much thought, *culture* is notoriously difficult to define. In chapter 3, we will examine this problem and consider it in a particularly theological frame. For now, it will do to refer to the influential definition of Clifford Geertz, who describes culture as "an historically transmitted pattern of meanings embodied in symbols, a system of inherited conceptions expressed in symbolic forms by means of which men communicate, perpetuate, and develop their knowledge about and attitudes toward life" (*The Interpretation of Cultures*, 3rd ed. [New York: Basic Books, 2017], 95).

since the 1970s, evangelical theologians have often either ignored or actively rejected this path. At its most benign, this has often meant viewing projects of "contextual theology" emerging in Asian, African, and Latin American churches as exotic but irrelevant theological adventures—something of interest for missiologists and missionaries in certain locales but of little import for the broader church.[2] At other times, the attitude has been outright skepticism or even rebuke. For example, a prominent conservative evangelical pastor and writer contends that "the 'contextualization' of the gospel today has infected the church with the spirit of the age." As a result, "the world now sets the agenda for the church."[3]

Most of the time, objections do not take quite such a polemical tone. At a gathering of evangelical professors and scholars from around North America held in Atlanta in 2010, one session focused on the emergence and significance of world Christianity. The presenters discussed how the cultural dynamics at play in Africa, Asia, and Latin America were impacting the thinking and practice of the growing evangelical churches in those regions, highlighting what North Americans could learn from their counterparts in the Majority World. Allen Yeh, who was moderating the session, recalls a member expressing their skepticism during the time for audience questions: "African theology. Asian theology. Latin American theology," the questioner started, "Aren't all these 'cultural' theologies just relativism? Why can't we just do 'pure' theology?"[4] Having attended the meetings that year, I remember the questioner adding another interesting sentiment: "We don't ask what the African perspective on gravity is," he added, "so why do we need to ask what the African perspective on biblical theology is?"

Many Christians, especially in the evangelical tradition, share with the questioner a concern that the turn to context in theology simply rests on a faulty premise: that the changing composition of the church should have significant impact on the nature and scope of Christian teaching. So before proposing a model for accounting for culture in the theological task, we

2. Thus, Robert J. Schreiter notes that, for decades, it was common for these projects to be considered not "'real' or genuine theology" but, instead, "hyphenated theolog[ies]"—theologies above which "reigned theology as theology, enthroned on its method" (*The New Catholicity: Theology between the Global and the Local* [Maryknoll, NY: Orbis Books, 1997], 2).

3. John MacArthur, "'Contextualization' and the Corruption of the Church," *Grace to You* (blog), September 22, 2011, https://www.gty.org/library/blog/B110922/.

4. Allen Yeh, *Polycentric Missiology: Twenty-First Century Mission from Everyone to Everywhere* (Downers Grove, IL: IVP Academic, 2016), 40.

must first grapple with the concerns evangelicals have historically harbored about such an enterprise. To be clear, I do not view these as mere "straw man" objections. Rather, they speak to serious concerns that come along with considering these issues in light of evangelical commitments. Moreover, in responding to them we will begin to recognize some of the ways that evangelical approaches to contextual theology can make a distinctive contribution to the ongoing discussion.

The Objection Stated: Theology, Like Science, Should Operate Independently of Culture

The foremost objection to contextual theology often goes like this: If theology consists primarily in speaking of God by reference to his self-revelation in Scripture and in Jesus, then it would seem to follow that the content of Christian doctrine should be generally independent of the cultural makeup of the church in any given time or place. Thus, the notion that theology must change in light of shifting demographics is as patently confused as a physicist claiming that the laws of matter, gravity, or thermodynamics are in need of revision because they have been developed mostly by privileged white men. This is nonsense precisely because the laws of physics are what they are, regardless of what we may want them to be or the culture of the person who discovers them. Similarly, if theology is a process of discovering and passing on the truth about the way things are—who God is, what he has said in Scripture, and so forth—then the location, culture, and identity of the church's leaders and theologians should make no material difference to the content of Christian teaching.

This way of thinking about theological method does not come to us out of nowhere. It is, essentially, the position articulated by an evangelical forefather, Charles Hodge. Writing from his Princeton study in the late nineteenth century, Hodge put it this way: "The true method of theology is, therefore, the inductive, which assumes that the Bible contains all the facts or truths which form the contents of theology, just as the facts of nature are the contents of the natural sciences. It is also assumed that the relation of these Biblical facts to each other, the principles involved in them, the laws which determine them, are in the facts themselves, and are to be deduced from them, just as the laws of nature are deduced from the facts of nature."[5]

---

5. Charles Hodge, *Systematic Theology* (1872; repr., Grand Rapids: Eerdmans, 1986), 1:17.

The analogy between theology and the natural sciences, as well as the notion that all the necessary ingredients for theological discourse lie embedded
in Scripture, was shared by many evangelical theologians in the twentieth
century. The influential dispensationalist theologian Lewis Sperry Chafer,
for example, had significant differences with Hodge regarding the content of
Christian teaching, but he espoused essentially the same theological method
and even used similar analogies. "The theologian creates none of his own
materials," he writes, "any more than the botanist creates the flowers or the
astronomer orders the stars."[6] With a "scientific attitude," the theologian is
in the business of "arranging and exhibiting the positive truth the inspired
Scriptures set forth."[7] If he does his job well, the theologian could be rightly
regarded as a "superscientist."[8]

Writing a few decades later, evangelical giant Carl F. H. Henry similarly
contended that theology should consist in arranging the propositional truths
revealed in Scripture "into a system of axioms and theorems."[9] The goal of
the theologian is to complete this process of "axiomization" once and for all,
just as mathematicians can comprehensively describe the truths of geometry
with a series of theorems.[10] While Henry is careful to clarify that no theology
this side of eternity can be infallible, he does envision the possibility of a
theology that is comprehensive and biblical enough to essentially complete
the theological task.

Responding to the Objection

It is worth pausing for a moment to note that Hodge, Chafer, and Henry
were very different thinkers. Despite the methodological similarities highlighted above, the content of their systematic theologies is remarkably
disparate. If the three were on a panel discussion together, they would
have lively and wide-ranging disagreements. But what is common to all
three, as well as to many evangelicals today, is an expectation that theology
should not be impacted by culture in significant ways, any more than a
biologist's, physicist's, or mathematician's accent, eye color, or ethnicity might impact their observations of the world. As Kevin Vanhoozer

6. Lewis Sperry Chafer, *Systematic Theology* (Dallas: Dallas Seminary Press, 1947), 1:8.
7. Chafer, *Systematic Theology*, 1:7–8.
8. Chafer, *Systematic Theology*, 1:8.
9. Carl F. H. Henry, *God, Revelation, and Authority* (Waco: Word Books, 1976), 1:240.
10. Henry, *God, Revelation, and Authority*, 1:240.

puts it, the apparent "glory of the inductive method" lies in the promise that "close observation allows the facts to emerge, regardless of who is doing the observing"; thus, "the location or situation of the interpreter is irrelevant."[11]

Yet as Vanhoozer and others have argued, while this vision of theology as inductive science may aim at something valuable, it ultimately leads us astray. First, it fails to consider the degree to which the practice of science is itself firmly rooted in specific paradigms of thought, social norms, and cultural priorities. This was perhaps best demonstrated by the Christian physicist and philosopher Michael Polanyi, who argued in the 1960s that science promises more than it can deliver in its claim to offer a unique and purely objective view of the universe. "Complete objectivity as usually attributed to the exact sciences," he contends, "is a delusion and is in fact a false ideal."[12] On the contrary, science, like all knowing, involves "a passionate contribution of the person knowing what is being known."[13] Polanyi is no relativist when it comes to truth—rather, he concludes that while scientists are right to aim toward *a kind of objectivity* (a notion we will soon explore further), they are no more able than anyone else to do the pure inductive reasoning we sometimes imagine to be their stock-in-trade.

Not only is scientific *method* more complicated than we might think, but scientific *practice* is in fact rather varied across time and place. The aims of various fields of science are constantly changing in response to what we learn about the universe (e.g., physicists must now grapple with the implications of quantum mechanics), as well as to the emerging needs of specific communities (e.g., many North American biologists today are especially concerned with the need for stronger antibiotics to respond to increasingly drug-resistant bacteria, while their counterparts in sub-Saharan Africa are especially focused on mitigating the ongoing impact of malaria and other mosquito-borne illnesses). David Clark notes that, contrary to the caricature of the scientist as a merely passive processor of data, scientists often rely

---

11. Kevin J. Vanhoozer, "On the Very Idea of a Theological System: An Essay in Aid of Triangulating Scripture, Church and World," in *Always Reforming: Explorations in Systematic Theology*, ed. A. T. B. McGowan (Downers Grove, IL: IVP Academic, 2007), 137.

12. Michael Polanyi, *Personal Knowledge: Towards a Post-Critical Philosophy* (Chicago: University of Chicago Press, 1962), 18.

13. Polanyi, *Personal Knowledge*, vii.

on their personalities, including their cultural backgrounds and imaginative abilities, in order to develop innovative theories.[14]

So science itself is more complicated than Hodge, Chafer, and Henry assume, and this must be considered when evaluating the degree to which it can be a model for theology. We may also wonder whether science is a well-suited analog for theological reflection at all. While theologians seek to foster commerce with every discipline of intellectual study—all truth is God's truth, after all—their most frequent trading partners have generally been in philosophy, history, and the study of language and culture, all of which are prerequisites for the close reading of Scripture, especially in its original languages. By necessity, then, theology may be less like the hard sciences or mathematics—which aim at describing concrete realities in ways that are verifiable through experimentation and proofs—and more like the humanities and arts—disciplines that seek to make the most of, rather than to minimize, the language and culture of their practitioners. To put it differently, just as the success of a musician is judged not only by her ability to master theory and technique but also by her ability to perform in a way that speaks to a particular audience in a certain moment, theologians are called not only to get the facts right but also to explain their implications in such a way that they can serve the mission of the church in particular times and places.

Thus, theology demands more (certainly not less!) than merely restating the data of Scripture. It does not function in a formulaic manner, in which there is always one right answer. Rather, it requires the faithful expression of Christian teaching in light of the history and ongoing needs of the church. Using the imagery of "theodrama" to describe the Christian story of God's redeeming work, Vanhoozer puts it this way: "The task of systematic theology is to train actors with good improvisatory judgment, actors who know what to say and do to perform and advance the gospel of Jesus Christ *in terms of their own cultural contexts*."[15] While Scripture thus remains the anchor and "concrete deposit of theodramatic wisdom"—we do not have *carte blanche* to say whatever we like about Christian doctrine—theology

14. David K. Clark, *To Know and Love God: Method for Theology* (Wheaton: Crossway, 2003), 50–51.

15. Kevin J. Vanhoozer, "'One Rule to Rule Them All?' Theological Method in the Era of World Christianity," in *Globalizing Theology: Belief and Practice in an Era of World Christianity*, ed. Craig Ott and Harold A. Netland (Grand Rapids: Baker Academic, 2006), 121, italics original.

has always functioned to point to "the way, the truth, and the life in terms that were faithful to the script yet fitting and appropriate" in the time, place, and culture of the local church.[16]

Hodge, Chafer, and Henry confirm this hypothesis themselves, at least in a minimal sense. Each writing in different times and cultural contexts, they explain the faith with different terminology, imagery, and analogies—communicating the judgments and implications of Scripture as clearly as possible for their respective audiences. They follow in the footsteps of the earliest Christians by using the language of their own time and place to express their theological conclusions, rather than insisting that believers use the Greek of Paul, the Aramaic of Jesus, or the Hebrew of Moses.

In at least this very basic sense, then, all theology is contextual theology. This is an important starting point. But it is also a very minimal understanding of contextual theology; no one, including Hodge, Chafer, or Henry (to my knowledge), has actually argued that Christian theology must use the Koine Greek of the biblical writers or the early church. Rather, those voicing this objection often detect in the call to contextualize or globalize theology an uncritical acceptance of contemporary cultural norms—a capitulation to the patterns of this world. This leads us directly to a second objection.

The Objection Modified: To Avoid Idolatry, Culture's Impact on Theology Must Be Kept to a Minimum

The second objection—which is, in some ways, a modification of the first—focuses on a pitfall attached to the process of translation or contextualization: the unhealthy mixture of Christian faith and those theological or ethical convictions that are endemic in the recipient culture. This is generally what is meant by *syncretism*,[17] and it is easy to see why this is such a concern. When

---

16. Vanhoozer, "'One Rule to Rule Them All?,'" 121–22. For further elaboration of this proposal, see Kevin J. Vanhoozer, *The Drama of Doctrine: A Canonical-Linguistic Approach to Christian Theology* (Louisville: Westminster John Knox, 2005), esp. 318–24.

17. Scott Moreau helpfully documents the history of the use of this word, including an important emerging debate about whether it should carry a strictly negative connotation and who gets to define its boundaries (A. Scott Moreau, "Syncretism," in *Evangelical Dictionary of Theology*, ed. Daniel J. Treier and Walter A. Elwell, 3rd ed. [Grand Rapids: Baker Academic, 2017], 850–52). Because, as Moreau notes, all religious expressions are to some degree or another a mixture of various cultural, linguistic, and religious traditions—and thus, in a broader sense, syncretistic—I will use other language (such as *idolatry of culture*) to highlight those expressions of Christian faith that are judged to be insufficiently distinct from their cultural backgrounds. This intentionally

Christians introduce their faith to a people group for the first time, one of the challenges they immediately face is the question of how to explain the language and concepts central to the gospel. Most of the time, they must use a common word for *God* in the recipient culture, even though it will, at least initially, carry associations with a being quite different from the God of Abraham, Isaac, and Jacob. To explain the atoning death of Christ, they may appeal to local myths or practices that are analogous to the Christian concept, then later try to clarify the ways in which the Christian understanding of atonement is unique. A constant risk in the process is that central Christian beliefs or practices will be diluted along the way.

Iconography provides an especially visible example of this phenomenon. Throughout the history of the church, Christian artists have consistently sought to depict Jesus as a person who looks like the people around them in their own culture. Thus, a Dutch artist naturally "portrayed a Dutch Jesus, an Italian one presented an Italian."[18] On one level, this would appear to be the most harmless kind of contextualization. After all, a major implication of the incarnation is that God has brought himself into fellowship with *all* of humanity, and it is only natural that artists would seek to express this truth by depicting Jesus in a way that honors their own experience of the human condition.

Yet this honorable effort often plays out in troubling ways. For example, because of the dominance of European imperialism, it is the Western European Jesus—with pale blue eyes, wavy brown hair, light skin, and pinkish cheeks—that became the most prominent image of God incarnate for centuries.[19] It is likely that the well-known depiction of Jesus with light skin and blue eyes arose in part from an anti-Semitic bias common in Western Europe in the era of European colonialism, encouraged along by a falsified ancient letter describing Jesus as a tall, attractive man with light skin.[20]

---

leaves aside questions of who has the authority to make such judgments and how they are to be made, which will be the subject of discussion in later chapters.

18. Joan E. Taylor, *What Did Jesus Look Like?* (New York: Bloomsbury, 2018), 15.

19. Taylor, *What Did Jesus Look Like?*, 15.

20. The document known as *The Letter of Lentulus* claimed to have been written by a Roman official at the time of Christ (Taylor, *What Did Jesus Look Like?*, 17). As Taylor argues in her book, it is no small irony that the letter's depiction of Jesus—good-looking by standards of the time, admirable, tall—is almost an exact negation of the descriptions found in Isaiah 53, which Christians from the earliest centuries regarded as applying (often literally) to Jesus: "He had no form or majesty that we should look at him, and no beauty that we should desire him. . . . And as one from whom men hide their faces he was despised, and we esteemed him not" (Isa. 53:2–3).

As a result, depictions of Jesus that may have originally been designed to build bridges between Christianity and local cultures—to contextualize the faith—can also end up functioning to sanctify one culture at the expense of perceived threats and rivals.

Such a dynamic was likely at work, sometimes consciously and sometimes not, in nineteenth- and twentieth-century America. Historians Edward J. Blum and Paul Harvey have documented the way Americans often gravitated toward depictions of a white Jesus and in so doing sanctified a vision of white superiority: "By wrapping itself with the alleged form of Jesus, whiteness gave itself a holy face. . . . With Jesus as white, Americans could feel that sacred whiteness stretched back in time thousands of years and forward in sacred space to heaven and the second coming."[21] Moreover, as Americans grew increasingly suspicious of Jewish and Catholic immigrants from Europe in the early twentieth century, Jesus was depicted as a particular kind of white person: "a blond-haired, blue-eyed, non-Semitic" one.[22]

Helpfully, Blum and Harvey also note that this history is complex and includes white Christians who appealed to the "white Jesus" to argue for the abolition of slavery and black Christians who saw in the "white Jesus" a liberator who suffered with and for them. Thus, it is far too simplistic to conclude that every racial group has formed Christ in their own image, so that all we have in the end are competing claims to a divided Christ.[23] Still, it is impossible to look at the history and ignore the ways that cultural idolatry—the exaltation of one's tribe or race by association with God—poses a serious threat to the integrity of Christian reflection.

Cultural idolatry need not find expression only in visual imagery. All theological discourse—and perhaps especially those approaches that are focused on building bridges between Christianity and the broader culture—must grapple with the possibility that culture may have an undue influence on our thinking about God and his works.

In the first few centuries after Jesus, Christians were constantly debating the degree to which they could accommodate prevailing cultural assumptions that seemed sympathetic to or compatible with Christian thinking. Theologians like Clement of Alexandria, who sought a synthesis of

---

21. Edward J. Blum and Paul Harvey, *The Color of Christ: The Son of God and the Saga of Race in America* (Chapel Hill: University of North Carolina Press, 2012), 8.

22. Blum and Harvey, *Color of Christ*, 10.

23. Blum and Harvey, *Color of Christ*, 19.

Christianity and Middle Platonism, were viewed as stretching the boundaries of what was acceptable. For example, Clement argued that Christians should think of pagan Greek philosophy as something like the Old Testament, preparing the way and creating the categories for Christianity. This meant urging his disciples to strive to embody a kind of "Christian Gnosticism," even as he fought against versions of Gnosticism that had strayed too far. Centuries after Clement's lifetime, Christian thinkers questioned the wisdom of his contextual judgments (along with those of his most famous student, Origen), arguing that he gave too much weight to Platonic thought. Where Clement saw bridges that could bring pagans to saving knowledge of Jesus, his critics argued that those bridges invited more traffic in the opposite direction, allowing the prevailing culture to shape the very foundations of the church.[24]

Today, some contend that the early church consistently sacrificed far too much in aligning the faith with Hellenistic convictions, especially after the conversion of the Roman Emperor Constantine, though recent scholarship has undermined the validity of such broad-brush accusations.[25] In chapter 6, we will examine in more detail the ways in which the early church's contextual judgments prove instructive for our work today. For now, we need only observe that, at least for Clement's critics, his work is an example of the damage done when culture gains undue influence in the theological process.

We need not travel back fifteen hundred years to see this phenomenon; examples from the more recent past also prove instructive. In India, a plethora of nineteenth- and twentieth-century thinkers proposed adumbrations of the faith that sought to integrate an Indian worldview and Christian convictions. These proposals have ranged from the very modest (e.g., treating baptism as the satisfaction of the unfulfilled longing for cleansing already present in Hinduism[26]) to the more radical (e.g., suggesting that Hindu

---

24. For an insightful analysis of Clement that is more sympathetic to his contribution to Christian theology, see Piotr Ashwin-Siejkowski, *Clement of Alexandria: A Project of Christian Perfection* (New York: T&T Clark, 2008).

25. The most ardent proponent of this idea—referred to as the "Hellenization thesis"—was Adolf von Harnack, who argued that almost all of the dogmatic development in early centuries was a result of the unhealthy Hellenization of Christianity (*Outlines of the History of Dogma*, trans. Edwin Knox Mitchell [New York: Funk and Wagnalls, 1893]). For an accessible and wise response to von Harnack, see Robert Louis Wilken, *The Spirit of Early Christian Thought: Seeking the Face of God* (New Haven: Yale University Press, 2003).

26. Roger E. Hedlund, "Indian Expressions of Indigenous Christianity," *Studies in World Christianity* 10, no. 2 (2004): 195.

texts can replace the Old Testament for Indian Christians[27]). Today, Indian Christians assess these movements in various ways, but those with broadly evangelical instincts have been skeptical of the more radical approaches. They argue that such strategies give too much ground to Hinduism, yielding a version of Christian doctrine too indistinguishable from prevailing Hindu assumptions, and possibly even extending the legacy of anti-Semitism in Christian thought.[28]

It is not our concern here to determine whether the critique sticks in this particular case. Our goal for now is simply to recognize the nature of this objection. In summary, the concern centers on the risk that seems to attend giving culture a significant role in theological reflection and formulation: the blurring of lines between cultural commitments and God's self-revelation in Scripture. If we allow culture to play a significant role in theological reflection and expression, we run the risk of allowing theology to be enslaved to idolatrous human instincts.

Responding to the Objection

This cautionary attitude about overly eager cultural accommodation is part of evangelical DNA. As Amos Yong notes, evangelicals historically distinguished themselves from more liberal counterparts at least partially by preserving a "cultural hermeneutic of suspicion that is always concerned about syncretism with the world."[29] This has shaped evangelical attitudes both in North America—where evangelicals have often seen themselves as a countercultural minority—as well as in the worldwide evangelical community, where missionaries have often exported a "Christ against culture" mentality. Yong notes, for example, how, in his evangelical Chinese context,

---

27. See D. S. Amalorpavadass, ed., *Research Seminar on Non-Biblical Scriptures* (Bangalore, India: National Biblical, Catechetical, and Liturgical Centre, 1974) and the helpful discussion of this issue in Timothy C. Tennent, *Theology in the Context of World Christianity: How the Global Church Is Influencing the Way We Think About and Discuss Theology* (Grand Rapids: Zondervan, 2007), 53–75.

28. E.g., Israel Selvanayagam critiques the replacement of the Old Testament with Hindu Scriptures as "confused" and argues that this move is motivated at least in part by the "anti-Semitic attitude of the early western theologies or of Hinduism" ("Waters of Life and Indian Cups: Protestant Attempts at Theologizing in India," in *Christian Theology in Asia*, ed. Sebastian C. H. Kim [New York: Cambridge University Press, 2008], 66).

29. Amos Yong, *The Future of Evangelical Theology: Soundings from the Asian American Diaspora* (Downers Grove, IL: IVP Academic, 2014), 104.

"converts to Christianity were expected to leave their cultural traditions behind in turning to Christ."[30]

Yet paradoxically, evangelicals have also found themselves in the vanguard of *contextualization*, defined broadly as the adaptation of "the forms, content, and praxis of the Christian faith so as to communicate it to the minds and hearts of people with other cultural backgrounds."[31] For example, evangelicals have often taken the lead in creating Bible translations that are readable and relevant to everyday people. This is work that Lamin Sanneh, a leading historian of world Christianity, regards as one of the most important forces propelling the growth of the churches in the Majority World.[32] As Craig Blomberg notes, despite evangelicals' generally conservative theological instincts, they are often more in favor of contextualization than other groups because they are passionate about sharing the good news in the clearest and most compelling terms possible.[33]

This impulse to contextualize the gospel is anchored squarely in the New Testament itself. Scholars have noted that Luke designed the book of Acts to model how the gospel may be shared and take root in various contexts. In a book that has set the agenda for discussions of contextualization and the New Testament, Dean Flemming writes, "Part of Luke's reason for writing Acts, then, was not only to encourage Theophilus and other Gentile Christians to participate in God's universal mission but also to give them programmatic examples of the church's Spirit-empowered witness to various groups of people."[34]

Thus, the way Paul narrates the gospel to the largely Jewish audience in Pisidian Antioch, offering a positive and relatively detailed retelling of Israel's history culminating in the Messiah's atoning death (Acts 13:13–52), is radically different from the way he narrates the gospel to the primarily Gentile audience in Athens, making little use of the Old Testament but in-

---

30. Yong, *Future of Evangelical Theology*, 20.

31. A. Scott Moreau, *Contextualization in World Missions: Mapping and Assessing Evangelical Models* (Grand Rapids: Kregel, 2012), 36.

32. See Lamin Sanneh, *Whose Religion Is Christianity? The Gospel beyond the West* (Grand Rapids: Eerdmans, 2003). It is notable, moreover, that the work of evangelical groups like the Summer Institute of Linguistics is regarded as leading the field in translation theory and best practices.

33. Craig Blomberg, "We Contextualize More Than We Realize," in *Local Theology for the Global Church: Principles for an Evangelical Approach to Contextualization*, ed. Matthew Cook et al. (Pasadena, CA: World Evangelical Alliance Theological Commission, 2010), 37–55.

34. Dean Flemming, *Contextualization in the New Testament: Patterns for Theology and Mission* (Downers Grove, IL: InterVarsity, 2005), 30.

stead relying on Greek religious thought and poetry (Acts 17:16–34). Both approaches, meanwhile, are distinct from the evangelistic speech in Acts 14:8–20, in which Paul makes use of only rudimentary natural theology to point the pagan audience away from worshiping himself and Barnabas and toward their creator. In all three cases, as Flemming demonstrates, Paul seeks to persuade his audiences to follow Christ by using their language, culture, and religious intuitions, while also challenging their thinking where fidelity to the gospel required it.[35]

The rest of the New Testament exhibits a similar impulse, often using profoundly local imagery to describe the loftiest theological ideas. John borrows the idiom of *logos* from contemporary Greco-Roman culture to communicate the unique relationship between the Son and the Father. The epistles refer to Jesus as the "chief Shepherd" (1 Pet. 5:4), the "great high priest" (Heb. 4:14), the "wisdom of God" (1 Cor. 1:24), or simply "Lord" (e.g., Phil. 2:11)—a word that, in addition to its resonance with the Old Testament's description of God, carried associations with Caesar. The atonement is variously depicted with legal, cultic, and relational metaphors. The Christian's struggle to live faithfully is described as an athletic competition, a military effort, and an agricultural endeavor.

The apostolic instinct to describe transcendent truths in such local, earthy terms is ultimately rooted in Jesus's own habit of speaking in metaphors and parables accessible to everyday people from all walks of life. Like Jesus, his disciples were willing to wager that the risk of some listeners mistakenly putting their trust in the medium (the local language, culture, and imagery) rather than the message (the good news of salvation) was outweighed by the benefit of communicating the good news to those ready to hear and respond in faith.

Evangelicals, then, are in good company in their willingness to embrace the risks associated with contextualization. This goes beyond merely recognizing that all theology is contextual; it suggests an active, positive partnership between theology and culture, even if such a partnership is fraught with the risk of cultural idolatry. But even when they have accepted that culture has a genuine role to play in theological reflection, evangelicals have

---

35. Flemming, *Contextualization in the New Testament*, 56–88. For an updated and expanded discussion that goes beyond Flemming's initial efforts, see Andrew J. Prince, *Contextualization of the Gospel: Towards an Evangelical Approach in the Light of Scripture and the Church Fathers* (Eugene, OR: Wipf & Stock, 2017), 72–114.

generally restricted its significance to the final step of theological reflection: making theological conclusions accessible and applicable to a particular audience. This limitation is important and leads us to a third objection.

The Objection Modified Again: Cultural Context May Help Us Apply and Express Theology, But It Should Not Affect Theology's Content

The third objection—which, again, can be thought of as yet another modification of the objection we have been considering all along—concedes that theologians must translate theological insights to make them understandable and accessible in various contemporary contexts, but it asserts that theologians must simultaneously ensure that Christian doctrine itself remains unaffected by this process of translation. In other words, the objective of any theological engagement with culture is simply the transference of the "deposit of faith," not theological innovation, growth, or transformation. Thus, while it may be right to speak of *contextualizing* theology, it is misguided to pursue the development of *contextual* theologies. While the former is simply a matter of making theology understandable in a contemporary context, critics see in the latter a force that threatens to pollute the purity of Christian doctrine and fragment the faith into hundreds of incommensurable theological systems.

According to this objection, the primary obligation of Christian theology as it relates to cultural context is to find culturally and linguistically appropriate ways of expressing established Christian doctrine. Thus, in an influential book on the subject, David Hesselgrave and Edward Rommen take it for granted that the task of the missionary, like any minister of the gospel, is to "present the supracultural message of the gospel in culturally relevant terms."[36] Grant Osborne echoes this approach, defining contextualization as "the crosscultural communication of a text's significance for today."[37] In this view, the sole intent of contextualizing Christian teaching is to make it more accessible to contemporary listeners, helping them to see how they can apply the faith to their lives. Contextualization is thus about the

---

36. David J. Hesselgrave and Edward Rommen, *Contextualization: Meanings, Methods, and Models* (Grand Rapids: Baker, 1989), 1.

37. Grant R. Osborne, *The Hermeneutical Spiral: A Comprehensive Introduction to Biblical Interpretation*, 2nd ed. (Downers Grove, IL: IVP Academic, 2006), 22.

communication and *application* of Christian doctrine but should not affect the *generation* of Christian doctrine.

Millard Erickson makes a version of this argument in a recent revision of his widely used textbook, *Christian Theology*. In a chapter entitled "Contextualizing Theology," he argues that the task of the theologian is to "state the gospel message in terms that will be understood in today's world," while leaving untouched the "substance" or "content" of biblical doctrine.[38] In order to contextualize theology appropriately, the first step is to "find the essential meaning underlying all particular expressions of a biblical teaching," a process that requires crystallizing what we learn from Scripture as a "timeless truth."[39] For example, the biblical teaching that God is "high above the earth" is fundamentally communicating that "God is transcendent," beyond the limitations of his creatures. Once we have a "universal didactic statement"—a principle that is not attached to a particular culture or perspective—we can then engage contemporary culture in order to make a suitable translation or application.[40] This process, with its firewall between the distillation of Christian doctrine on the one hand and the contextualization of that teaching on the other, is designed to ensure that while the "form of expression of a truth" can change with language, culture, and time, the "essence" of Christian doctrine can remain unaffected by such translation.[41]

For Erickson, this is the only way to preserve a happy balance between theology and human cultures. It rejects the naivete of traditionalists, who claim that contextualization of Christian doctrine is entirely unnecessary, failing to recognize their own cultural conditioning. But it also refuses the doctrinal innovation advocated by "transformers," who are too willing to trade in the substance of Christian teaching for something more palatable to contemporary audiences. In connection with a "transformer" approach, Erickson highlights the danger of the view that culture might "do more than merely guide the form" of Christian teaching, that it might "contribute to the content itself."[42] Giving culture a place in generating the content of Christian theology would amount to rejecting "the faith that was once for all delivered to the saints" (Jude 3).[43]

---

38. Millard J. Erickson, *Christian Theology*, 3rd ed. (Grand Rapids: Baker Academic, 2013), 68.
39. Erickson, *Christian Theology*, 80.
40. Erickson, *Christian Theology*, 80, 83.
41. Erickson, *Christian Theology*, 78.
42. Erickson, *Christian Theology*, 84.
43. Erickson, *Christian Theology*, 84.

Erickson's thinking about theology and culture is hardly unique among contemporary evangelicals. Walter Kaiser, for example, has defended a method of deriving theology from Scripture through principlizing or abstraction. The theologian is to find in any biblical passage the "focal point" and state the underlying ideas being taught in terms of a timeless principle.[44] And while Wayne Grudem does not explicitly endorse a particular vision of the relationship between theology and culture in his widely used systematic theology textbook, his approach generally matches up with Erickson's and Kaiser's thinking. The theologian's task is "the collection and then the summary of the teaching of all the biblical passages on a particular subject,"[45] and while contemporary culture may shape how we *apply* what we learn from Scripture, it need not influence the substantive work of assembling and summarizing the biblical text and its principles. As a result, Grudem does not conceive of his systematic theology as particularly "local" or "contextual," though he would likely recognize that his examples and points for application are drawn mostly from North America.

This way of conceiving the theological task is perhaps the most significant reason for the collective shrug offered by some Christians in response to the question of the implications of the worldwide shifts in the balance of Christianity. After all, if cultural context is to shape *only the expression and application* of theology, then a North American pastor or scholar need not be very concerned with how a Nigerian pastor is reading the language of sacrifice in Hebrews, or with how a Chinese theologian is conceiving justification in terms of shame and honor. Whatever is substantive in such proposals will be unrelated to the culture in which it emerged, and whatever is "contextual" will be irrelevant to someone in a different culture—except, perhaps, as a missiological case study. Thus, in this view "contextual theologies" are desirable as attempts to communicate clearly in any given time and place, but not as instruments for deepening or expanding our understanding of God or his Word.

44. Walter C. Kaiser Jr., "A Principlizing Model," in *Four Views on Moving beyond the Bible to Theology*, ed. Gary T. Meadors (Grand Rapids: Zondervan, 2009), 21–24; Walter C. Kaiser Jr., *Toward an Exegetical Theology: Biblical Exegesis for Preaching and Teaching* (Grand Rapids: Baker, 1981), 149–64.
45. Wayne Grudem, *Systematic Theology: An Introduction to Biblical Doctrine* (Grand Rapids: Zondervan, 1994), 23.

Responding to the Objection

Clearly, this is the most nuanced objection to the project of contextual theology we have encountered so far. It acknowledges that theology is not quite as purely analytical as theoretical mathematics or physics; rather, it involves genuine entanglement with local language and culture. In the face of the clear danger that this entanglement creates, evangelical theologians seek to safeguard Christian doctrine from the dual dangers of cultural fragmentation and theological discontinuity. By the former, we refer to the notion that our theological reflection may be so profoundly embedded in human cultures that we can never escape enough to actually verify whether our view of things matches up with reality, or to determine which theological views are actually correct when disagreements arise. By the latter, we refer to the concern that if Christian theology undergoes substantive—not just superficial—change every time it enters a new culture, we can easily lose the thread that connects all Christian expressions regardless of time, culture, and location, making it impossible to unify around shared commitments, or even to say which expressions of the faith are faithful to the gospel and which are not.

To protect against these two dangers, Erickson and others argue that one step in the theological process—that of abstracting timeless, decontextualized principles (or what is sometimes referred to as a "gospel core") from the biblical text—must remain protected from cultural and contextual influence, thereby securing the autonomy of Christian doctrine against its enslavement to fallen human cultures. While this objection is right in its intent, it ultimately misdiagnoses the disease and prescribes a flawed remedy.

First and foremost, this objection simply fails to reckon adequately with the reality that all theology is contextual, even if Scripture is indeed "universal" in the sense of being understandable and transformative in all places and times. As David Clark notes, the shaping force of context applies as much to the process of principlizing or abstracting lessons from Scripture as it does to the expression and application of those principles. Indeed, even the notion that *principles* (as opposed to narratives or poetic expressions, for example) are the best way to summarize the truth of Scripture is a culturally embedded way of thinking about the calling of the theologian.[46]

---

46. Clark, *To Know and Love God*, 90–98.

In reality, we learn about and speak of God with a particular language, within the framework of a specific culture, and in the context of social and geographical networks. As a result, the meaning of even the simplest theological affirmations—"Jesus is my healer," for example—is shaped in important ways by cultural commitments (e.g., a "healer" may be something like a Western medical doctor, a shaman, a supernaturally gifted monk, or something else entirely).[47] More importantly, this particularity is the divine design; in Scripture and in Christ, God chooses to use local languages, genres, and cultures to reveal himself, rather than communicating with us in some supracultural or supralinguistic mode.[48] The reversal of Babel on the day of Pentecost is accomplished through the redemption of diverse languages and cultures rather than through their abolition, and the perfected humanity in Revelation 7 praises the Lamb in a diversity of tongues rather than leaving their cultural baggage altogether behind.[49] In short, the quest to distill from Scripture a set of acultural, timeless truths is not just a futile theological endeavor; it actually represents the rejection of the gifts of God intended for the edification of his people.[50]

If culture is a resource for theology, then we must address the threats of cultural fragmentation and theological discontinuity in some other way. While theology need not—and cannot—be culture-free, evangelicals know that theology must also be in some sense *free from culture*. That is, our talk of God must not be so dominated by culture that we merely reaffirm what our communities already believe. Moreover, evangelicals who have thus far been skeptical of "contextual theologies" are right to wonder how we can ensure that there is doctrinal continuity across space, culture, and time if we are not to rely on an acultural, timeless "kerygmatic kernel" underneath so many cultural husks.

47. This example comes from Matthew Cook, "Contextual but Still Objective?," in *Local Theology for the Global Church: Principles for an Evangelical Approach to Contextualization*, ed. Matthew Cook et al. (Pasadena, CA: World Evangelical Alliance Theological Commission, 2010), 79.

48. More than three decades ago, D. A. Carson put it this way: "From the perspective of human perception and formulation *there is no supracultural core*. However the heart of the gospel be conceived by human beings, it is conceived in a particular linguistic, cultural, philosophical and religious framework" ("Church and Mission: Reflections on Contextualization and the Third Horizon," in *The Church in the Bible and the World: An International Study*, ed. D. A. Carson [Grand Rapids: Baker, 1987], 249).

49. Justo L. González and Catherine G. González, "An Historical Survey," in *The Globalization of Theological Education*, ed. Alice Frazer Evans, Robert A. Evans, and David A. Roozen (Maryknoll, NY: Orbis Books, 1993), 13–22.

50. Vanhoozer, *Drama of Doctrine*, 316–17.

Addressing these concerns will be the burden of subsequent chapters, which seek to provide a framework for constructing an evangelical theology that makes the most of the church's diverse cultural contexts while preserving the coherence of the church and of Christian teaching. For now, we can register a reminder that Christians have always affirmed that while Scripture and the Christian teaching it generates are irreversibly and unquestionably embedded in human culture, God's sanctifying grace allows these finite and fallen tools to yield true knowledge of and communion with him in all his plenitude. So, though we can never fully escape it, culture is not rightly understood ultimately as a prison but rather as a locus for God's work of transformation and sanctification. If this is right, then the invitation to contextual theology is far more than a contemporary fad—it is a summons to hear Scripture better, to know God more deeply, and to be transformed increasingly into the likeness of Christ.

Conclusion: Toward a Chastened "Theological Science"

At the start of this chapter, I said that the objections voiced here have important things to teach us. While I have argued that none of these objections get things quite right, it should be clear by now that the theologians raising them have some good reasons to be cautious. As we will see more clearly in the next chapter, many of the articulations of contextual theology that have emerged since the 1970s have come attached to worldviews in which Scripture has diminished authority and even ability to speak to us *extra nos* (from outside of us).

So, evangelicals have been fighting an instinct, brewing at least since Immanuel Kant, that suggests that theology can do little more than describe *human experiences of God*, that it cannot describe God himself.[51] The appeal to science is a way of pushing back against this notion, demanding that theology maintain a kind of "objectivity"—that theologians, like scientists, describe what is real, rather than merely our own thoughts and wishes. Lesslie Newbigin, a theologian deeply sensitive to the interplay of culture and Christian doctrine, argues that while we must acknowledge that the gospel is always

---

51. For one of the most important and early efforts to rework the task of theology as a reflection on human experience rather than on God's speech and actions in the world, see Friedrich Schleiermacher, *Brief Outline of Theology as a Field of Study*, 3rd ed., *Revised Translation of the 1811 and 1830 Editions*, trans. Terrence N. Tice (Louisville: Westminster John Knox, 2011).

culturally conditioned, it "is not an empty form into which everyone is free to pour his or her own content."[52] Therefore, as David Clark notes, it is perfectly right that theology should aim to "put us in touch with God *as God truly is*," not in the sense that such theology will be perfect, exhaustive, or "God's-eye" in its point of view, but in the sense that, by means of reflection on God's self-revelation, theology can result in "genuine, truthful, even if limited and imperfect, knowledge of God's own self."[53]

This is a real and legitimate goal, and so evangelicals are correct to demand that theologians "should embody virtues and practice methods that permit them to lay aside their own preferences and to see the object of their study for what it is."[54] One way to hold on to this instinct while also acknowledging and embracing the shaping force of our cultural context is by developing a chastened "theological science"—one that acknowledges that we never "see things whole"[55] but that strives nevertheless toward faithful, contextually formed witness to the self-revelation of God in Scripture and in Christ.

T. F. Torrance's articulation of "theological science" is helpful here. On the one hand, Torrance acknowledges that theology can never be a purely inductive process: "Whether we like it or not, theology is always inextricably involved in culture, past or on-going, if only because theology must use language, and language is rooted in society and the physical universe of space and time in which we live."[56] On the other hand, he recognizes that "we only know God truly as we allow our own inventions and fictitious presuppositions to be unmasked before the direct disclosure of the Truth of God."[57] When we subject our prior beliefs to critical questioning and "allow ourselves to be detached from all preconceptions and prejudgments," we remove the idols of our heart that obscure the true God.[58] Like Carl Henry, Torrance sees theological reflection as an echo of mathematics, though not

52. Lesslie Newbigin, *The Gospel in a Pluralist Society* (Grand Rapids: Eerdmans, 1989), 152–53.

53. Clark, *To Know and Love God*, 50, italics original.

54. Clark, *To Know and Love God*, 50. For further reflection on this, including an account of how his mind has changed over the years on the question of what "objectivity" in theology must mean, see Cook, "Contextual but Still Objective?"

55. William A. Dyrness, *Learning about Theology from the Third World* (Grand Rapids: Zondervan, 1990), 185–88.

56. T. F. Torrance, *Christian Theology and Scientific Culture* (New York: Oxford University Press, 1981), 12.

57. T. F. Torrance, *Theology in Reconstruction* (Grand Rapids: Eerdmans, 1966), 91–92.

58. Torrance, *Theology in Reconstruction*, 92.

in the sense that we can expect to achieve detached and once-for-all re-sults. Rather, as mathematicians seek in their proofs to "echo the inherent rationality of the universe," so also theologians are engaged in "the kind of knowing in which our minds fall under the compulsive impact of what they seek to know and are obedient to what is known in accordance with its own inherent witness and order."[59]

In this chapter, we have argued that the mistake of evangelical theological engagement with culture has not been its insistence that our descriptions of God must rely upon and speak of something above culture and time—a God beyond any human context. To be sure, evangelicals' confidence in God's effective and gracious communication is what makes them uniquely positioned to do theology in a global context with joyful conviction. Rather, the problem has been the assumption that our submission to God's eternal and unchanging nature is inconsistent with also acknowledging the con-textual nature of our speech about him. As Henri Blocher elegantly puts it when addressing the matter of theology and culture, we must affirm that we worship "the Rock of Ages, *tsur ʿolamim* (Isa. 26:4), who changes not," while also acknowledging that "the Rock is not immobile; he is the Living Rock, and Paul can strikingly write that he would accompany his people through the desert wanderings (1 Cor. 10:4)."[60] If we can bear witness to these two things at the same time—that the God we worship makes himself known in and through cultural forms, *and* that he is himself above them all—then we will have a unique contribution to make to contextual and catholic theology.

59. Torrance, *Theology in Reconstruction*, 95.

60. Henri Blocher, "Permanent Validity and Contextual Relativity of Doctrinal Statements," in *The Task of Dogmatics: Explorations in Theological Method*, ed. Oliver D. Crisp and Fred Sanders (Grand Rapids: Zondervan, 2017), 111, 128.

2

A Word Very Near

Contextual Theology and Christian Scripture

> But the word is very near you. It is in your mouth and in your heart, so that you can do it.
>
> —Deuteronomy 30:14

In the previous chapter, we explored several common objections to the marriage of culture and theology, arguing that while evangelicals have rightly sought to protect theology from the threat of cultural hegemony, this quest is more complicated than simplistic solutions suggest. Rather than casting culture as the enemy of "pure doctrine," we must recognize it as one among God's many gifts that enable us to learn and speak well of him. If Scripture is the soul of theology, culture provides flesh and bones, enabling finite creatures to come to know and speak of the triune God in their own languages and in the context of concrete, local communities. In this sense, all theology should be locally shaped, making the most of the cultural resources in its native environment; this is what makes theology *contextual*. Yet to achieve its purpose of tutoring the church in a life of authentic discipleship, theology must attend not only to its local context—for no local church is an island—but also to the contextual judgments of the universal church, including contemporaries around the globe as well as fathers and mothers in the faith; this is what makes theology *catholic*.

The subsequent chapters will explore this vision in greater detail. But this conception of contextual theology does not emerge in a vacuum, so before explaining it further, we will take some time to map the growing number of proposals regarding how theology and culture should interact. We will see that a central element of perennial debate is the manner in which Scripture and culture should work together to inform the theological process. After surveying the landscape, I will argue for the first of five theses that inform the approach I want to advocate—namely, that *evangelical contextual theologies must look to Scripture as their magisterial authority, even as they increase their appreciation for the crucial ministerial role of culture for the theological task.* Finally, we will round out the chapter with a case study exploring how the approach sketched here might shape an assessment of theologies of liberation. These may be the most prominent products of the turn to contextual theology, and they provide an insightful view of the way in which diverse approaches to Scripture have resulted in contrasting visions of what it means to do theology informed by local cultural context.

Defining Our Terms

Before getting into the history of contextual theologies, we must first address a matter of definition. In the previous chapter, we saw that all theology is rooted in a cultural milieu and is therefore, in some sense, contextual. No theology is, after all, supracultural. What, then, do we mean when we speak of *contextual theologies*? At best, the term seems redundant; at worst, it could suggest that the theologies emerging from younger or less powerful parts of the church are *ethnic* or *cultural* theologies, while the work of North American and European thinkers is simply *theology*, universal in scope and relevance.

So it is clear that the adjective *contextual* can apply to theology in more than one way. In one sense, all theology is unquestionably contextual, bound up with the culture and language in which it is conceived and expressed. This is appropriate, since God has chosen to reveal himself to his people in and through culture rather than above and beyond it. As a result, Christians from the earliest centuries recognized it is God's desire to see the church flourish and find a home in every language and culture on earth.

Yet it is also the case that theologians have always engaged the resources of their cultural contexts in different ways—with varying levels of intentionality and desire to honor the positive contribution of these resources to the theological task. For example, in the first centuries of the church, theologians like Tertullian sought to downplay the connection between the Christian faith and their local cultures, highlighting the vast differences between the Christian ethic and worldview and the wider culture. Meanwhile, others, such as Justin Martyr and Clement of Alexandria, looked for connections and bridges with their cultural contexts, suggesting at times that Christianity was essentially a culmination of their culture's philosophy and literature.[1] Later theologians modulated between these extremes. All along, everyone was doing contextual theology in the weak or descriptive sense of the term, including those who were polemicizing against their local or host cultures (after all, they had to use language and cultural norms to critique their cultures!).

With that caveat, for the sake of clarity, we will refer to contextual theologies as *those theological efforts that intentionally make use of local cultures and languages as key resources for the theological task.* We can make a few observations about this definition. First, such theologies often emerge in the service of Christian mission because they are often generated in order to serve a key Great Commission task: demonstrating how the gospel connects with but also corrects local cultural beliefs and customs for the sake of helping the Christian faith become more at home in a place where it is considered foreign.[2] This is part of the reason that contextual theologies have, in the last few decades, generally been associated with the growing and vibrant churches in the Majority World. However, this definition does not preclude anyone anywhere from doing contextual theology. At times—even in places with long histories of Christianity—theologians do contextual theology (in the sense described here) to critique current cultural trends or to help Christians think theologically about changes in their cultural milieu.[3]

1. I draw these examples from the work of Kwame Bediako, whose work we will consider in more detail in a case study at the end of chapter 6. See Kwame Bediako, *Theology and Identity: The Impact of Culture upon Christian Thought in the Second Century and in Modern Africa* (Oxford: Regnum, 1992), 1–222.

2. On the missional thrust of contextual theologies, see Timoteo D. Gener, "Doing Contextual Systematic Theology in Asia: Challenges and Prospects," *Journal of Asian Evangelical Theology* 22, no. 1 (2018): 49–68.

3. A good example here is William A. Dyrness, *The Earth Is God's: A Theology of American Culture* (Maryknoll, NY: Orbis Books, 1997).

Second, this definition allows us to recognize that all theological work falls on a spectrum of greater or lesser intentional engagement with culture as a theological resource, rather than falling into one category or the other (intentionally engaged with cultural resources or not). It might be helpful to think about culture in a similar way to Christian tradition. In a sense, all theology—even the sort that proclaims "no creed but the Bible"—is engaged with tradition and uses what has been handed down from generations of other Christians in order to perform the theological task. However, some theologians intentionally search the old books and the creeds to enrich and support their theological work, while others may neglect tradition or even spend a great deal of time showing why all Christians of past generations were wrong about a particular doctrine. The movement to develop contextual theologies in recent decades thus has parallels with efforts to recover and revitalize the role of Christian tradition for the theological task. In both cases, advocates believe that they are highlighting a resource for the theological task that is underutilized and deserves more attention (even if they would also contend that other theological sources must similarly be accounted for).

Finally, this definition intentionally leaves many disputes about contextual theology unresolved. For example, it acknowledges that contextual theologies may sometimes look like simple translations of previously developed systems of Christian thought, while in other cases they may propose more radical suggestions, revising even the organization of our theological systems. This openness is intentional, designed to account for the variety of approaches that will sometimes be needed in the theological process.

A Brief History of Contextual Theologies

With this methodological element out of the way, we can now consider the recent history of what have come to be called *contextual theologies*. About thirty years ago, Robert Schreiter noted the vast variety of theological activities that function under the broad rubric of "contextual theologies." Such endeavors emerge in remarkably different cultures and languages, and they often have different aims; some seek to translate "imported theologies" into local parlance, while others focus their reflection on "how the Gospel is taking root in local circumstances amid shifting realities"; some aim at small communities or people groups, while others seek "to articulate theologies for whole regions and even continents."[4] Three decades later, some of these efforts have fizzled out, while others have grown to maturity and produced new lines of inquiry of their own. In the meantime, scores of new projects, as well as new conceptions of the task of contextual theology, have also emerged, making it more difficult than ever to exhaustively describe the diversity of contextual theologies. Such a task is beyond the limited scope of this chapter, but we do need to examine enough of the picture to understand where the current proposal fits among relevant alternatives.[5]

The story of contextual theology in the twentieth century begins with the Roman Catholic Church. In the 1960s, the Second Vatican Council, the first assembly of its kind in over a hundred years, launched a major overhaul in Catholic thinking about the relationship between theology and culture. *Lumen Gentium*, one of the council's key documents, tasks the church with ensuring that "whatever good lies latent in the religious practices and cultures of diverse peoples, is not only saved from destruction but is also cleansed, raised up and perfected unto the glory of God, the confusion of the devil and the happiness of man."[6] This was not necessarily a novel move—recall, after all, that Jesuit missionaries to China and India were contextualizing the gospel message hundreds of years earlier—but it did transfer the impulse toward contextualization (often called *inculturation* or *adaptation* in Roman Catholic theology) from the fringe of Catholic missionary work to the center of official teaching. Equally important, in addition to declaring the importance of conducting mass in local languages and the accommodation of local customs, the documents also emphasized that the Church is enriched when it enters and accommodates a new culture.[7]

---

4. Robert J. Schreiter, foreword to *Models of Contextual Theology*, by Stephen B. Bevans (Maryknoll, NY: Orbis Books, 1992), ix.

5. Readers will also benefit from the overview offered by Victor Ezigbo in "Contextual Theology: God in Human Context," in *Evangelical Theological Method: Five Views*, ed. Stanley E. Porter and Steven M. Studebaker (Downers Grove, IL: IVP Academic, 2018), 95–97.

6. *Lumen Gentium: Dogmatic Constitution on the Church* (Vatican II, November 21, 1964), 17, Vatican Resource Library, https://www.vatican.va/archive/hist_councils/ii_vatican_council/documents/vat-ii_const_19641121_lumen-gentium_en.html.

7. *Lumen Gentium*, 23. On inculturation in the Roman Catholic church in general, see Robert A. Hunt, *The Gospel among the Nations: A Documentary History of Inculturation*, American Society of Missiology Series, no. 46 (Maryknoll, NY: Orbis Books, 2010). On the impact of Vatican II specifically, see Julian Saldanha, "Vatican II and the Principle of Inculturation," in *Vatican II: A Gift and a Task*, ed. Jacob Kavunkal, Errol D'Lima, and Evelyn Monteiro (Mumbai: Bombay Saint Paul Society, 2006), 195–211.

This final point in particular prompted theologians to go beyond merely accommodating traditional Christian teaching to local language, culture, and customs and toward a process whereby theologians consciously find in local cultures a partner and tool for understanding and explaining Christian doctrine. In Roman Catholic circles, this call to action soon started bearing fruit, first at the grassroots level—most notably in the flourishing of liberation movements and theologies—and then in influential works of theological literature.[8]

Meanwhile, nudged by the maturation of churches in Asia, Africa, and Latin America, Protestants were embarking on a similar journey. In 1972, Shoki Coe, an influential Taiwanese theologian, famously coined the term *contextualization*, calling theologians not only to adapt Christian doctrine to local culture and language (which was widely called *indigenization* in Protestant circles at that time) but also to respond to the rapid social changes brought about by technology and globalization.[9] Mainline Protestant work approaching precisely those tasks soon emerged around the globe.[10]

As we noted in the previous chapter, evangelicals came late to the contextual theology party because they were skeptical about the strings attached to the invitation. Many scholars correctly noted that Protestant and Roman Catholic efforts toward developing contextual theology often had the effect of minimizing the unique authority of Scripture and the need for the particularities of Christ's teaching. Yet, as early as the 1970s, several leading evangelical voices affirmed the need to address the influence of culture in theological reflection while maintaining fidelity to evangelical commitments.[11]

---

8. E.g., Raimon Panikkar, *The Unknown Christ of Hinduism: Towards an Ecumenical Christophany*, rev. ed. (Maryknoll, NY: Orbis Books, 1981); Robert J. Schreiter, *Constructing Local Theologies* (Maryknoll, NY: Orbis Books, 1985); Jon Sobrino, *Spirituality of Liberation: Toward Political Holiness*, trans. Robert R. Barr (Maryknoll, NY: Orbis Books, 1988); Agbonkhianmeghe E. Orobator, *Theology Brewed in an African Pot: An Introduction to Christian Doctrine from an African Perspective* (Nairobi, Kenya: Paulines Publications Africa, 2008).

9. Theological Education Fund, *Ministry in Context: The Third Mandate Programme of the Theological Education Fund (1970–77)* (London: Theological Education Fund, 1972), 20–21.

10. E.g., John S. Mbiti, *New Testament Eschatology in an African Background: A Study of the Encounter between New Testament Theology and African Traditional Concepts* (New York: Oxford University Press, 1971); Kosuke Koyama, *Waterbuffalo Theology* (Maryknoll, NY: Orbis Books, 1974); Justo L. González, *Mañana: Christian Theology from a Hispanic Perspective* (Nashville: Abingdon, 1990).

11. This is perhaps best expressed in the 1978 *Willowbank Report* (Lausanne Committee for World Evangelization, *The Willowbank Report on Gospel and Culture*, in *Making Christ Known: Historic Mission Documents from the Lausanne Movement 1974–1989*, ed. John Stott [Carlisle, UK: Paternoster, 1996], 73–113).

At present, while most evangelicals increasingly recognize the impact of culture on all theological discourse and are likewise open to translating the substance of Western theological texts to make them more usable and relevant in non-Western churches, there is still a great deal of skepticism about how culture might play a constructive role in the theological process. Nevertheless, an increasing number of important contributions are emerging from evangelical quarters, mostly from theologians who hail from or have lived for long periods in the Majority World.[12]

Mapping the Terrain: Taxonomies of Contextual Theologies

Having briefly laid out the history of contemporary contextual theologies, we can now try to find some patterns and order through which to understand them.[13] Rather than starting from scratch, we can begin with the influential work of Stephen Bevans, who, more than two decades ago, developed a typology of contextual theologies that remains widely used. Bevans describes six types, or models, of contextual theology.

Four of the models can be characterized by their pessimism or optimism about the relationship between Christianity and human culture. On one side of the spectrum are those approaches that are optimistic about finding significant theological insight through dialogue with local cultures. Thus, what Bevans calls the *anthropological model* is characterized by a search for "God's revelation and self-manifestation within the values, relational patterns, and concerns of a culture."[14] Rooted in a robust emphasis on the goodness of creation and the Spirit's ongoing work in cultures and communities outside of the traditional church, theologians using this model hope to articulate

12. E.g., Samuel Waje Kunhiyop, *African Christian Theology* (Grand Rapids: Zondervan, 2012); Simon Chan, *Grassroots Asian Theology: Thinking the Faith from the Ground Up* (Downers Grove, IL: IVP Academic, 2014); Amos Yong, *Renewing Christian Theology: Systematics for a Global Christianity* (Waco: Baylor University Press, 2014); Gene L. Green, Stephen T. Pardue, and K. K. Yeo, eds., *Majority World Theology: Christian Doctrine in Global Context* (Downers Grove, IL: IVP Academic, 2020). Notable as well is an emerging class of commentaries focused on reading Scripture in light of various cultural contexts. See Tokunboh Adeyemo, ed., *Africa Bible Commentary* (Grand Rapids: Zondervan, 2006); Brian C. Wintle, ed., *South Asia Bible Commentary: A One-Volume Commentary on the Whole Bible* (Grand Rapids: Zondervan, 2015).

13. Note that these typologies are about the relationship between *theology* and culture, which is a slightly different matter than the broad question of how *Christians in general* should relate to culture. This issue will be treated in the next chapter, which will include interaction with the influential work of Richard Niebuhr in this area.

14. Stephen B. Bevans, *Models of Contextual Theology* (Maryknoll, NY: Orbis Books, 1992), 49.

"a theology which, while radically different from traditional formulations, earnestly claims authentic fidelity to its deepest spirit."[15]

On the other side of the spectrum are models that are less optimistic. For example, Bevans describes the *countercultural model*—his label for theological approaches that primarily seek to critique cultures through "critical analysis and gospel proclamation."[16] Slightly more optimistic is the *translation model*, which focuses on finding dynamic equivalents that can communicate the substance of Christian belief in new cultural forms.[17] Bevans associates this view with most Protestant evangelicals and with Roman Catholics in the mold of Pope John Paul II, who see in this model a way of accommodating new cultures while cautiously seeking to preserve historic Christian belief.[18]

Bevans also presents the *synthetic model* as a kind of halfway point between the anthropological (more optimistic about culture) and countercultural and translation (less optimistic about culture) models. This approach attempts to engage in a genuine, dialectical conversation between Christian tradition and local cultures.[19] Bevans associates this model with two creative Asian theologians, Kosuke Koyama and José M. de Mesa, both of whom combine cultural analysis, theological acumen, and humor to generate a productive dialogue between theology and culture.[20]

Bevans's final two models are not necessarily committed to any single theory of Christianity and culture but instead focus, respectively, on praxis and religious experience. The *praxis model*, rather than focusing primarily on conceptual engagement between Christian doctrine and cultural frameworks, emphasizes fostering prophetic, liberating action.[21] This model is best represented by liberation and feminist theologians who aim in their theological work to support and empower in-the-trenches social transformation on behalf of the oppressed.[22] Finally, Bevans presents the *transcendental*

---

15. Bevans, *Models of Contextual Theology*, 1992, 57.

16. Bevans associates this view especially with thinkers like Lesslie Newbigin and Lamin Sanneh (Stephan B. Bevans, *Models of Contextual Theology*, rev. ed. [Maryknoll, NY: Orbis Books, 2002], 119). Note that this model was only added in the second edition of the book.

17. Bevans, *Models of Contextual Theology*, 1992, 31–33.

18. Bevans, *Models of Contextual Theology*, 1992, 37–44.

19. Bevans, *Models of Contextual Theology*, 1992, 81–87.

20. See, e.g., Koyama, *Waterbuffalo Theology*; José M. de Mesa and Lode L. Wostyn, *Doing Theology: Basic Realities and Processes* (Manila: Claretian, 1990).

21. Bevans, *Models of Contextual Theology*, 1992, 63–65.

22. Bevans notes that it is difficult to find many examples of this model because it is focused more on action than conceptual reflection; nevertheless, he points in particular to the work of

model, which shifts the focus altogether away from broad cultural and social trends and seeks instead to express an individual's "experience of God, as experienced in a particular spatio-temporal or cultural milieu."[23]

While Bevans's typology has been remarkably resilient, many authors have sought to add to and clarify the various ways that Christians have engaged culture in theological and missiological reflection. For example, Scott Moreau, a leading evangelical missiologist, has argued that so much diversity lies buried within the translation and countercultural models—the models overwhelmingly favored by evangelicals—that more specificity is needed to do justice to the remarkable differences between the many variations of these approaches.[24] Moreau does an admirable job of summarizing various proposals to modify or replace Bevans's typology, focusing especially on those suggested by evangelical scholars.[25] In addition, Moreau has offered his own map of evangelical approaches to contextual engagement, describing how evangelical practitioners aim to function either as "facilitators," "guides," "heralds," "pathfinders," "prophets," or "restorers."[26] Each approach is governed in part by distinctive convictions about the degree to which culture can provide positive resources for Christian doctrine, as well as a discernment of the strategic paths that are most likely to aid the acceptance of Christian faith in particular times and places.

While both Bevans and Moreau do a great service by offering intelligent assessments of the existing territory, none are quite adequate for our task here. As Moreau rightly notes, Bevans's models work as far as they are designed to go, but like a world map that merely labels the continents, they exclude important complexities.[27] Similarly, Moreau's categories are useful taxonomies, but they focus primarily on the missiological task, shedding light only obliquely on the task of constructive theology.

---

several feminist theologians, such as Virginia Fabella, Elsa Tamez, and Mercy Amba Oduyoye as representatives (Bevans, *Models of Contextual Theology*, 2002, 76–77).

23. Bevans, *Models of Contextual Theology*, 1992, 101. Bevans associates this model with North American theologian Sally McFague and Latin American theologian Justo González.

24. A. Scott Moreau, *Contextualization in World Missions: Mapping and Assessing Evangelical Models* (Grand Rapids: Kregel, 2012), 44–45.

25. Moreau, *Contextualization in World Missions*, 325–68.

26. Moreau, *Contextualization in World Missions*, 203–324.

27. As Moreau notes, this is also true of the work of Robert Schreiter, which elides many of the complexities evangelicals engaged in mission are likely to find important. See Schreiter, *Constructing Local Theologies*; Robert J. Schreiter, *The New Catholicity: Theology between the Global and the Local* (Maryknoll, NY: Orbis Books, 1997).

In a recent work, Victor Ezigbo highlights the need for a clear distinction between *explanatory* and *constitutive* approaches to contextual theology. By the former, Ezigbo has in mind approaches in which "theologians merely use local metaphors and thoughts to explain the Christian faith to a present-day community."[28] In his view, most missiological typologies remain focused primarily on this type of work—the discovery of helpful translations or local expressions of the faith. In contrast, Ezigbo advocates for *constitutive* contextual theology, which is defined by its belief in "the context of a present-day Christian community as an essential theological source that should contribute both to the form and content of Christian theology."[29]

Getting us closer to a taxonomy for constructive theology is the approach offered by Marc Cortez, which proposes a modification of Bevans's models that is more sensitive to the complexity of the various tasks to which theologians are called. At times, Cortez argues, theologians simply seek to "understand the biblical paradigms as they were and are given in the text, and to communicate those paradigms in a new cultural situation . . . with an emphasis on accurately communicating the original sense of the paradigm."[30] For example, the worldview-shaping statement "Jesus is Lord" needs to be translated into local language in a way that is sensitive to the local context while also remaining faithful to the original biblical assertion. In such situations, something like Bevans's translation model serves well.[31]

At other times, however, Cortez argues that theologians will need to embrace other approaches. For example, we must grapple not only with Scripture's direct assertions but also with all that it implies; the doctrine of the Trinity, for example, is an indirect but necessary implication of the Bible's claims.[32] Articulating these implications requires the use of analogies that can build a bridge between complex or culturally distant notions (e.g., Jesus's atoning work on our behalf) and locally accessible ideas (e.g., a courtroom in which a defendant receives a pardon).[33] Thus, when dis-

---

28. Victor I. Ezigbo, *The Art of Contextual Theology: Doing Theology in the Era of World Christianity* (Eugene, OR: Cascade Books, 2021), 10.

29. Ezigbo, *Art of Contextual Theology*, 11. For more on Ezigbo's particular arrangement of the theological sources, see pp. 14–35.

30. Marc Cortez, "Context and Concept: Contextual Theology and the Nature of Theological Discourse," *Westminster Theological Journal* 67 (2005): 97.

31. Cortez, "Context and Concept," 97.

32. Cortez, "Context and Concept," 95.

33. Cortez, "Context and Concept," 98. Cortez refers to such analogies as *models*, drawing especially from influential theological articles that use this terminology in a specific way ("Context

cussing biblical inferences and theological analogies, theologians are called to do something more than mere translation: they must allow the imagery and concepts of local cultures to shed light on theological reality. This may involve simply translating the language of biblical metaphors, but it is likely also to require the generation of new analogies suitable to the local situation (e.g., relating Jesus's work on our behalf to the work of ancestors in some African worldviews). For this reason, Cortez contends that an approach more like Bevans's synthetic model—in which local cultures play an active role in shaping theological concepts—is needed when operating at this level.[34]

Finally, Cortez contends that at times theologians must move yet another level beyond merely translating biblical assertions or synthesizing analogies that integrate Scripture's necessary implications. In such cases, theology requires "speculation"—that is, "a thoughtful deduction from or extension of [biblical] assertions and inferences."[35] While this includes what we often think of as metaphysical speculation (e.g., the development of theories about how the trinitarian persons interact, theories that are not *necessary* inferences from Scripture but are intended to help us think about the relationship between the Bible's various assertions about the Father, Son, and Spirit and the implications of those assertions), it also includes the kind of reflection that leads to concrete behaviors. Thus, when theologians call the church to particular actions on the basis of Scripture (e.g., to respond in a particular way to injustice), they are "speculating" in the sense that they are seeking to integrate all that Scripture says and all that it implies and to relate that faithfully to the demands of the contemporary context. Cortez argues that at this level of theological reflection, we need something along the lines of Bevans's praxis model—a way of approaching contextual theology that is interested not only in translating biblical paradigms and analogies but also in adopting actions that are suitable in a given culture or society.[36]

To sum up, then, Cortez argues that theologians should adopt different postures toward local contexts depending on the primary task they are performing: whether *translating* biblical assertions, *synthesizing* analogies that bridge the gap between biblical implications and locally accessible ideas,

---

and Concept," 91–93). However, since Bevans and others in this conversation use *model* to refer to something different—i.e., the various theological approaches used for relating context and theology—we here use the language of *analogy*.

34. Cortez, "Context and Concept," 99.
35. Cortez, "Context and Concept," 95.
36. Cortez, "Context and Concept," 100–101.

or *theorizing* the connections between abstract theological concepts and concrete actions. As we move further away from the mere restatement of biblical assertions and toward the development of theories and specific actions, we allow for increasing weight to be given to local culture and context, though (even in the third model) Scripture must remain the ultimate norm.[37]

Even if one does not find concord with every detail of Cortez's proposal, it no doubt adds important depth and complexity in helping us conceive what contextual theology must be. In addition to reminding us that no single model is sufficient for all theological reflection (this was also a point Bevans made decades earlier), it alerts us to the reality that theologians must constantly make decisions about how to weight various sources and pursue particular strategies in line with their specific calling and location.

We have now surveyed a bewildering array of typologies and systems for categorizing various approaches to contextual theology. Despite this diversity, we can recognize that at least two characteristics mark advocates of every model of contextual theology. First, they all share a conviction that our cultures penetrate the theological process not only in the final step (when we communicate the message in terms that will be understandable in our local context) but all the way through. Culture shapes how we select, interpret, and frame biblical texts. We bring different questions to the texts because of the differences in our cultural contexts and even because of how our language shapes our conceptual world. And culture continues to influence our judgments to some degree as we discern where to draw theological boundaries and how to guide the church in its pursuit of faithful obedience.

Second, in each of these cases *contextual theology* denotes an intention not merely to *tolerate* diverse human cultures and languages but to find in them *critical resources* for clarifying, reflecting upon, and responding to divine revelation. As we translate Scripture into contemporary languages and do theological reflection in new contexts, our grasp of the gospel is widened and deepened.

This does not require a Pollyanna-like naivete about the compatibility of human cultures with the divine order. As we will see in the next chapter, while culture is one way in which humans reflect the divine image, like all our image-bearing activities, it is marred by the fall. Indeed, because it often

---

37. Marc Cortez, "Creation and Context: A Theological Framework for Contextual Theology," *Westminster Theological Journal* 67 (2005): 358–59.

operates at a subconscious level, culture can be one of the most insidious barriers to full obedience to the gospel. Yet ultimately, this expectation that culture can contribute to theological discernment, rather than merely inhibiting it, is rooted in God's prior activity—namely, that in his grace and providence the triune God has elected to work in and through (rather than outside, against, or above) the cultures and languages of the nations. As we seek to know and speak of our redeemer, we are similarly called to embrace these cultures and languages as blessings rather than burdens for the theological journey.

Beyond these broad points of agreement, however, visions for contextual theology diverge based on the way theologians answer a range of other, more disputable questions, such as the following:

- Should we focus on the contributions of our local cultures or emphasize their shortcomings (which the gospel promises to correct)?
- To what degree should Christians of a particular time and place focus on solving their local, occasional theological problems, and to what degree should they pay close attention to the challenges of the church beyond their cultural context?
- Must theology attend primarily to systematic questions about Christian doctrine, or should it focus more on the practical, ethical, and missiological issues facing everyday Christians, especially those living with persistent and significant suffering?

These questions all play a role in shaping the ultimate form that contextual theology must take. Yet there is a question that is above all of these, and it is to that question that we now turn.

Discerning a Path: The Role of Scripture in Contextual Theological Reflection

How should Scripture and culture each inform the theological task? This question is so fundamental that it is, in certain ways, as old as the church itself. As we have already seen, Christians in the first few centuries of the church had vigorous arguments about how much space to give local culture in their theological formulations, with some choosing to place it almost alongside Scripture as an equally weighted source (e.g., Clement of Alexandria), and others highlighting the countercultural nature of the Christian calling (e.g., Tertullian). In the present moment, the dividing lines are drawn somewhat differently, but we can still generally place theological proposals along a spectrum in terms of their optimism or skepticism about culture and their views of Scripture's authority.

In a recent book, Rubén Rosario Rodríguez seeks to chart a path between "theologians of culture," who assign diverse cultures a substantial role in the theological task, and proponents of a "Scripture-centered theology," who focus their theological efforts on understanding revelation rather than the church's diversity.[38] Rodríguez recognizes the need for this mediating path in part because of an ironic tension: while the "nascent theological movements" emerging from the Majority World church do clearly highlight the importance of local culture for theology, Christians in these movements also overwhelmingly tend to view Scripture as an authoritative "locus of divine revelation."[39] So while theologians of culture generally see themselves aligned with the Majority World church, the reality is that most Christians in these churches tend to honor Scripture's authority more highly than the theology-of-culture approach would allow. At the same time, a Scripture-centered approach naive to the impact of culture also misses the mark, failing to consider the degree to which theology in these various contexts actually does reflect diverse cultural flavors and accents. This means that both the Scripture-centered and the culture-centered theological proposals that have emerged in Western twentieth-century theology are ultimately poor fits for the emerging world Christianity of the twenty-first century. In response, Rodríguez calls for a middle way between these two extremes.

To understand his proposal, it helps to know a bit more about each side of the debate he seeks to address. On one side are theological methods shaped by Paul Tillich, who advocates an approach that correlates Christianity and culture as a way of allowing Christianity to remain relevant, especially in the increasingly post-Christian culture of Europe and North America. Crucially, Tillich adopts an approach in which "experience as the inspiring presence of the Spirit is the ultimate source of theology."[40] For Tillich, this

38. Rubén Rosario Rodríguez, *Dogmatics after Babel: Beyond the Theologies of Word and Culture* (Louisville: Westminster John Knox, 2018), xiii–xiv.

39. Rodríguez, *Dogmatics after Babel*, xvii.

40. Paul Tillich, *Systematic Theology*, vol. 1 (Chicago: University of Chicago Press, 1973), 45.

is grounded in a confidence in humanity's capacity for hearing from God in a variety of contexts—not only throughout the diverse body of Christ but even beyond the Christian community. As such, Tillich argues that "being open for new experiences which might even pass beyond the confines of Christian experience is now the proper attitude of the theologian."[41]

On the other side stand theologies shaped especially by Karl Barth, who was born the same year as Tillich but has a diametrically opposed approach to theology. Barth and those influenced by him bristle at the notion that Christian theology should be driven primarily by religious experience (whether of Christians or non-Christians), contending that this is a sure path to idolatry. Rather than projecting our experience, speculation, and wishes onto God, the only sure way forward for theology in modernity is to focus on what God has actually spoken in revelation—especially the Christian Scriptures—and to help the church respond in obedience.

Thus, Barth responds to Tillich at the start of his *Church Dogmatics* by stating that while reflecting on the phenomena we associate with "culture" may be interesting, and may even be worthwhile, we "must not imagine that in so doing it has even touched the task of theology," which lies instead in reflection on God's revelation in Christ and in Scripture.[42] While "God may speak to us through Russian Communism, a flute concerto, a blossoming shrub, or a dead dog," theology at its best must always ensure that it remains focused on the revelation of God in Christ.[43]

It would be incorrect to suggest that Barth's approach to theological reflection is entirely devoid of reflection on culture and experience. He recognizes that culture shapes the theological task in various ways, and he seems to have had room for the notion that cultural achievements can be redeemed.[44] Yet, unquestionably, Barth offers a vision of the theological task that spurns

41. Tillich, *Systematic Theology*, 1:45. Tillich does not wish to jettison Scripture as a theological source and norm entirely, but he views it primarily as a generative source with which the Christian theologian must construct theological criteria and norms. For more on Tillich's approach to culture and theological method, see Paul Tillich, *Theology of Culture*, ed. Robert C. Kimball (New York: Oxford University Press, 1959); Russell Re Manning, ed., *The Cambridge Companion to Paul Tillich* (Cambridge: Cambridge University Press, 2009).

42. Karl Barth, *Church Dogmatics* I/1, 55, study ed., ed. G. W. Bromiley and T. F. Torrance (New York: T&T Clark, 2009). The page numbers I cite for Barth's *Church Dogmatics* are those that appear in the margins of the study edition, as these correspond to the pagination of the classic fourteen-volume set.

43. Barth, *Church Dogmatics* I/1, 55–56.

44. Barth discusses culture in a somewhat more positive light in *Church Dogmatics* IV/3, 795–830. For an insightful argument that Barth has more to say about theology and culture than

the anthropological preoccupation he saw in Tillich and his disciples, contending that the church is at its best when rooted in revelation rather than in anthropology.

Rodríguez argues that neither side of this debate has it completely right and presses us to move beyond "the false dichotomy characteristic of both anthropological and revelational theologies—which favor either experience or revelation but are unable to bring both together."[45] Instead, he proposes that we give God's self-revelation priority in our theological reflection (affirming Barth's insights) but at the same time acknowledge that God's nature remains fundamentally hidden and mysterious. This leads to a "methodological humility" that encourages—even requires—Christians to look beyond their own canon of revelation for insight into God's being and work.[46] Theologians should look for the liberating work of the Spirit wherever it is to be found and recognize "divinely inspired acts of justice, compassion, and liberation" as revelatory.[47] Specifically, Rodríguez highlights what Christian theology may gain from the revelation to be found in Judaism and Islam, as well as from contemporary movements of liberation, such as the Black Lives Matter movement.[48]

In sum, Rodríguez proposes to address the challenge of Babel—the problem of diversity and plurality that divides humanity and the church—by giving divine revelation centrality while also acknowledging that God reveals himself in many and diverse ways and that cultures and religions of all sorts may turn out to be revelatory in a manner and to a degree that we have thus far failed to recognize. He calls for contextual theological reflection that is marked by "religious pluralism, comparative theology, and interreligious cooperation" as theologians seek to recognize God's voice "beyond the walls of the church" and seek "justice, compassion, and solidarity with fellow human beings who have been denied their basic dignity as creatures made in the image of God."[49]

What should we make of this proposal? Unquestionably, Rodríguez is right in recognizing a false dichotomy that has often emerged in Western

---

we often assume, see Jessica DeCou, "Barth and Culture," in *The Oxford Handbook of Karl Barth*, ed. Paul Dafydd Jones and Paul T. Nimmo (New York: Oxford University Press, 2019), 609–21.

45. Rodríguez, *Dogmatics after Babel*, 143.
46. Rodríguez, *Dogmatics after Babel*, 143.
47. Rodríguez, *Dogmatics after Babel*, 168.
48. Rodríguez, *Dogmatics after Babel*, 148–75.
49. Rodríguez, *Dogmatics after Babel*, 185–86.

theology in the last two centuries, pitting theologies of culture against theologies that prioritize divine revelation. There is no reason that theologians should have to choose between regarding Scripture as authoritative and acknowledging (even celebrating) the contribution of culture to the theological task. In fact, given that God speaks in Scripture through human authors bearing very local cultural attitudes and norms, paying close attention to the biblical text should only deepen our appreciation for the formative and informative role of culture.[50]

Similarly, there is no reason that the church's remarkable expansion into new cultural territory, which has prompted it to reckon with the shaping role of culture in theology, must undermine Scripture's relevance for God's people. In fact, what is remarkable about Christian expansion in the last two centuries is the degree to which it has resulted in stunning diversification that is still held together *especially* by a common loyalty to the Christian Scriptures, which have been translated into hundreds of languages and cultures.[51]

Rodríguez may ultimately be correct in directing theologians to consider the ways God may have revealed himself outside of the Scriptures and to recognize the work of the Spirit in unexpected places.[52] Yet there are powerful reasons to insist that, even when we consider all the other sources that inform the theological task, Christian Scripture must play a uniquely normative and definitive role. This is because, unlike other tools at the theologians' disposal—the company of fellow saints, the spiritual disciplines, the Great Tradition, the gift of reason, the insights of culture—Scripture is God's life-giving communication to his people, and as such is uniquely generative of and authoritative over the theological task.

---

50. This case is made well in two representative books: Dean Flemming, *Contextualization in the New Testament: Patterns for Theology and Mission* (Downers Grove, IL: InterVarsity, 2005); Jerry Hwang, *Contextualization and the Old Testament: Between Asian and Western Perspectives* (Carlisle, UK: Langham Global Library, 2022).

51. See Lamin Sanneh, *Whose Religion Is Christianity? The Gospel beyond the West* (Grand Rapids: Eerdmans, 2003).

52. No one has made the case more extensively for this approach to contextual theology than Amos Yong, who contends that "any viable constructive Christian theology for the foreseeable future will need to be essentially in comparative dialogue with other faiths" ("Preface to the 2018 Reprint Edition," in *Discerning the Spirit(s): A Pentecostal-Charismatic Contribution to Christian Theology of Religions* [2000; repr., Eugene, OR: Wipf & Stock, 2018], 2). For further development, see Amos Yong, *Beyond the Impasse: Toward a Pneumatological Theology of Religions* (Grand Rapids: Baker Academic, 2003); Amos Yong, *Hospitality and the Other: Pentecost, Christian Practices, and the Neighbor* (Maryknoll, NY: Orbis Books, 2008).

Evangelicals have long viewed adherence to this principle as a key stipu-
lation for the development of local or contextual theologies. This is reflected
in the 1978 *Willowbank Report*, in which evangelical leaders from around the
world voiced support for contextually reflective interpretation of Scripture
provided that "Scripture remains always central and normative."[53] Similarly,
when representatives from evangelical churches in Asia, Africa, and Latin
America met in Seoul in the 1980s to discuss the relationship between the
Bible and culture, one of the few things they were able to agree on was a
mutual commitment to "building our theology on the inspired and infallible
Word of God, under the authority of our Lord Jesus Christ, through the
illumination of the Holy Spirit."[54] Today, leading Majority World theologians who advocate for the role of culture in the theological task continue
to regard Scripture's uniquely authoritative role in theological reflection
to be a nonnegotiable element of their theological method.[55] As essential
as cultural savvy may be in the theological task, evangelical theology's *sine
qua non* is acquaintance with and submission to Scripture. This leads us
to our first thesis regarding an evangelical contextual theology: *evangelical
contextual theologies must look to Scripture as their magisterial authority, even
as they increase their appreciation for the crucial ministerial role of culture for
the theological task.*

Shrewd readers will recognize trouble on the horizon here. After all, if
culture shapes our theological thinking "all the way through," as we saw in

53. Lausanne, *Willowbank Report*, Section 4B. Importantly, attendees at the Willowbank con-
sultation included many of the luminaries who would shape the next generation of contextual
theological efforts in the Majority World, such as Saphir Athyal (India), Kwame Bediako (Ghana),
and René Padilla (Ecuador).

54. Bong Rin Ro and Ruth Eshenaur, eds., *The Bible and Theology in Asian Contexts: An Evangelical Perspective on Asian Theology* (Taiwan: Asia Theological Association, 1984), 24. A few years
later, theologically conservative biblical scholar D. A. Carson likewise voiced hearty support for
the development of contextual theologies, so long as these were defined as "attempts by nationals to
construct a *biblically controlled* theology each for its own language, culture and generation" ("Church
and Mission: Reflections on Contextualization and the Third Horizon," in *The Church in the Bible and
the World: An International Study*, ed. D. A. Carson [Grand Rapids: Baker, 1987], 255, italics added).

55. To cite just a few recent examples: Robert Chao Romero, *Brown Church: Five Centuries
of Latina/o Social Justice, Theology, and Identity* (Downers Grove, IL: IVP Academic, 2020), 216;
Timoteo D. Gener, "Divine Revelation and the Practice of Asian Theology," in *Asian Christian
Theology: Evangelical Perspectives*, ed. Timoteo D. Gener and Stephen T. Pardue (Carlisle, UK:
Langham Global Library, 2019), 13–37; Kunhiyop, *African Christian Theology*, 13–42. See also
point 6 of *The Cape Town Commitment*, a document produced through the collaboration of a
worldwide movement of evangelical churches (Third Lausanne Congress, *The Cape Town Commitment: A Confession of Faith and a Call to Action* [Cape Town: Lausanne Movement, 2011], https://
lausanne.org/content/ctc/ctcommitment).

chapter 1, then even our interpretation of Scripture must be affected by our cultural context. And if we wear cultural lenses even as we read Scripture, then are we not doomed simply to project our own cultural biases onto it, or at least to be blinded to the parts disagreeable to us? This is a species of what is commonly called the "hermeneutical circle": our preunderstandings can circumscribe what we are willing and able to see in Scripture, and our reading of the text can then act to confirm those preunderstandings.

This is a real problem that has vexed philosophers and theologians for centuries. It is tempting to look for some process or hermeneutical technique that could safeguard the meaning of a text from the influence of the reader's culture. But while exegetical methods can and should discipline our tendency to read sloppily and unfaithfully, modernity has generally trained us to overestimate the ability of method to lock out all complicating factors. For example, we should acknowledge that because reading is an inherently moral process, we need not only good exegetical methods but also fitting character—habits of heart and mind that will enable us to listen patiently and obediently to the text.[56]

Yet neither excellent exegetical method nor strength of moral character is sufficient to ensure that we hear God's voice in Scripture rather than our own. Ultimately, the church's saving grace is that the Father sends the Spirit so that we can hear the Word aright, and hear it in all of its terrible judgment and shocking mercy toward us and our communities.[57] This is an extension of the logic at work in Deuteronomy, where God declares that "this commandment that I command you today is not too hard for you, neither is it far off. . . . But the word is very near you. It is in your mouth and in your heart, so that you can do it" (Deut. 30:11, 14).

This gracious work is achieved through the power of the Holy Spirt, who cultivates in us the mind of Christ and leads his people into truth, usually by means of careful study that makes the most of all the tools at our disposal. As a result of God's illuminating work, while culture always shapes our

56. See Kevin J. Vanhoozer, *Is There a Meaning in This Text? The Bible, the Reader, and the Morality of Literary Knowledge* (Grand Rapids: Zondervan, 1998); Stephen T. Pardue, "Athens and Jerusalem Once More: What the Turn to Virtue Means for Theological Exegesis," *Journal of Theological Interpretation* 4, no. 2 (2010): 295–308.

57. See Daniel J. Treier, *Introducing Theological Interpretation of Scripture: Recovering a Christian Practice* (Grand Rapids: Baker Academic, 2008), 157–86; J. Todd Billings, *The Word of God for the People of God: An Entryway to the Theological Interpretation of Scripture* (Grand Rapids: Eerdmans, 2010), 105–48.

reading of the Bible, God can speak through culture and even show us where it stands under divine judgment. We can gain further insight into what it means to attend to culture while also submitting our contextual theological reflection to Scripture by considering theological developments emerging from Latin America since the 1970s.

Case Study: Liberation Theology and Integral Mission in Latin America

Unquestionably, one of the most important effects of the "cultural turn" in theological studies has been the development of *theologies of liberation*. Today this label functions as an umbrella term referring to a wide variety of Protestant and Roman Catholic contextual theologies that have emerged all over the world, "in which the experience and circumstances of the interpreters are given a prime importance as the first step in seeking to be a disciple of Jesus."[58] In particular, theologies of liberation press the church to consider what we come to understand about God from the perspective of the poor and marginalized, and to put theology into action. Rejecting "detached reflection on scripture and tradition," they argue that theology must begin from and respond to the devastating effects of poverty and suffering, including oppression based on gender or ethnic identity.[59]

In a narrower sense, *liberation theology* originally referred to a specific movement in Latin America that emerged in the 1970s. In a defining work originally published in 1973, Peruvian Roman Catholic theologian Gustavo Gutiérrez explains that liberation theology starts with "an attempt at reflection, based on the gospel and the experiences of men and women committed to the process of liberation in the oppressed and exploited land of Latin America." It is not merely a political ideology disguised as a theological system, but an effort "to reconsider the great themes of the Christian life within this radically changed perspective and with regard

---

58. Christopher Rowland, "Liberation Theology," in *The Oxford Handbook of Systematic Theology*, ed. John Webster, Kathryn Tanner, and Iain Torrance (New York: Oxford University Press, 2007), 634.

59. Rowland, "Liberation Theology," 636. To see the diversity in contemporary appropriations of liberation, note that *The Cambridge Companion to Liberation Theology* includes chapters on movements in Asian, black, and feminist theology, among others (Christopher Rowland, ed., *The Cambridge Companion to Liberation Theology* [New York: Cambridge University Press, 1999]).

to the new questions posed by this commitment."[60] Gutiérrez argues that liberation theology ultimately is "not so much a new theme for reflection as a *new way* to do theology," as it "does not stop with reflecting on the world, but rather tries to be part of the process through which the world is transformed."[61]

In explaining the origins of the movement, Gutiérrez cites the confluence of several factors: a fresh vision in the Roman Catholic church for the importance of charity put into action, a deepened sense of the need for theology to address the human condition, trends in philosophy focusing on concrete action over mere speculation, "the influence of *Marxist thought*, focusing on praxis and transformation of the world," and "the rediscovery of the *eschatological dimension* in theology."[62] Gutiérrez clearly captured the mood of the moment. His book was soon followed by a slew of new and creative works written by him and a host of others.[63] Far from merely producing new literature, these theologians gave voice to and helped fan grassroots movements of activism on behalf of the poor and, in the process, awakened the conscience of the worldwide church.[64]

Gutiérrez and those who followed after him intentionally sought not only to address the dire situation in Latin America but also "to contribute to the life and reflection of the universal Christian community."[65] Wisely, Gutiérrez recognized that while such a contribution would come from engaging with and learning from the local situation, refusing to stop there and instead seeking to engage the wider church would produce something "*unique*, both particular and universal, and therefore fruitful."[66] Thus, liberation theology as envisioned by Gutiérrez was a contextual theology committed to local perspective and action, with an eye toward bringing the whole church into a deeper and truer faith.

---

60. Gustavo Gutiérrez, *A Theology of Liberation: History, Politics, and Salvation*, rev. ed. (Maryknoll, NY: Orbis Books, 1988), xiii.

61. Gutiérrez, *Theology of Liberation*, 12.

62. Gutiérrez, *Theology of Liberation*, 6–9, italics original.

63. See, e.g., José Míguez Bonino, *Doing Theology in a Revolutionary Situation* (Philadelphia: Fortress, 1975); Leonardo Boff, *Jesus Christ Liberator: A Critical Christology for Our Time*, trans. Patrick Hughes (Maryknoll, NY: Orbis Books, 1978); Sobrino, *Spirituality of Liberation*.

64. For a thoughtful overview of the development and implications of liberation theology in Latin America from its start to the 1990s, see David Tombs, *Latin American Liberation Theology* (Boston: Brill, 2002).

65. Gutiérrez, *Theology of Liberation*, 11.

66. Gutiérrez, *Theology of Liberation*, 11, italics original.

After two very productive decades, Latin American liberation theologies would encounter substantial challenges, in part because of consistent opposition from more conservative Christians, and in part because of political developments that made Marxist-aligned movements far less appealing.[67] On the latter point, it is worth noting that liberation theologians generally sought to use Marxism only as a tool of social analysis, rather than as a controlling authority in their thought (much as all theologians use tools of philosophy and anthropology to understand the world). Yet some thinkers were more disciplined in this regard than others. For example, Singaporean theologian Simon Chan highlights a prominent Asian theologian who extolled the glories of China's "'social, economic and political achievements . . . in which the suffering of the masses is largely eliminated'—this at the height of the Cultural Revolution, which even by the most conservative estimates led directly to the death of at least two million Chinese!"[68]

In general, the most fruitful expressions of liberation theology were those that sought to integrate the insights of their contexts while also attending carefully to the biblical witness as a source of revelation and authority. The work of Mexican biblical scholar Elsa Tamez is an eye-opening example of reading Scripture from the perspective of the marginalized and oppressed, often yielding new insight into the meaning of biblical texts and theological concepts. In one book, for example, Tamez sets out to offer "a rereading of justification by faith from the perspective of Latin America," arguing that "a biblical-theological rereading of justification in light of our reality can illuminate our understanding of Christian life and faith."[69]

Specifically, Tamez argues that the doctrine of justification by faith is inseparable from our understanding of sin, which must in turn be informed by (among other things) the experiences of profound suffering and poverty in Latin America. There, we see that sin is not only an individual problem but also a seemingly "indestructible power," wreaking deadly and dehumanizing havoc

67. For a helpful summary of these challenges, see Tombs, *Latin American Liberation Theology*, 271–92.

68. Chan, *Grassroots Asian Theology*, 22. Chan here quotes Taiwanese theologian Choan-Seng Song in an article in which he also compares the Maoist revolution to the events of the exodus ("New China and Salvation History: A Methodological Enquiry," *Southeast Asia Journal of Theology* 15, no. 2 [1974]: 52–67).

69. Elsa Tamez, *The Amnesty of Grace: Justification by Faith from a Latin American Perspective*, trans. Sharon H. Ringe (Nashville: Abingdon, 1993), 13.

on society and all of creation.[70] "Experience teaches," she writes, "that a life of marginalization gnaws away at the intimate spaces of a person to the point of making him or her feel unworthy and insignificant in his or her own eyes, in the eyes of others, and even before God."[71] Tamez carefully demonstrates that as we deepen our grasp of sin by attending to the experience of the oppressed (and to the individuals and systems that perpetuate oppression), so also we have the opportunity to glimpse in a brighter way the nature of God's justice and the broad scope of his work of *justifying*, in the sense of "making righteous."

The constructive work of Spanish theologian Antonio González, who boldly confronts the weaknesses of first-generation liberation theologies, is in a similar vein. Despite decades of high-minded work, these theologies have failed to win over the teeming masses they claim to represent, who have found hope instead in the gospel-centered message of Pentecostal evangelicals. After a careful examination of the causes of this failure, González notes that these Pentecostal churches have discovered things that liberation theology lacked, such as "a call to personal faith," a concrete connection to a "community of disciples," and direct access to "a risen Messiah who rules directly over his people."[72]

González argues that liberation theology was, in a sense, "not sufficiently radical," as it focused far too much on social utopianism and failed to attend to the biblical story of Jesus and the kingdom he announced.[73] To survive, González argues, liberation theology will need "a radical, biblical vision of social change," in which new communities are formed of people "who by God's grace are willing to return good for evil, washing their own clothes in the blood of the Lamb, for they believe that only thus will a way to liberation be opened that no Babylon in our history will be able to close."[74] Much of González's work, then, is spent demonstrating how a truly biblical theology offers a far more solid footing for the goals of liberation theology than its earlier iterations, which often treated the biblical text superficially. The result is a fresh hearing of the good news that is biblically rich and deeply thoughtful about its approach to practical engagement.[75]

70. Tamez, *Amnesty of Grace*, 43.
71. Tamez, *Amnesty of Grace*, 40.
72. Antonio González, *The Gospel of Faith and Justice* (Maryknoll, NY: Orbis Books, 2005), 168.
73. González, *Gospel of Faith and Justice*, 165.
74. González, *Gospel of Faith and Justice*, 170.
75. In addition to *The Gospel of Faith and Justice*, see also Antonio González, *God's Reign and the End of Empires* (Miami: Convivium, 2012); Antonio González, "The Trinity as Gospel," in

René Padilla and Integral Mission

What eluded the first-generation liberation theologies—a lasting ecclesial movement of and for the poor that also shaped the trajectory of Christian theology more broadly—was achieved by a small group of evangelical theologians and leaders who remain less well-known than their counterparts in the Roman Catholic and mainline Protestant churches.[76] In many ways, the work of these leaders represented contextual theology at its best: it sought to make the most of local cultural resources and to address the (very urgent) needs of its community while never undermining or neglecting the authoritative and powerful role of Scripture as the soul of theology. And even as it focused on the local church, it self-consciously sought to remain in dialogue with the global community of Christians in order to gain from and contribute to the people of God from every nation, tribe, and tongue.

One of the most important of these leaders was René Padilla, an Ecuadorian theologian who grew up in an actively evangelical family. Given the politics of the time, this meant that he and his family were the subjects of remarkable persecution from the Roman Catholic majority, and Padilla himself had been the subject of multiple assassination attempts by the time he was eighteen.[77] Reflecting later on his experiences and the political and social environment of the era (the 1970s were a period of remarkable turmoil and ferment in nearly every Latin American nation), Padilla "recalled 'longing to understand the meaning of the Christian faith in relation to issues of justice and peace in a society deeply marked by oppression, exploitation, and abuse of power.'"[78]

As Padilla grew up and increasingly took on leadership roles in the Latin American church, he and others in his community came to lament the degree to which the dominant theological approaches available to them were unworkable for leading the church forward. Evangelical theology, while

Majority World Theology: Christian Doctrine in Global Context, ed. Gene L. Green, Stephen T. Pardue, and K. K. Yeo (Downers Grove, IL: IVP Academic, 2020), 48–59.

76. It is gratifying to see this story being told and filled out in new ways. See Daniel Salinas, *Latin American Evangelical Theology in the 1970's: The Golden Decade* (Boston: Brill, 2009); J. Daniel Salinas, *Taking Up the Mantle: Latin American Evangelical Theology in the 20th Century* (Carlisle, UK: Langham Global Library, 2017); David C. Kirkpatrick, *A Gospel for the Poor: Global Social Christianity and the Latin American Evangelical Left* (Philadelphia: University of Pennsylvania Press, 2019).

77. David C. Kirkpatrick, "C. René Padilla and the Origins of Integral Mission in Post-War Latin America," *Journal of Ecclesiastical History* 67, no. 2 (2016): 360.

78. Kirkpatrick, "C. René Padilla," 360.

biblically rich and informed by a robust spirituality, was strictly set against admitting that the church had any role to play in social or cultural transformation. Yet liberation theology, as advanced at the time, was a poor fit for the evangelical church, as it was not sufficiently rooted in the biblical text and its unique authority and power.

Sharing a commitment to biblically engaged theology that could address the needs of the time, in 1970 Padilla and others formed the Fraternidad Teológica Latinoamericana (Latin American Theological Fellowship, or FTL), which would turn out to have remarkable influence throughout Latin America and beyond. Padilla and the group soon "became engaged in the development of a contextual theology, a theology 'forged in the heat of Evangelical reality' in Latin America [and] in faithfulness to the Word of God.'"[79] It is impossible to read the early documents of the group without recognizing that its primary uniting characteristic was the members' affection for Christian Scripture. The Fellowship's first common document, "The Evangelical Declaration of Cochabamba," focuses almost entirely on the nature of Scripture and its adequacy for guiding Christians in the theological task. Noting the difficulties facing Latin America and the absence of a fitting response from the evangelical church, the document firmly calls for "a new evaluation of our situation," which involves "returning to the Bible and the Lord who reigns through it." The document clearly presses for change, but only under the rubric of obedience "to the clear demands of the Word of God," of following Jesus, and of "becom[ing] a community which expresses the spirit of justice, kindness, and service" in response to the good news.[80]

Padilla soon came to articulate a theological perspective that sought to fuel just such a movement, coining the term *misión integrale* (integral mission). According to Padilla, the concept "regards being, doing and saying as inseparable dimensions of the witness to Jesus Christ as Lord and Savior."[81] In advancing the concept of integral mission, Padilla rejected the restrictive visions of Christian salvation that generally held sway among conservative evangelicals in North America. Such views resulted in part from the intellectualization and privatization of religion in those regions, producing

---

79. Salinas, *Latin American Evangelical Theology in the 1970's*, 10. The quotation is from Samuel Escobar, "Biblical Content and Anglo-Saxon Trappings in Latin American Theology," *Occasional Bulletin of the Latin American Theological Fraternity*, no. 3 (1972): 2.

80. Salinas, *Latin American Evangelical Theology in the 1970's*, 200.

81. C. René Padilla, *Mission between the Times: Essays on the Kingdom*, rev. ed. (Carlisle, UK: Langham Monographs, 2010), 17.

theology that was "insulated from socio-political reality, indifferent to the needs and the suffering of the poor." Because the Christian God is acting in our world to accomplish salvation of whole persons, not merely souls, "in the context of poverty and oppression, theology . . . must be liberating—it must be a denunciation of systemic evil and an annunciation of God's kingdom of justice and righteousness."[82]

Yet Padilla also rejected the views of more left-leaning liberation theologies, which too often failed to read the Bible "on its own terms" and allowed their ideology "to force it into an ideological straitjacket." As a corrective, Padilla advocated for a more critical reception of the tools liberation theologians tended to use, and he called for greater attention to Scripture. "Theology," Padilla writes, "is the reflection on praxis in the light of faith for the sake of obedience to the whole counsel of God."[83] This does not require reading Scripture without attention to our local situation—which would be neither possible nor desirable. But it does require that Scripture be "allowed to judge freely" our commitments and previous views. Padilla argues that when theologians do their work under the authority of Scripture and with a keen eye to the context, we gain "a richer and deeper understanding of Scripture," which leads in turn to "a deeper and richer understanding of the context" and to genuine, Spirit-empowered transformation.[84]

These assertions may strike readers today as relatively unremarkable. If so, it is precisely because the work of Padilla and the FTL gained such wide acceptance and impact in the years since the 1970s.[85] Yet in those early years, their perspective was initially treated with skepticism and suspicion. Some claimed their work had been compromised because they allowed the Latin American context to drive their reading of Scripture. In retrospect, it is much easier to see now that Padilla and others in the FTL were in fact advancing a contextual theology that discerned the context

82. C. René Padilla, "Liberation Theology: An Appraisal," in *Freedom and Discipleship: Liberation Theology in an Anabaptist Perspective*, ed. Daniel S. Schipani (Maryknoll, NY: Orbis Books, 1989), 43.
83. Padilla, "Liberation Theology," 47.
84. Padilla, "Liberation Theology," 48.
85. Kirkpatrick notes that "'Integral Mission' is utilized as the official phrase and model by nearly 600 mission and relief agencies," and the concept is now "widely assumed within diverse communities of global evangelicalism" (*A Gospel for the Poor*, 142). Kirkpatrick's monograph details the surprising path by which this movement moved from the periphery of the worldwide church to penetrate its most influential decision-making bodies.

and allowed it to yield insight into the nature of the Christian faith while simultaneously remaining committed wholeheartedly to the authority and power of Scripture.

The result was an approach to Scripture and theology that genuinely met the needs of the local context, in which poverty, oppression, and violence were the norm. By God's grace, the efforts of this small group of evangelical theologians led to the establishment of a spiritually vital movement of Christians that is still growing today. Importantly, the contextual theology developed there met a crucial need in the global church, offering a broader perspective on the gospel that had been largely forgotten or neglected in the North American and European evangelical church.

Conclusion

In this chapter, we have started to come to a clearer sense of the distinctive contribution and vision of evangelical contextual theologies. Such efforts will seek to build on what has gone before, acknowledging the wisdom of early efforts to integrate cultural context as a resource that is not only inescapable but also helpful. Yet because of their confidence in and allegiance to the self-revelation of God in Christian Scripture, they will approach that task with a different emphasis and accent than counterparts in other parts of the church.

This dependence on Scripture is certainly not simplistic. Cultural context impacts our reading of Scripture just as much as any other aspect of theological inquiry, and so epistemic modesty and self-awareness remain essential. But a commitment to submitting ourselves unswervingly to the testimony of Scripture—even as we seek to be more aware of the contributions of our local cultures—allows evangelicals to produce contextual theologies that are more balanced than other prevalent approaches. As the example of Padilla and the FTL demonstrates, such theology is not just a valuable intellectual advance; it can help fuel a remarkable process of transformation and renewal that reaches far beyond the confines of the local context where it started.

Clearly, culture is a key element of this story. Padilla and others recognized not only that their theology needed to meet the needs of their local contexts but also that their cultural contexts helped them to see things that Christians from other cultures had been failing to recognize. Yet, in order to learn from their example, we need a better understanding of how this process works. What, exactly, do we mean when we speak of *culture*? And why should we expect that culture is part of God's design for leading his church into truth and transformation? It is to these questions that we will turn our attention next.

3

The Wealth of the Nations Shall Come to You

How Culture Matters for Theology

Then you shall see and be radiant;
   your heart shall thrill and exult,
because the abundance of the sea shall be turned to you,
   the wealth of the nations shall come to you.

—Isaiah 60:5

We have so far made the case that evangelical theology must engage world Christianity more fruitfully, and we have surveyed a range of present efforts seeking to do this well. We have also encountered the first of five theses that seek to give shape to the evangelical version of contextual theology: *evangelical contextual theologies must look to Scripture as their magisterial authority, even as they increase their appreciation for the crucial ministerial role of culture for the theological task.* The burden of this chapter is to articulate and defend a second thesis, arguing that engagement with cultural resources—in addition to being *inevitable*—is *desirable* for the theological task. Thus, we will

63

contend here that *evangelical contextual theologies must acknowledge culture as a material theological good, a gift from God designed for the benefit of the church.*

Supporting this thesis will require first clarifying further what it means theologically to speak of "cultures," as well as how Christian theology can give sufficient attention to this creational reality without being distracted from its primary task and thus becoming something other than itself. Scripture offers crucial aid to us here by focusing our eyes on the prophets and apostles, and—most of all—on Christ; in each of them, we see models of the marriage of culture and revelation that should inform our understanding of these matters.

Finding Our Place in the Christ and Culture Debates

To begin, we should recall that the nature of culture and its relationship with Christianity was a point of interest for Christian writers long before the modern discussions of contextualization and contextual theology. For example, in one of the earliest samples of Christian writing that we have, the *Epistle to Diognetus*, an anonymous second-century author identified as "a student of the Apostles" writes to a nonbelieving acquaintance about the Christian way of life. Early in the letter, he describes the unusual relationship between Christians and their local cultures: "Christians are not distinguishable from other people either by country, language, or customs. For nowhere do they live in their own cities, speak some unusual dialect, or practice an uncommon lifestyle. . . . They live in their native countries, but only as outsiders. They participate in everything like citizens and tolerate all things as foreigners. Every foreign place is their homeland, and every homeland is foreign."[1] From this brief quotation, we can get a glimpse of how in the second-century world—where culture, nationality, and religion were typically tightly intertwined—Christians charted a different path. This was one of the early Christians' distinctives: they were unusually ready to use local languages in prayer and worship, even translating the sacred texts of Scripture into various local languages as the church spread, resulting in a dynamic, polycentric faith.[2] To study the cross-cultural transmission of

---

1. *Epistle to Diognetus* 5. The quotation is from Clayton N. Jefford, ed., *The "Epistle to Diognetus" (with the "Fragment of Quadratus"): Introduction, Text, and Commentary* (New York: Oxford University Press, 2013), 145.

2. Lamin Sanneh, *Translating the Message: The Missionary Impact on Culture*, 2nd ed. (Maryknoll, NY: Orbis Books, 2009).

the Christian faith over the centuries is to see a faith consistently finding new expression in relation to its host cultures.[3]

Yet while the conversation about Christianity and culture is thus in some ways as old as the faith itself, the development of the field of cultural anthropology, the decline of *Christendom* (a state of affairs in which Christianity had a longstanding and dominant influence in broader public life), and the growth of the modern missions movement have conspired to instigate renewed and deeper interest in the interplay between culture and Christian faith in the last several decades.

A primary touchstone in almost every treatment of this subject matter is Richard Niebuhr's *Christ and Culture*.[4] In this influential work, the mid-twentieth-century theologian articulates five ways in which Christians tend to think about the relationship between culture and Christianity. On one side of the spectrum lies the Christ-*against*-culture perspective, which asserts that Christians must primarily be in conflict with and subversive of their cultures. On the other side of the spectrum is the Christ-*of*-culture perspective, promoting an assimilation of Christianity into prevailing cultural norms and trends. The other three positions that Niebuhr outlines stand in between these two poles: synthesists (Christ *above* culture), dualists (Christ and culture *in paradox*) and conversionists (Christ *the transformer of* culture). Niebuhr regards these three as the primary approaches Christians have used in their engagement with culture through the centuries.[5]

Synthesists contend that there is a fundamental compatibility between the world and Christian faith, seeing Christ as fulfilling cultural aspirations and then advancing them yet further through his supernatural gifts.[6] Dualists, by contrast, recognize a tension between the demands of Christ and the demands of their local cultures, each of which require a kind of loyalty.[7] Finally, conversionists—the type that Niebuhr depicts with the most nuance, and with which he seems to have the most sympathy—recognize both

---

3. See the excellent and still very relevant work in Andrew F. Walls, *The Missionary Movement in Christian History: Studies in the Transmission of Faith* (Maryknoll, NY: Orbis Books, 1996); Andrew F. Walls, *The Cross-Cultural Process in Christian History: Studies in the Transmission and Appropriation of Faith* (Maryknoll, NY: Orbis Books, 2002).

4. H. Richard Niebuhr, *Christ and Culture* (New York: Harper & Row, 1951).

5. Niebuhr, *Christ and Culture*, 40.

6. Niebuhr, *Christ and Culture*, 42. Niebuhr cites Thomas Aquinas as the clearest example of this type.

7. Niebuhr, *Christ and Culture*, 42–43. Niebuhr cites Luther as the primary proponent of this type.

commonality with and antithesis to human cultures, but seek the "turning of men from self and idols to God" in and through human culture and society.[8]

Though Niebuhr delivered his lectures more than seventy years ago, his work remains remarkably influential in both popular and academic reflection on culture. Recently, for example, John Stackhouse has applied a modified Niebuhrian approach to contemporary aspects of the church's engagement with culture.[9] Stackhouse's assessment of Niebuhr is careful, and it yields often-overlooked insights. Helpfully, Stackhouse reminds readers that Niebuhr did not intend for any of the types to be authoritative but recognized that each was a partial element of faithful Christian engagement with the world.[10] Moreover, Stackhouse contends that wise engagement in the present moment will require a more balanced sort of "conversionism" than we have so far specified—one that allows for the reality of redemptive work in the present moment (eschewing total withdrawal from cultural engagement) while still resisting a utopianism that presumes we can conquer all of society's institutions in the name of Christ.[11]

Biblical scholar D. A. Carson likewise engages Niebuhr's work as an entryway to help us "work out a more comprehensive vision, a canon-stipulated vision" of the relationship between Christ and culture.[12] Carson critiques Niebuhr's typology for being anemic in its engagement with the Bible and argues for several modifications given Scripture's guidance in the area of cultural engagement. For example, he contends that any prescription for Christian engagement with culture must grapple seriously with the remarkable diversity in how God's people in Scripture interacted with their wider world. Taking seriously both creation and fall, kingdom and exile, conquest and persecution—to name a few—should protect against the greatest extremes in the debate (indeed, Carson argues that Niebuhr's two extreme positions are largely untenable in light of Scripture), while also allowing flexibility for Christians in various contexts to emphasize the biblical teachings that

---

8. Niebuhr, *Christ and Culture*, 43. Niebuhr associates this view with Augustine and Calvin.

9. John G. Stackhouse Jr., *Making the Best of It: Following Christ in the Real World* (New York: Oxford University Press, 2008), 13–42.

10. Stackhouse, *Making the Best of It*, 38–40. See also Niebuhr, *Christ and Culture*, 230–31.

11. Stackhouse, *Making the Best of It*, 309–10. An analysis in the same vein, arguing that Christians in North America in particular must be willing to chasten their expectations with regard to changing culture, is James Davison Hunter, *To Change the World: The Irony, Tragedy, and Possibility of Christianity in the Late Modern World* (New York: Oxford University Press, 2010).

12. D. A. Carson, *Christ and Culture Revisited* (Grand Rapids: Eerdmans, 2008), 43.

are most important in their time and place.[13] We would also be remiss not to note the serious critiques of Niebuhr's work coming from Anabaptist theologians, who have made a compelling case that Niebuhr's treatment of the Christ-against-culture model is unfair and naive, though the argument of this chapter does not require that we adjudicate these disputes in detail.[14]

Yet as helpful as Niebuhr's work may be for framing various ways in which Christians might engage their social and cultural worlds, his lectures were composed with a very different set of challenges in mind than the ones we seek to address here. At the time of their writing, the issues of multicultural collaboration and globalization were not even on the horizon. Instead, the major change Niebuhr sought to address was the debate in post–World War II America about how Christians should or should not assert themselves in American public life through state institutions, or to what degree they should accept secularization of those institutions in light of specifically American commitments and norms.[15] As a result, Niebuhr's focus is on how Christians should engage the organs of society and state, rather than on how the practice of theology might benefit from the resources of local culture.

In addition, the sense of the word *culture* has subtly changed since Niebuhr's time. Where most of Niebuhr's work focuses on Christian engagement with the *products of* human cultivation—e.g., literature, art, philosophy, governmental structures—culture is today conceived also as an ongoing *process* and a *lens* through which human perceptions are formed and expressed. Indeed, Niebuhr's formulation of Christ *and* culture can make sense only if culture is understood primarily as something *out there*—society at large and its products and structures—against which Christianity can conceive itself.[16] Today, scholars instead tend to think of culture as a web of patterns through which we live and see everything, including the Christian faith itself.[17] In addition to pressing us to find other resources, these distinctions

13. Carson, *Christ and Culture Revisited*, 59–65.

14. See, e.g., Stanley Hauerwas and William H. Willimon, *Resident Aliens: Life in the Christian Colony* (Nashville: Abingdon, 1989); Craig A. Carter, *Rethinking "Christ and Culture": A Post-Christendom Perspective* (Grand Rapids: Brazos, 2006). For a judicious defense of Niebuhr against the most extreme Anabaptist critiques, see Stackhouse, *Making the Best of It*, 30–42.

15. Niebuhr, *Christ and Culture*, 1–2.

16. Thus, D. Stephen Long highlights the necessary disjunction in Niebuhr's work between culture and nature, and the potential problems this introduces to the discussion (*Theology and Culture: A Guide to the Discussion* [Cambridge: James Clarke, 2010], 13–14).

17. See Kathryn Tanner, *Theories of Culture: A New Agenda for Theology* (Minneapolis: Fortress, 1997), 25–37; Lalsangkima Pachuau, *God at Work in the World: Theology and Mission in the Global Church* (Grand Rapids: Baker Academic, 2022), 147–51.

should alert us to the need to deepen our sense of what culture is as we seek to identify its usefulness for the theological task.

The Dynamics of Culture

According to a widely used definition from anthropologist Clifford Geertz, a culture is "an historically transmitted pattern of meanings embodied in symbols, a system of inherited conceptions expressed in symbolic forms" that people use to "communicate, perpetuate, and develop their knowledge about and attitudes toward life."[18] This definition has the benefit of being widely used and relatively comprehensive. Yet, as we look more closely, we need to highlight some limitations of this narrow account.

The field of cultural anthropology has, since Geertz's time, become far more divided about the nature of culture and even about the legitimacy of maintaining that there is a thing we might rightly call *culture*. Four caveats are worth noting here before we pursue further the question of how exactly culture fits into the Christian theological picture.[19]

First, critics of early anthropologists' conception of culture have high-lighted how the origins of the culture concept are ultimately linked with efforts in the twentieth century to highlight the "civilization" of European (primarily white) societies and the "primitiveness" of the rest of the world. In this context, "culture" was something to be cultivated and displayed in par-ticular kinds of literature, manners, and art. By contrast, to be "uncultured" was to be "uncivilized"—to lack an understanding and appreciation of these very particular ways of being in the world. In rejecting this notion, the first generation of cultural anthropologists rescued the culture concept by argu-ing that Western "civilization" could claim no monopoly on culture. Franz Boas, a seminal leader in modern anthropology, was known for defending

---

18. Clifford Geertz, *The Interpretation of Cultures*, 3rd ed. (New York: Basic Books, 2017), 95. The first edition of this book was published in 1973.

19. For a more robust but still very accessible account of the critique of early definitions of culture, see John Monaghan and Peter Just, *Social and Cultural Anthropology: A Very Short Introduction* (New York: Oxford University Press, 2000), chap. 2. For an analysis of culture that situates this history within a broader understanding of the Christian faith, see Brian M. Howell and Jenell Williams Paris, *Introducing Cultural Anthropology: A Christian Perspective*, 2nd ed. (Grand Rapids: Baker Academic, 2011), 27–50; William A. Dyrness, *The Earth Is God's: A Theology of American Culture* (Maryknoll, NY: Orbis Books, 1997), 59–65; Tanner, *Theories of Culture*, 3–24.

the truth that all peoples, no matter how "primitive" they may appear by European standards, have cultures—symbolic forms and actions used to communicate "their knowledge about and attitudes toward life" (as Geertz puts it)—and that their cultures are equally worthy of our close attention, as each has something to teach us about the human person. No society can thus be said to be devoid of "culture."[20]

As much as this is an unquestionably better position than the previous notion of culture as the unique possession of European elites, critics still have valid concerns. They point out that early anthropologists tended to study cultures as fascinating and exotic objects; while they often purported to highlight the dignity and wisdom of non-Western cultures, they still regarded themselves as those with a "God's-eye" view of the world, standing over and above their subjects in some sense. The ethnographer, by classifying and categorizing, is the one ultimately running the show.[21] Which leads to a second critique: it is difficult to describe other cultures without in some way exercising a kind of unwarranted authority in the process.

Third, scholars have questioned the degree to which cultures are rightly understood as discrete systems.[22] While we may think and speak of cultures as independent entities (e.g., Filipino culture, American culture), real life tells us that cultures are constantly colliding and overlapping, borrowing from and impacting each other in dynamic ways. To illustrate the point, think for a moment about your own cultural identity. Even if you have spent your entire life in one country or even one small town, you likely live at the intersection of multiple cultural identities rooted in your ethnic heritage, religious identity, generational cohort, and other biographical details. At different times in your life—or even in different contexts—you likely reflect various aspects of these cultures in your thinking and behavior. This is even more self-evident if you, like an increasingly large percentage of the world's population, have lived part of your life in a multicultural city or in more than one country.

20. For a seminal work making this case, see Franz Boas, *The Mind of Primitive Man* (New York: Macmillan, 1922).
21. See, e.g., Néstor Medina, *Christianity, Empire and the Spirit: (Re)Configuring Faith and the Cultural* (Boston: Brill, 2018), 2–3.
22. See, e.g., Robert J. Schreiter, *The New Catholicity: Theology between the Global and the Local* (Maryknoll, NY: Orbis Books, 1997), 46–61; Tanner, *Theories of Culture*, 38–58.

Fourth, and in a similar vein, contemporary anthropologists have often emphasized that conceiving of cultures as singular, coherent systems can obscure the reality that any single "culture" typically encompasses a whole host of realities that are not all necessarily consistent with or connected to one another. Thus, a young person working a corporate job in downtown Nairobi will have a remarkably different—and in some cases totally opposing—way of seeing and navigating her world than her uncle working as a farmer a hundred miles from the nearest city. Which one better represents the culture of Kenya, or even of their ethnic group? As the young person changes in response to global trends, moreover, does she become less authentically *Kenyan*? Not necessarily. This is because Kenyan (or even Kikuyu) culture is not a single, monolithic entity, but is itself a constantly changing reality encompassing a variety of attitudes, judgments, and ways of being in the world. Moreover, as individuals make their way in the world, they construct a kind of bricolage of their own using various aspects of the cultures in which they find themselves—and this, in turn, creates new cultural trends and identities.[23] William Dyrness brings together these various insights well when he describes culture as "that changing set of communal practices and assumptions that serve as a repertoire of a people's actions, and by which they express their identity."[24]

It can be tempting to focus so much on the caveats and complexities that we despair of the culture concept's ability to do any good work for us. Most anthropologists agree that this would be a mistake, noting that, even if we cannot discuss it perfectly, the analysis of culture is ultimately worthwhile and insightful.[25] Yet, as we think about the relationship between Christianity, theology, and culture, we will be better off if we recall that cultures are plural, overlapping, and dynamic realities, and that our grasp of them is always limited. If we can keep these dynamics in mind as we find our way forward, we will be much better equipped to consider the implications of culture for Christian theology.

23. This notion, that culture involves individuals piecing together various inherited materials, was first appropriated by Claude Lévi-Strauss and has been used by cultural anthropologists seeking to explain the complex and changing reality of culture. See Monaghan and Just, *Social and Cultural Anthropology*, 45–46.

24. Dyrness, *Earth Is God's*, 67.

25. See, e.g., Regna Darnell, "The Anthropological Concept of Culture at the End of the Boasian Century," *Social Analysis* 41, no. 3 (1997): 42–54; Monaghan and Just, *Social and Cultural Anthropology*, 47; Howell and Paris, *Introducing Cultural Anthropology*, 44–47.

Placing Culture Biblically

The gifts of cultural anthropology in helping us understand culture are significant, and we have only scratched the surface here.[26] But remember where we started: we wanted to understand how culture can inform theology, and specifically how culture can rightly be understood as a material theological good. To answer this question, we need to look at culture from the perspective of Scripture and Christian teaching.

If we approach the Christian Scriptures with an understanding of culture as "that changing set of communal practices and assumptions that serve as a repertoire of a people's actions, and by which they express their identity,"[27] the first thing that should strike us is that the existence of Scripture itself is a potent sign that God is interested in engaging human cultures for divine purposes. After all, while God can reveal himself in myriad ways—telepathically, for example, or through the creation of an entirely new language and culture—he chooses instead to reveal himself through the means of ordinary and already existing words, images, and practices. Indeed, Christians have always marveled at how the triune God chooses to reveal himself in earthy and local ways, finding in human languages and cultures a vessel that is clumsy and imperfect but made sufficient through the working of divine grace.[28]

Culture and Covenant

In addition to this general reality, we can also learn from the way that culture figures in the specific drama of redemption. From the start, Genesis notably highlights God's use of speech to accomplish his purposes. Creation is accomplished through words (rather than through a physical act); and, in addition to dwelling with Adam and Eve in the garden, God speaks to

---

26. For a deeper analysis of the culture concept and its intersection with Christian mission and the practice of Christian faith, see Schreiter, *New Catholicity*, 46–61; Henning Wrogemann, *Intercultural Theology*, trans. Karl E. Böhmer, vol. 1, *Intercultural Hermeneutics* (Downers Grove, IL: IVP Academic, 2016).

27. Dyrness, *Earth Is God's*, 67.

28. Perhaps the most creative and engaging thinker on this topic is Augustine of Hippo, who was trained as a rhetorician before his conversion and often reflected on the nature of language as a limited instrument that nevertheless serves God's purposes of revealing himself. For an introduction to his thought on this subject, see Carol Harrison, *Beauty and Revelation in the Thought of Saint Augustine* (New York: Oxford University Press, 1992), 54–96; Philip Burton, *Language in the "Confessions" of Augustine* (New York: Oxford University Press, 2007).

communicate his will and intentions.[29] Even if God's creative speech is best understood as metaphorical, Genesis soon features divine engagement with specific languages. When God calls Abram in Genesis 12, he reaches him in his own ancient Near Eastern tongue. Later, he uses imagery from Abraham's local cultural repertoire to confirm his covenant with him. Representing himself with a torch and smoking fire pot, he himself walks between the cut-up pieces of animals, adopting a local practice designed to confirm the "cutting" of a covenant (Gen. 15:1–21). In this very particular moment and very culturally located ceremony, the triune God is initiating a program of redemption with a global, or even cosmic, scope—a plan of action that, according to the Christian reading of Scripture, is still being carried out now, thousands of years later.

Here we see the shadow of a pattern that will be repeated throughout Scripture: God uses local, even parochial, cultural resources as vehicles to reveal himself and achieve global redemptive purposes. In what may be Scripture's most important distillations of this point, the tabernacle and temple—the distinctive homes of God's holy presence—are constructed from many of the same resources that neighboring ancient Near Eastern cultures would have used in their own religious and cultural constructions, not from sacred materials dropped from on high or by using cultural forms utterly unique to Israel. Indeed, the gold used in the construction of the ark of the covenant and the tabernacle is the very gold given to the Israelites by the Egyptians upon their exit from bondage (Exod. 3:22; 12:36; 25:1–7). Augustine of Hippo saw in this plundering of the Egyptians a metaphor for what Christians must regularly be doing with the cultural and intellectual resources of their non-believing neighbors: making use of their best insights as they learn to speak of and worship the triune God.[30]

Babel and the Acceleration of Human Culture-Making

Augustine could well have also grounded his point in Scripture's development of the imagery first introduced in the Tower of Babel narrative. In Genesis 11 we find the capstone of the first part of the book of Genesis, a hinge passage that bridges the "primordial history"—describing creation, the patriarchs,

29. For further reflection on this point, see Moisés Silva, *God, Language, and Scripture: Reading the Bible in the Light of General Linguistics* (Grand Rapids: Zondervan, 1990), 20–21.

30. Augustine, *On Christian Teaching* 2.40.60.

and the flood—and the rest of the book, which focuses on God's designs to bless "all the families of the earth" through the seed of Abraham (Gen. 12:3). Directly before and after the brief Babel narrative itself (Gen. 11:1–9), the reader is presented with several genealogical lists, likely designed to highlight the increasing multiplication of humanity in fulfillment of the command of Genesis 1:28, as well as to advance the plot to the key character of Abram.

Nestled within the laundry lists of names, however, is the somewhat puzzling account of humanity attempting to build a city and a tower and God intervening by "confus[ing] their language" and then dispersing them "over the face of all the earth" (Gen. 11:7–8). The biblical text never clearly identifies the problem with humanity's actions in the passage. But narrative clues suggest that both idolatry and refusal of the divine command to "fill the earth" (Gen. 1:28) are at issue.[31] Similarly, there is ambiguity in the nature of the divine response, which could either be read as a judgment or as a more neutral act intended to ensure that the plan of redemption carries forward.[32]

Clearly, there is some element of tragedy in the text, and it is tied up with the development of culture as an element in the process of redemption. Culture in the older sense of the word—the artifacts and structures that result from human cultivation of creation—here become the tools of self-aggrandizement instead of the worshipful service commanded in the garden, foreshadowing the idolatrous habits that will permeate and warp the rest of human history. Humans develop new technology, and their first instinct is to use it to protect and project their dominance over all things.

At the same time, culture, in the anthropological sense of the term—to repeat Dyrness's definition from above, that "set of communal practices and assumptions that serve as a repertoire of a people's actions, and by which they express their identity"[33]—is clearly in view as well. Language, the most

---

31. The passage highlights the arrival of people "from the East," which is associated in the Genesis narrative up to this point with Cain and Shem, and the actions of the people seem to be an attempt at achieving equality with God, echoing the decision of Adam and Eve in Eden.

32. The dominant reading in the literature is that this is a judgment of the people's pride. See, e.g., the summary treatment in Victor P. Hamilton, *The Book of Genesis: Chapters 1–17*, New International Commentary on the Old Testament 1 (Grand Rapids: Eerdmans, 1990), 349–52. However, there are alternative views. For example, Theodore Hiebert raises a number of good questions about the legitimacy of this reading and ultimately argues that the text presents God's actions as neutral, reflecting the divine will rather than anger or frustration at humanity's alleged rebellion ("The Tower of Babel and the Origin of the World's Cultures," *Journal of Biblical Literature* 126, no. 1 [2007]: 29–58).

33. Dyrness, *Earth Is God's*, 67.

essential element of culture in this sense of the word, is presented as both problem and solution. And, nestled in a section of Genesis that reflects on the diversification of humanity, the Babel story addresses not only linguistic diversity but also cultural or ethnic variety.

The ambiguities of the text should constrain us from taking it as a purely positive or purely negative judgment of language and culture. On the one hand, the text gives voice to the tragic origins of cultural diversity, and the preceding table of nations seems designed to emphasize that humanity is not only spreading but splintering into various factions.[34] Original readers would have been well aware of the enmity that eventually arose between these various families, tribes, and nations, and they would have seen in the Babel narrative the shadow of inter-ethnic conflict.[35] The divine decision to confuse and to scatter results in a painful human cost: relationships are broken, clans are pulled apart, and alliances are destroyed. On the other hand, the text does seem to sanction linguistic and cultural diversity as some element of the divine design. It is only through the diversification of humanity's languages and cultures that they will be able to overcome their fear of being scattered and carry out the divine command to fill the earth. Thus, even if its origins are tragic, the ultimate effect of the diversity instigated at Babel is salutary and merciful. From another angle, Carson sums up the good and bad of Babel: "We human beings can corrupt the unity and turn it into rebellion, and we can corrupt the diversity and turn it into war."[36]

---

34. Commentators have rightly noted that there may have been a diversity of languages prior to Babel, given the repeated reference to languages, clans, and nations in Gen. 10:5, 20, and 31. It is thus possible that the introduction to the Babel narrative indicates a society with a *lingua franca* rather than a truly monolingual world. Even so, the narrative reports the *acceleration* of diversity after God's intervention, and thus its significance for linguistic and cultural diversity.

35. The extreme version of this interpretation—that cultural diversity is pure tragedy—has been used in attempts to justify the cordoning off of various cultures from one another. Thus, during apartheid in South Africa, the Dutch Reformed Church initially refused to condemn the racist and unjust system in part because of their understanding of Babel, in which they saw a warning against forced inter-ethnic unity (*Human Relations and the South African Scene in the Light of Scripture* [Cape Town: Dutch Reformed Church, 1976], 16). Within a decade of that publication, however, they would come to repudiate this view and develop a theology of reconciliation that recognized the calling of Christians to value intercultural unity. For an overview of this history, see Russel Botman, "The Church Partitioned or the Church Reconciled? South Africa's Theological and Historical Dilemma," in *Race and Reconciliation in South Africa: A Multicultural Dialogue in Comparative Perspective*, ed. William E. Van Vugt and G. Daan Cloete (Lanham, MD: Lexington Books, 2000), 105–19.

36. Carson, *Christ and Culture Revisited*, 74.

Throughout the rest of the Old Testament, there is little further commentary on the Babel event. We learn in the call of Abram that God intends to bless "all the families of the earth" (Gen. 12:3), which is probably a subtle reference to the divine plan to bless the scattered clans and nations forged at (and before and after) Babel. As the drama of Israel's redemption plays out, we learn that their interactions with those outside Israel are designed to make them a "light for the nations," attracting those of every nation to the glory of YHWH (Isa. 49:6). To accomplish this, Israel is called to build a culture unique among its neighbors, distinctive because of its rejection of all forms of idolatry and its holy love for God and neighbor. Yet this culture is not *de novo* or *ex nihilo*; instead, it arises out of and borrows heavily from the world of the ancient Near East, using language, customs, and ways of being that were ordinary in their time and place.[37]

Pentecost and Revelation 7: Babel Recapitulated and Undone

It is in the New Testament that we receive two significant clues as to how we should read the Babel event in retrospect, as we learn more about what the triune God has been up to all along. The first clue comes in Luke's narration of the day of Pentecost. There we have a kind of mirror image of Babel.[38] Luke tells us that the disciples are "all together in one place" (Acts 2:1) and are acting "with one accord" (1:14), setting up a parallel to the gathering of a unified people in Genesis 11. But rather than building something that will attempt to reach heaven, they wait patiently for divine direction.[39] While at Babel God intervenes to confuse tongues and prevent communication and cooperation, at Pentecost he gives "tongues" of fire, and the disciples speak in other "tongues" that allow for supernatural communication and cooperation.[40]

37. John H. Walton, *Ancient Near Eastern Thought and the Old Testament: Introducing the Conceptual World of the Hebrew Bible*, 2nd ed. (Grand Rapids: Baker Academic, 2018).

38. These observations are not new by any stretch; interpreters at least as early as Augustine have noted the parallels between Babel and Pentecost. For a fascinating overview of the connections that previous generations traced, see Tristan Major, *Undoing Babel: The Tower of Babel in Anglo-Saxon Literature* (Toronto: University of Toronto Press, 2018), 50–77.

39. Here Augustine sees a contrast between the pride of humanity in Genesis 11 and the submission and humility of the apostles: "Through proud men, languages were divided; through humble apostles, languages were gathered together. A spirit of pride dispersed the languages, the Holy Spirit gathered languages together" (*Enarrationes in Psalmos* 2:54.11.20–25, as quoted in Major, *Undoing Babel*, 67–68).

40. The Greek word *glōssa* is used in Acts 2 to refer to the "divided tongues as of fire" (v. 3) as well as the "other tongues" the disciples are able to speak (v. 4). The same word is used throughout

In an apparent effort to underscore the parallel, Luke not only relays that "devout men from every nation under heaven" were present (2:5), but he actually lays out a long list of geographic areas represented, echoing the table of nations that accompanies the Babel narrative in Genesis.[41] Moreover, while Pentecost seems to have involved diaspora Jews visiting Jerusalem for the feast of weeks (a celebration of the wheat harvest)—and is, therefore, not yet a full integration of all people into the redeemed community—it identifies the global scope of the Holy Spirit's mission and presages the inclusion not only of scattered Jews but of people from throughout Judea, Samaria, and the "end of the earth" (1:8). As with Babel, Pentecost's effect is ultimately for the participants to scatter and fill the earth, but here the scattering is accomplished through the miraculous communication in various languages rather than through divinely ordained confusion.

The second clue regarding how to interpret the Babel event in light of Christ comes in the vision of the church in Revelation 7. Here, John sees a great multitude worshiping the slain Lamb (Jesus) in unison. He notes that the multitude is "from every nation, from all tribes and peoples and languages" (Rev. 7:9), an indication that these are the redeemed people mentioned in the song of the elders in 5:9–10. The scene is described as the fulfillment of a rich variety of Old Testament texts that speak of the banishment of human misery in the care of the perfect shepherd (7:15–17). It is also the completion of the project begun at Pentecost—the drawing of people from every tribe on earth into relationship with the triune God.

Here is what is significant about the biblical depiction of Pentecost and the heavenly multitude: in both cases, Babel is undone not through a return to a monolingual, monocultural past but through a redemption of vast cultural and linguistic diversity. This is a surprise in the biblical story.

Since the call of Abram, God had invested heavily in a single group of people, and their identity—the combination of religious, linguistic, and cultural resources they borrowed from elsewhere and cultivated into a unique culture—was the location of and vehicle for God's long-term redemptive work. And so even when the apostles recognized that Christ was bringing access to God to a broader group of people, and even when we take into

---

Gen. 11 in the Septuagint (the Greek version of the Old Testament with which Luke and his readers would have been familiar), where the word *language* is used in most English translations.

41. Craig Keener, "Why Does Luke Use Tongues as a Sign of the Spirit's Empowerment?," *Journal of Pentecostal Theology* 15, no. 2 (2007): 181.

account such globally focused prophecies as Isaiah's prediction that the "nations shall come to your light" (Isa. 60:3), the expectation in the apostolic era would certainly have been for the reversal of Babel to take place by uniting the world around the history, culture, and language of the Jewish people.

Instead, Babel is redeemed through the giving of a Spirit who perfects cross-cultural communication rather than eliminating it through reversion to a common tongue and culture. The scattering to the corners of the earth is once again repeated, but instead of God's redemptive work focusing on one clan in the table of nations, the Spirit of Pentecost works in and through all nations, unifying among them a single people through his holy power. Finally, in Revelation, we see this new people in one place, experiencing what the settlers of Shinar ultimately longed for and needed: fellowship with the triune God. Yet here they remain culturally and linguistically distinct, and it is precisely in and through this distinctiveness, blessed by the Spirit of Pentecost, that they are able to sing with one voice to the triune God.

Placing Culture Theologically

This is a mere thumbnail sketch of how Scripture must inform our understanding of culture's place in the long drama of redemption.[42] Though incomplete, this sketch prompts us to consider what sort of a thing culture is in theological terms, which in turn helps us understand the ways in which it should—and should not—impact the task of theology.

Culture as Good Creation and Common Grace

A fine starting point is to locate any theological analysis of culture in connection to God's good creation. Long before the sharp rise in interest in culture in the mid-twentieth century, Dutch thinkers Abraham Kuyper and Herman Bavinck argued that we must understand culture in precisely this way. As Bavinck puts it, culture arises out of the command for humans to "have dominion" over the earth and all that is in it (Gen. 1:26–28). As we govern creation as God's vice-regents and enjoy its rich provision, we cultivate order and beauty, particularly through the twin paths of scholarship

---

42. For further reflection, see Lucien Legrand, *The Bible on Culture: Belonging or Dissenting* (Maryknoll, NY: Orbis Books, 2000); Medina, *Christianity, Empire and the Spirit*, 51–97.

and the arts.[43] Following John Calvin, Bavinck notes that, like all good gifts, the knowledge and beauty discovered and created in scholarship and the arts must never be despised, since they are from God; even when they are discovered or cultivated by pagans, the gifts of culture are ultimately the gifts of God.[44] In this way of thinking, culture is definitively an element of *common grace*—those gifts that God distributes to all creatures, not just to his covenant people.

Kuyper, who was about twenty years older than Bavinck, is perhaps best known for his argument that Christ is ultimately sovereign over every sphere of creation, including human affairs; he famously told the audience at the inauguration of a university in Amsterdam that "There is not one square inch of the entire creation about which Jesus Christ does not cry out 'This is mine! This belongs to me!'"[45] Because of Christ's sovereignty over all things, Kuyper and the tradition after him have argued that every aspect of culture—the arts, science, construction, agriculture, technology, politics—must be understood as the execution of the original mandate to fill, subdue, and have dominion over the earth.[46]

Eight decades later, the Roman Catholic Church would make a similar assessment of culture in a key Vatican II document, *Gaudium et Spes*. There, the council describes culture as a tool for discovering the varied and diverse goods of creation, through which "man himself is more clearly revealed and new roads to truth are opened."[47] Thus, when a carpenter shapes a beautiful piece of furniture, or a philosopher builds a good argument; when a mathematician unlocks an elegant proof, or an artist paints an arresting scene—whenever we cultivate God's creation in a way that brings about goodness, truth, and beauty—we recognize culture functioning like what

43. Herman Bavinck, *Reformed Ethics*, ed. John Bolt (Grand Rapids: Baker Academic, 2019–21), 1:162.

44. Bavinck, *Reformed Ethics*, 1:162–63. See Calvin, *Institutes* 2.2.15.

45. Abraham Kuyper, "Sphere Sovereignty (1880)," in *Abraham Kuyper: A Centennial Reader*, ed. James D. Bratt (Grand Rapids: Eerdmans, 1998), 489.

46. Kuyper lived this out in surprising ways. Refusing merely to serve as a member of the clergy, he also embraced various "public" roles as a politician, labor union leader, and the founder of a state-sponsored university. For an accessible introduction to his thought, see Richard J. Mouw, *Abraham Kuyper: A Short and Personal Introduction* (Grand Rapids: Eerdmans, 2011). See also Bruce Riley Ashford, *Every Square Inch: An Introduction to Cultural Engagement for Christians* (Bellingham, WA: Lexham, 2015).

47. *Gaudium et Spes: Pastoral Constitution on the Church in the Modern World* (Vatican II, December 7, 1965), 1.4.44, Vatican Resource Library, https://www.vatican.va/archive/hist_councils /ii_vatican_council/documents/vat-ii_const_19651207_gaudium-et-spes_en.html.

Scripture identifies as Wisdom, bringing creation to its intended end.[48] As William Dyrness summarizes, culture is most basically the wise cultivation of creation, a special calling for humanity as the image of God, and a result of God's Spirit, who works generally to assist humanity in this calling.[49] As a result, nothing—not even the brokenness of sin—can stop "creation and culture from constituting a theatre in which God's glory is somewhere to be seen and where the Spirit is everywhere active."[50]

Culture as Location and Agent of Brokenness

Yet in the same breath that we affirm the cultural optimism of Kuyper and *Gaudium et Spes*, we must also call attention to culture's dark underbelly. After all, much human cultivation of creation is exploitative, idolatrous, or ruinous. This is clearly the case with arts and scholarship, where the products of culture are generally reflective of deep goodness, beauty, and truth but also include the admixture of elements clearly at odds with divine intentions for creation. In Genesis, this is at least one implication of the culture-making described long before Babel. Cain's descendant Lamech seems to have a family that thrives in terms of technological and musical advancement (Gen. 4:20–22), but this advancement culminates in the first song in Scripture, in which Lamech uses the gift of music to proclaim his violent and brazen exploits (Gen. 4:23–24).[51] Throughout Israel's history, its artisans are called upon to use their skills to craft the tabernacle and temple, but these same skills are also perverted toward the creation of endless streams of idols.

This highlights an ironic and insidious reality: to the degree that arts and scholarship are glorious and powerful enough to inspire worship of the triune God, they can also harness that power and glory to direct the human soul precisely away from its intended ends.[52] In our own time, universities are an interesting example of this phenomenon. While the concept of the university initially grew out of the church's own cultivation of learning, throughout the modern era they have been transformed (with notable exceptions) into

48. *Gaudium et Spes*, 2.2.57.
49. William A. Dyrness, *Poetic Theology: God and the Poetics of Everyday Life* (Grand Rapids: Eerdmans, 2011), 38.
50. Dyrness, *Poetic Theology*, 73.
51. I am indebted to my colleague Andrew Heyd for highlighting this connection.
52. For further reflection on the uneasy relationship between the arts and theology, see William A. Dyrness, *Visual Faith: Art, Theology, and Worship in Dialogue* (Grand Rapids: Baker Academic, 2001), 11–24.

some of the most powerful engines humanity has ever found for severing the glory of creation from the worship of its creator.

Yet it is not just culture in the sense of *arts and scholarship*—the artifacts and results of human cultivation of creation—that is subject to the corruption of the fall. Sin also infects culture in the *anthropological* sense—those shared practices and assumptions that communities use to form networks, codify values, and shape identities. In other words, common language and culture make it possible for communities to work toward common goods, but they also facilitate the contagion of corruption. Racist and sexist norms could not persist or even come to be "norms" in the absence of the shaping power of cultures, through which such damaging perceptions and postures are taught, entrenched, and spread. Similarly, cultures often prove to be powerful insulators of an unjust status quo—allowing for the persistent abuse of women, for example, or frustrating steps that would serve the greater good, such as when cultural norms of special treatment for friends and acceptance of bribery allow only the highly connected to prosper and engage in commerce.

These norms and patterns are often deeply embedded in our cultures, reflected in the most basic elements of language and daily life, which makes it difficult even to identify the places where our own cultures are facilitating corrupted norms. For example, in South Asian contexts, caste is not only a fact of life; it is woven into linguistic and social norms. In many cultures the world over, women are referred to with diminutive appellations that often serve, intentionally or not, to prevent men from regarding them as co-equal image-bearers. All cultures include axioms that drive home distinctively anti-biblical principles, but precisely because they are axiomatic, they function at a level of consciousness that makes it hard to see their negative influence on our ways of thinking and living.[53]

To make matters worse, corrupted culture has its own cloaking mechanism. Like a clever computer virus, it has a way of concealing the damage it is doing, even from those who should be trained to spot it, such as Christian leaders and theologians. Thus, upon closer examination, we find that

53. E.g., "God helps those who help themselves" is a common bedrock axiom for those in North America and is often applied—by Christians—in ways that are totally incompatible with a biblical perspective on grace. Similarly, the notion of *bahala na*, translated roughly as "what will be will be," is a Filipino axiom that at least some of the time absolves humans of genuine responsibility. See, e.g., Timoteo D. Gener, "Fatalism," in *Global Dictionary of Theology: A Resource for the Worldwide Church*, ed. William A. Dyrness et al. (Downers Grove, IL: IVP Academic, 2008), 315–17.

Kuyper's defense of culture as the glorious cultivation of God's creation comes attached to a commitment to European cultures in particular as the most evolved or developed versions of such cultivation.[54] In a similar manner, critics argue that *Gaudium et Spes* evinces a kind of positivity about modernity and modern cultures that at times appears naive to the ways in which these worldviews involve commitments that are deeply at odds with Christian belief.[55] This is not a unique failure of Kuyper or Vatican II—it is the nature of culture that it fosters a kind of blindness to its own failings and subversions, leaving us all dangerously inattentive to our own culture's failings.

Culture as Instrument of Providence, Revelation, and Redemption

Yet the Christian perspective is that culture does not remain mired entirely in the moral disorder of Lamech and Babel. While it is true that all cultures (in the anthropological sense of the word) and even the artifacts of culture (arts and scholarship) are tainted by the brokenness of the fall, redemption likewise extends "far as the curse is found." This truth is reflected in the church's robust commitment from its earliest days to see the gospel take root in any and all cultural soils, using the church's diverse cultural gifts to understand and proclaim the good news of Jesus.

Theologically, this posture is rooted in the triune God's own willingness to get his hands dirty. He reveals himself in existing human languages, using divine titles (with the exception of the tetragrammaton) that are borrowed from local cultures, even willing to risk confusion and syncretism. When "the word of the Lord" comes to prophets and apostles, the grammar is not otherworldly but draped in the linguistic quirks of the prophet himself—and

54. In Kuyper's influential Stone Lectures, in which he lays out his understanding of Calvinism, he argues (in line with many scientists of his time) that humanity is on an upward trajectory since its beginning in Africa, with European Calvinist Christianity at the top of that evolutionary development (Abraham Kuyper, *Calvinism: Six Stone-Lectures* [Amsterdam: Höveker & Wormser, 1899], 37–45). See also Cornelis van der Kooi, "The Concept of Culture in Abraham Kuyper, Herman Bavinck, and Karl Barth," in *Crossroad Discourses between Christianity and Culture*, ed. Jerald D. Gort, Henry Jansen, and Wessel Stoker (New York: Rodopi, 2010), 42.

55. Thus, Tracey Rowland argues that *Gaudium et Spes* (and a whole line of thinking connected to it) is fundamentally mistaken in its assessment of modern culture as either neutral or conducive to the flourishing of Christian faith. She suggests that contemporary Roman Catholic theologians should be far more skeptical of modernity than they have generally been. See Tracey Rowland, *Culture and the Thomist Tradition: After Vatican II* (New York: Routledge, 2003), 1–50.

so God's perfection is revealed through clumsy language that nevertheless accomplishes divinely intended ends. He provides for access to his presence through materials curated by artisans wielding their distinctive, local skills, so that his holiness is mediated through a culturally embodied beauty that somehow manages to communicate transcendence. In the incarnate Christ, he unites himself permanently with all humanity through uniting himself with the culture of a particular tribe and clan; thus, God himself learns to speak with a particular accent and cultivates a distinctive set of tastes in beauty, music, and food. The clearest revelation of God turns out not to be an acultural set of principles but, rather, a human life and death that can only be understood in its connection to a particular culture and time.

Rather than interpreting this as an indication that first-century Jewish culture is the pinnacle of cultural evolution, with Pentecost looming large in their origin story, Christians have historically regarded all of this as an indication that any culture can serve as an adequate vehicle for revelation— through the translation of Scripture—and a potential host for the flourishing of the good news. Because the Father, Son, and Spirit have first moved to accept the risks of deep cultural engagement in order to cultivate connection, understanding, and communion with humanity in all its wild diversity, Christians have sought to embody a pan-ethnic and pan-cultural mode of existence. As we saw at the start of this chapter with the *Epistle to Diognetus*, the earliest Christian documents lay claim to this conception of the relationship between culture and faith; but in the winds of modernity, which brought a pervasive instinct to flee from cultural particularity, this model was perceived as a threat rather than an asset to the faith.

At this point, we must introduce a theological distinction: while there is a sense in which all cultures are subject to divine blessing and the Spirit's work of revelation, this "common grace" is distinct from the special work of revelation in which God's word comes directly to the people of God through the mouths of the prophets and, ultimately, in the person of Christ. Thus, God gives good gifts to all, so that all cultures enjoy the benefits of common grace and distributed or general revelation; yet the fullness of God's self-revelation emerges in the context of distinctive covenant relationships with his people. This distinction is crucial because this fuller, clearer revelation of God must be used as a plumb line for recognizing the seeds of truth scattered abroad. Without giving priority to Scripture and Christ as the clearest word from God, it is impossible to tell which aspects of our cultures bear the fingerprints of the triune God and which are the handiwork of his enemies.

This does not mean that Greco-Roman culture or (before that) ancient Near Eastern cultures obtain special status as entities uniquely unstained by sin or naturally connected to the triune God; Greek, Hebrew, and Aramaic are not, as it were, the languages of heaven. Like the people of Israel, the prophets and apostles—and their languages and cultures—are chosen in divine freedom and not based on their special merits (Deut. 7:6–11). Thus, while Christians owe a special kind of attention to these languages and cultures to better understand the unique self-revelation that the triune God accomplished in and through them—and indeed, the medium and the message are inseparably intertwined—what is *special* in special revelation is the revelation, not its cultural or linguistic media.

At the same time, it is notable that, in the first centuries of Christianity, many Christians regarded Greco-Roman culture broadly as a *preparatio evangelica* (preparation for the gospel). Though they recognized that it was replete with brokenness and idolatry, they also saw in this culture—in the thinking of Plato (several centuries before Christ) and Plotinus (two centuries after Christ), for example—intimations pointing toward the true God, and a rich array of vocabulary and images that were necessary (or at least useful) for understanding and articulating the unique revelation of Christ. This understanding of culture could be construed maximally or minimally— each one bringing its own attendant dangers—but, in theological terms, Christians were making a claim about God's providential working within these cultures, allowing them to become fertile soil for a new stage of revelation and redemption.[56] Similarly, as Christians observed the gospel taking root in cultural contexts beyond the Greco-Roman world, they discerned that the Spirit had providentially come along beforehand, tilling the soil and

56. Augustine argues that Platonic philosophy has "recognized the true God as the author of all things, the source of the light of truth, and the bountiful bestower of all blessedness" (*City of God* 8.5, in *A Select Library of Nicene and Post-Nicene Fathers of the Christian Church*, 1st series, ed. Philip Schaff, vol. 2, *St. Augustine's "City of God" and "Christian Doctrine"* [Grand Rapids: Eerdmans, 1956]). Then, in his spiritual autobiography, he explains that his previous reading and training in Platonism gave him important pre-understandings that could later be completed— and corrected—as he encountered Scripture and Christ (*Confessions* 7.9–21). Augustine was the most influential early theologian to make this argument, but he was following a long tradition of Christian thinkers before him who made similar claims. For an elegant account of this stream of thought in antiquity, see Robert Louis Wilken, *The Spirit of Early Christian Thought: Seeking the Face of God* (New Haven: Yale University Press, 2003).

dispersing seeds that would eventually allow for the flourishing of Christian witness.[57]

This agricultural analogy can prove useful in discerning what exactly is at play when Christian faith finds expression in a cultural context for the first time. Does the church bring a new cultural "plant" to replace one that is being uprooted or cut down? Or is it grafting the gospel onto the existing flora of any given culture, completing the partial glimpses of revelation that were already present?[58] Both of these metaphors must be partially right, but they are also partially flawed. As we have already noted, neither Israel in the Old Testament nor the church in the New Testament endeavor to create a new culture *ex nihilo*; instead, they use resources that are almost entirely borrowed from cultural neighbors and languages, partly out of necessity and partly (in the case of the apostolic-era church) because of their calling to make disciples of all nations, which requires the adoption of local languages and concepts. Yet even if Christians use the linguistic and cultural tools already available, they use them to say things that have not been said before and to describe a God whose image has been obscured and distorted by the very language and cultural imagery that is now being taken up to translate God's self-revelation. Thus, even if the Christian works only with pre-owned materials, she is cultivating something new, and this is true whenever the gospel is taking root in any new place or time. Kenyan theologian John Mbiti describes this paradox especially well: "Cultural identities are temporary, serving to yield us as Christians to the fullness of our identity with Christ. Paradoxically, culture snatches us away from Christ, it denies that we are His; yet when it is best understood, at its meeting with Christianity, culture drives us to Christ and surrenders us to Him, affirming us to be permanently, totally and unconditionally His own."[59] To better understand this dynamic that Mbiti elegantly summarizes, it will help to look closely at a theologian

57. Over the centuries, Christians have often discussed whether Greco-Roman culture was unique in its suitability for Christian witness, and similar debates continue today. One of the best and most important contemporary engagements with this discussion is the work of Kwame Bediako, who contends that the soil of African primal religions was more of a *preparatio evangelica* than most have previously realized (*Christianity in Africa: The Renewal of a Non-Western Religion* [Maryknoll, NY: Orbis Books, 1995]).

58. This imagery is used in the Vatican document *Evangelii Praecones*.

59. John Mbiti, "African Indigenous Culture in Relation to Evangelism and Church Development," in *The Gospel and Frontier Peoples*, ed. R. Pierce Beaver (Pasadena, CA: William Carey Library, 1973), 94, quoted in Kwame Bediako, *Theology and Identity: The Impact of Culture upon Christian Thought in the Second Century and in Modern Africa* (Oxford: Regnum, 1992), 441.

in the Majority World church who is consciously wrestling with the way that his local culture can and should shape his theological reflection.

Case Study: Theology, Culture, and Chinese Christians

Carver T. Yu is a Chinese theologian based in Hong Kong. Aside from founding and, for many years, leading a key seminary in the region, Yu has written widely in both Chinese and English. His approach to theology begins with a robust view of revelation as the ultimate arbiter of theological development. "Theology," he writes, "has to follow the inner logic of the revelation of the sovereign God, who chose to reveal himself by his Word—the Word spoken to us through prophets, and ultimately as the Word incarnate."[60] Yet because he constantly operated in multiple cultures and lived through a season of rapid cultural transition in Hong Kong, Yu developed a keen awareness of the shaping force of culture for Christian theology. As a result, Yu is more insightful than most in reflecting on how we can attend to culture as a shaping force for theology while at the same time ensuring that it remains focused on the triune God revealed in Scripture and in Christ.

Culture matters for the theologian because it is a crucial component of humanity, God's image-bearers who have the unique ability and calling among God's creatures to bring order to and cultivate his good creation.[61] Every culture seeks in some sense to fulfill the mandate to "till and keep" (Gen. 2:15 NRSV), and seeks a measure of "wholeness for human existence."[62] Culture fosters communication and communion, and is an arena for God's "preserving and redeeming grace."[63] Even in cultures that vigorously reject the Christian doctrine of God and creation, we hear echoes of God's goodness, justice, and glory. For this reason, Yu argues that culture is a promising and essential partner in the theological task.

Yet the fall alters the picture. Just as the land once required only tilling, but after the fall it requires wrestling with thorns and thistles, so also

---

60. Carver T. Yu, "Theology in a Context of Radical Cultural Shift: A Chinese Reflection," in *Asian Christian Theology: Evangelical Perspectives*, ed. Timoteo D. Gener and Stephen T. Pardue (Carlisle, UK: Langham Global Library, 2019), 298.

61. Carver T. Yu, "The Bible and Culture in the Shaping of Asian Theology," *Transformation* 15, no. 3 (July 1998): 19.

62. Carver T. Yu, "Culture from an Evangelical Perspective," *Transformation* 17, no. 3 (2000): 82–83.

63. Yu, "Bible and Culture," 19.

"the distortion of humanity sets in and permeates every aspect of culture."[64] Cultures develop norms and structures that violate rather than promote human integrity; that alienate instead of fostering communion; that offer honor and obedience to idols rather than to the triune creator. The created goodness of culture remains, and God sustains and preserves even through these distortions. But every culture is now a mixture, containing within it "God's original promise" alongside human rebellion and confusion.[65]

Thus, Yu notes that part of the theological task must be "identifying God's preserving and redeeming grace at work in culture."[66] This is what many efforts at contextual theology get right, offering an important corrective to approaches that either ignore culture or treat it as a threat to doctrinal purity. Theologians should be ready to search for echoes of the Christian story in the art, writing, and practices of non-Christian cultures, recognizing these as genuine "spiritual resources for the attainment of human wholeness."[67]

Yet because of sin's pervasive distorting effects, Yu explains, "affirmation is not enough." In fact, approaches to contextual theology that uncritically affirm cultures in their entirety, often in the name of preserving social harmony, "have not taken culture seriously enough."[68] Further still, to turn a blind eye to culture's distortions is to miss the heart of the good news—that God does not leave us in our cultural bondage but liberates us through the redeeming and reconciling work of Christ.

So theology always requires cultural intelligence and discernment. We must understand the dynamics of our cultures and the cultures in which we minister; this is a prerequisite for our work of recognizing where the image-bearing power of God shines through and where the power of sin is at work to undermine God's good purposes. Without cultural understanding, the theologian cannot aid the church in its divinely assigned work of "real-life transformation."[69] At the same time, theology cannot and must not be reduced to cultural studies. Its most basic contribution is its studious (even "scientific") attention to God himself and his definitive self-revelation in the written and incarnate Word. Yu demonstrates that theology done with cultural discernment and exegetical care can be a powerful force.

---

64. Yu, "Culture from an Evangelical Perspective," 83.
65. Yu, "Culture from an Evangelical Perspective," 83.
66. Yu, "Bible and Culture," 19.
67. Yu, "Bible and Culture," 20.
68. Yu, "Bible and Culture," 20.
69. Yu, "Theology in a Context of Radical Cultural Shift," 298.

In a recent essay, Yu addresses the present state of affairs in mainland China, where decades of rapid development and social change have sown widespread confusion and disagreement about the future of Chinese society. He highlights two tendencies in contemporary Chinese culture: one to push for ever-expanding capitalism at all costs, and the other to press toward the recovery of the Chinese cultural past. Yu notes that throughout much of its recent history, Christians in China have largely ignored social issues like these. At times, they have even exacerbated the challenges—for example, when, for decades, Western missionaries promoted a vision of Western superiority that only reinforced the notion that Christianity is fundamentally a Western faith incompatible with genuine expressions of Chinese culture. More broadly, Christians have generally not viewed the social crises facing wider society as a *theological* problem.[70]

In contrast, Yu proposes that Christian theology is precisely the tool needed to offer a uniquely positive vision for the future of Chinese society amid its current crises. In brief, we can note two fruitful aspects of his proposal. First, Yu highlights the truth and beauty in the Confucian tradition's conception of human flourishing. For example, he notes that in the Confucian use of the concept of *ren* ("life-communion with the aim of enriching one another"[71]) we gain a vision for human flourishing that is richer and in fact more biblical than the notion of salvation as it is often conceived. *Ren* gestures at the reality that "the human being, to accomplish full humanity, has to participate with heaven and earth to transform and nourish all things under heaven, thus coming into union with all."[72] Yu argues that this concept gets something right about the biblically sanctioned vision for human well-being and can help evangelicals gain a deeper and wider sense of God's redemptive work, which we often consider narrowly and individualistically. This is not only an occasion to deepen our understanding of our own faith; it also serves to affirm that the Chinese cultural past has genuine gifts to offer the modern context.

At the same time, Yu does not shy away from judging the Confucian tradition where it is found wanting. "From the Christian perspective," he writes, "the Confucian tradition has a serious flaw in its lack of awareness of human

---

70. Yu, "Theology in a Context of Radical Cultural Shift," 302.
71. Móu Zōng-sán, *Lì Shǐ Zhé Xué* [Philosophy of history] (Taiwan: Student Press, 1976), 178, quoted in Yu, "Theology in a Context of Radical Cultural Shift," 308.
72. Yu, "Theology in a Context of Radical Cultural Shift," 308.

depravity." Lacking a robust sense of sin and the captivity it creates, Confucianism promotes liberation "not from transcendent power, but from self-reflection and self-discipline." The Christian can thus affirm that the Confucian tradition gets something right in its full-orbed vision of human flourishing, but this must not lead her to hold back in "proclaiming the reality of human sinfulness as well as the inability of human beings to save themselves."[73]

Yu commends a similar approach for engaging the current crisis in Chinese society as it relates to market capitalism. He documents the way in which China's extremely rapid economic growth since the 1980s has yielded many goods while also cultivating a system in which "efficiency and functionality" have become "the measure of all value."[74] One result of this shift has been the increasing tendency in Chinese society to treat institutions like marriage and family as contractual affairs, designed to facilitate "the exchange of commodities and rational calculation of maximum benefits."[75] While many Chinese recognize the threats of this approach to relationships that have historically been maintained as sacred, they are in need of a moral framework that can remain relevant in the present moment while also preserving these crucial social structures.

Yu argues that the Christian concept of covenant, and especially of God's covenantal love, can make a key contribution: "Here, the narrative of the covenantal nature of God's being and action, the gravity of covenantal love as manifested in Jesus Christ, the covenantal nature of the human person as the image of God, and the covenantal nature of the whole creation is highly relevant for upholding the integrity of Asian cultures in general and Chinese culture in particular. For the Christian tradition, unconditional covenantal love is the highest value, the measure of all values. In fact, covenant is the structure of created reality."[76]

What is important to see is that Yu's approach acknowledges the essential role that culture plays in the theological task. Yu clearly acknowledges the supremacy of the good news, letting Scripture be both the outer boundary and the driving force of his theological reflection. At the same time, he does not relegate culture to the final stages of the theological process. Instead, he shows how the local context raises the basic theological questions that the Chinese

73. Yu, "Theology in a Context of Radical Cultural Shift," 308.
74. Yu, "Theology in a Context of Radical Cultural Shift," 309.
75. Yu, "Theology in a Context of Radical Cultural Shift," 311.
76. Yu, "Theology in a Context of Radical Cultural Shift," 311.

church must address, and he acknowledges the ways in which Confucian language and concepts help us grasp important aspects of salvation and human flourishing that are often neglected in other cultural expressions of the faith.

Conclusion

In this chapter, we have tried to specify more clearly what we mean when we speak of "culture." We started by highlighting several caveats that should warn us against simplistic accounts of culture, noting that our cultures are constantly changing and overlapping with one another. Even if the "culture concept" in its current expression is relatively new, we saw that the idea is ultimately an important factor in Christian Scripture and theology. It is because humans are image-bearers of the God who creates, orders, and cultivates that they are capable of creating cultures. Culture is the site of human corruption and rebellion, but also of God's redemptive work, which does not abolish but perfects cultural distinctives. Both Pentecost and the multitude in heaven point to the reality not only that culture is unavoidable in our preaching and witness but also that it is, in fact, a material gift for the church to use in its common life of discipleship. Thus, culture matters for theology—that task of helping the church give disciplined attention to speaking of, worshiping, and living before the triune God.

Thus, we have argued that Christians stand ready to adopt and adapt anything and everything in culture that is amenable to redemption, especially those instances of goodness, truth, and beauty that are the result of God's common grace. In doing so, they seek to recognize areas of culture that are especially suitable for the grafting on of Christian faith, hunting for seeds of truth ready to be activated by the gospel of Christ. At the same time, Christians turn the tools of all cultures against themselves, at times using a culture's most potent forms to condemn its dearest achievements as falling under the judgment of a holy God. Knowing the blinding power of culture, Christians depend on the wisdom of the wider church—especially the church in other cultures and the church in ages past—to ensure that their uses of culture are not ultimately at odds with the church's service to Christ. This turn to the wider church leads us naturally to our next task: to specify more clearly *how* culture matters for theology, and especially how it can influence theology in a way that honors the church's remarkable diversity while preserving its authentic unity.

4

A Great Multitude from Every Tribe and Tongue

Grounding Contextual Theology in the Doctrine of the Church

> After this I looked, and behold, a great multitude that no one could number, from every nation, from all tribes and peoples and languages, standing before the throne and before the Lamb, clothed in white robes, with palm branches in their hands, and crying out with a loud voice, "Salvation belongs to our God who sits on the throne, and to the Lamb!"
>
> —Revelation 7:9–10

In the previous chapter, we investigated the idea of culture—first clarifying what we mean by the concept, and then highlighting culture's place in the biblical narrative and in a basic theological framework. Now the heart of the matter lies before us as we begin to specify the way in which Christian doctrine propels, shapes, and delimits the force of culture in theological reflection.

As we saw in the first chapter, theologians concerned with protecting the evangel, the good news, should rightly wish to ensure that, whatever attention we grant to cultural realities, we insist tenaciously on speaking of and worshiping the one and holy triune God of the gospel. Thus, whatever an evangelical contextual theology is, it must be so rooted in Christian doctrine that its magnetic north is not distorted by culturally constructed idols. At the same time, we have noted that human cultures—while imperfect and marred by the fall—are brimming with gifts from God designed to build the community of the kingdom and to clarify the gospel. In the real world, these forces sometimes act as two engines pulling in opposite directions: one propels theology to focus on the once-for-all good news of Jesus's work for all people, and the other spurs the church toward attention to the wild diversity it invites and cultivates as the gospel spreads into new contexts.[1]

The stakes here are significant. If theologians attend too much to cultural diversity or give it too much authority in the process, they risk not only the idolatry of cultural identity (worshiping whatever the local culture exalts as praiseworthy) but also the splintering of the church into thousands of isolated "sandboxes" that will struggle to experience the fellowship of the Spirit. Yet if fear of cultural hegemony, political correctness, or disunifying diversification pushes us to ignore the diversity of the church in order to protect the unity and purity of Christian doctrine, we are sure to fail as well. Not only will we miss the fresh insight into the gospel that the Spirit gives as the church grows into its full maturity in Christ; we will also almost certainly wind up baptizing the most prevalent cultural forms of Christianity (whether American, Korean, Brazilian, etc.), confusing these cultural instantiations of the faith with the gospel itself.

To succeed in holding on to these two dynamics—the animating power of the good news for all people and the gifts of local, specific cultures— evangelical contextual theologies need a trustworthy framework that can guide the process along. For assistance, theologians should look to the store-house of Christian doctrine to guide us; after all, we are hardly the first generation of Christians to grapple with the challenges of finding unity amid flourishing diversity.

This chapter will contend that *evangelical contextual theologies should look to the Christian doctrine of the church in order to coordinate the once-for-all of the*

---

1. In an insightful analysis of these dynamics, John Stott notes that this tension may be inherent to evangelical faith and can ultimately be a source of productive discipline as we learn to become "gospel people" (John Stott, *Evangelical Truth: A Personal Plea for Unity, Integrity and Faithfulness*, rev. ed. [Carlisle, UK: Langham Global Library, 2013], 16–18).

gospel and the remarkably diverse expressions of the faith that emerge in the real world. A robust ecclesiology must ultimately be the doctrinal anchor for the project of contextual theology because theology is, after all, a calling given to and for the benefit of the church—that special creature which Word and Spirit bind together across space, time, culture, and language—as it seeks to hear, proclaim, and respond to the being and work of the triune God.

To recognize the value of this approach, we will first identify and explore three other concepts that often serve to ground the church's attention to the gifts of cultural diversity and particularity: the process of globalization, the doctrine of the Trinity, and the doctrine of the incarnation. As we will see, while each of these concepts gestures in a helpful direction, each is ultimately unsuitable for underwriting the project of a gospel-oriented contextual theology. Understanding their shortcomings will help clarify what it must mean for the church to follow its calling to do theology in light of the great multitude God is gathering from every tribe and tongue.

Globalization and the Problem of "Global Theology"

For decades, scholars have sought to foster greater attention to the diversity of the global church, and many have urged the church to turn this diversity into a source of substantial theological gain. One of the most common modes of calling theologians forward in this regard has to do with globalization, that process by which "more people become more closely connected across larger distances, and grow more aware of their connections as well."[2] The concept originates as a description of specific economic dynamics that rapidly accelerated in the late twentieth century. As international travel, world trade, and migration exploded, supply chains and marketplaces that were once isolated and local became cross-continental and cross-cultural, with effects on everyone: suppliers now had new opportunities but also new competition; freed from the constraints of any one community, multinational companies could arrange sprawling empires that prioritized efficiency; and, at least according to advocates of globalization and free trade, customers benefitted from the new world order by gaining access to better and more affordable goods.

---

2. Frank J. Lechner and John Boli, "General Introduction," in *The Globalization Reader*, ed. Frank J. Lechner and John Boli, 6th ed. (Hoboken, NJ: Wiley-Blackwell, 2019), 1.

If one adopts this optimistic view of economic globalization, it is easy to see how it may be understood as an ideal model for the global church's theological development. A famous 1958 essay advocating for the free movement of goods highlights the way in which a product as simple as the modern yellow pencil benefits from innumerable people around the globe with different abilities and various goods to contribute to the process. One group fells the trees, another mines the graphite (depending on thousands of others who created their tools and developed the techniques), and scores of others collaborate to turn the raw materials into a final product whose simplicity belies the complex process of cooperation underlying it.[3] In the same way, we might imagine the global church working together, assembling the best insights and practices of thousands of local churches in order to produce a globalized theology. Such an approach to contextual or global theology could conceive of itself as a modern application of the apostle Paul's description of the body of Christ, in which various parts have diverse functions but work together in harmony. While such collaboration was once a merely local endeavor, the interconnectedness of the modern world allows us to widen the circle of cooperation, leading to better theology and improved practice.[4]

Despite the positive analogies between economic globalization and the potential for fruitful theological exchange, there are powerful reasons to reject globalization as the primary warrant or conceptual framework for contextual theological reflection. First, despite globalization's many positive deliverances, it has also proved uniquely powerful at accelerating old injustices and creating new ones. Global demand for cheap goods has often led to the ruinous and unsustainable capture of natural resources, the development of exploitative and inhumane labor practices, and a loss of local particularity to the new homogenous world order. Contextual theology that takes economic globalization as its anchoring metaphor, therefore, must face the likelihood of analogous deformities. For example, it may easily yield a consumerist-driven process in which "tastemaker" Christians from prosperous churches pick the theological insights from abroad that they most appreciate and develop these raw materials into a "global theology" that is

---

3. Leonard E. Read, "I, Pencil," *The Freeman*, December 1958.
4. For a thoughtful and fairly early account of how globalization may affect theology, see Robert J. Schreiter, *The New Catholicity: Theology between the Global and the Local* (Maryknoll, NY: Orbis Books, 1997), 1–27.

then exported everywhere as the latest and greatest theological composition, displacing important local efforts to understand and apply the faith.

In the world of markets and economics, the backlash against the most exploitative forms of globalization is well established, yielding, among other things, a cottage industry that aims to produce the same benefits as Walmart and McDonald's—access to the bountiful riches of the global supply chain for consumers—without the deleterious effects. This has produced the world of fair-trade coffee and movements to prioritize the purchase of local goods and one-of-a-kind artisanal handiwork rather than the homogenous products of multi-national corporations. But this hardly provides a better model for theological reflection. While they may be more humane and less exploitative, such approaches do not fundamentally alter the dynamics of poorer suppliers catering to the desires of well-to-do consumers. An echo of such movements in the world of theology would fare only modestly better.[5]

Laying aside the shortcomings of this approach, we would do well to acknowledge that those calling for the globalization of theology are onto something important. It is indeed the case that the increasing interconnectedness of the world provides unprecedented opportunities for churches of diverse cultures to unite in fellowship, cooperative practice, and theological exchange. Moreover, in calling for mutual accountability and exchange between worldwide churches, scholars calling for the globalization of theology are making a vast improvement over other proposals, such as those that deny the importance of culture for theology altogether, those that pursue a colonialist approach to theology (whether implicitly or explicitly), or those that seek to develop radically local theology that has nothing to do with the wider church.[6] In the end, the problem with globalization as a model for contemporary contextual theologies is not that it is entirely wrong, but rather that it is incomplete and lacking in orientation. Rooted in principles

5. See the work of Joerg Rieger, who notes that globalization has always been a part of the Christian story and that responses to it will require more creative engagement than we often initially assume (Joerg Rieger, *Globalization and Theology* [Nashville: Abingdon, 2010]).

6. Along these lines, see the essays in Craig Ott and Harold A. Netland, eds., *Globalizing Theology: Belief and Practice in an Era of World Christianity* (Grand Rapids: Baker Academic, 2006); Jeffrey P. Greenman and Gene L. Green, eds., *Global Theology in Evangelical Perspective: Exploring the Contextual Nature of Theology and Mission* (Downers Grove, IL: IVP Academic, 2012); Charles R. Ringma, Karen Hollenbeck-Wuest, and Athena O. Gorospe, eds., *God at the Borders: Globalization, Migration and Diaspora* (Mandaluyong, Philippines: OMF Literature, 2015); Pui-lan Kwok, Cecilia González-Andrieu, and Dwight N. Hopkins, eds., *Teaching Global Theologies: Power and Praxis* (Waco: Baylor University Press, 2015).

of global trade (or in social-scientific critiques of power)—rather than in Scripture or Christian tradition—it is theologically anemic, incapable of offering a deeply Christian vision for theology in the twenty-first century.

Trinity as a Theological Anchor for Unity amid Diversity

An alternative approach that appears more promising is to anchor contextual theologies in doctrines that are native to Christian theological soil: the Trinity and incarnation. These doctrines form the very core of the Christian faith, and each of them attends in its own way to the challenges of universality and particularity that surface when we consider how to balance the local and global aspects of Christian theology in an era of world Christianity. It is reasonable to hope that these doctrines can provide not only theological warrant but also a model for the church's effort to pursue genuine locality while also preserving unity.

We can begin with the doctrine of the Trinity, which contemporary theologians have applied to the matter of unity and diversity in two primary directions. The first is primarily intellectual and begins as an attempt to grapple with the problems created by the growing awareness of diversity and particularity brought about by modernity. Since the Enlightenment and scientific revolution, the library of human knowledge has expanded exponentially, revealing more and more not only about the created order but also about the vast variety with which humans interpret reality and organize their values. This heightened awareness of diversity has been accompanied by an increasingly acute anxiety that, to borrow from the Irish poet W. B. Yeats, "the centre cannot hold,"[7] that our apprehension of reality, or perhaps reality itself, is hopelessly fragmented.

In this context, the Trinity offers a distinctively Christian way of understanding plurality that is no threat to the unity (and comprehensibility) of truth. Put differently, the concepts developed by Christian theologians for understanding the plurality and unity in the Godhead point to a strategy for engaging the wild diversity of cultures and the created order discovered in modernity with hope instead of despair.[8] A thicket of proposals apply

---

7. W. B. Yeats, "The Second Coming," in *The Oxford Book of English Verse*, ed. Christopher Ricks (New York: Oxford University Press, 1999), 525.

8. On this application of the Trinity generally, see esp. Colin E. Gunton, *The Promise of Trinitarian Theology* (Edinburgh: T&T Clark, 1991); Colin E. Gunton, *The One, the Three, and the*

this insight specifically to the challenge of Christian engagement with other religions.[9]

The second application of the doctrine of the Trinity has to do with the ordering of human social life. In the latter half of the twentieth century, scholars began arguing with increasing frequency that this doctrine is an underappreciated tool for understanding the divine design for organizing society. Construed in the broadest terms possible, the idea is that the Trinity provides a grounding for healthy political arrangements. Thus, whereas a monadic, singular deity might suggest a society that finds unity through the oppressive application of hierarchy and homogeneity, in the Trinity we encounter a model of social interaction that prizes equality and unity while simultaneously respecting diversity.[10] Pioneering Brazilian theologian Leonardo Boff points in this direction, arguing that "a society that takes its inspiration from trinitarian communion cannot tolerate class differences, dominations based on power (economic, sexual or ideological) that subjects those who are different to those who exercise that power and marginalizes the former from the latter."[11]

Boff takes this point further by applying it specifically to God's people; the church is called to be a society that mirrors the mutuality in diversity of the triune God. "Ecclesial communion," Boff explains, "expresses trinitarian communion: each Person is distinct, but accepts the others and surrenders fully to the others."[12] In a similar proposal that also draws some distinctions from Boff's, Catherine Mowry LaCugna argues that "the reconception of God's monarchy from a trinitarian perspective was

---

Many: God, Creation, and the Culture of Modernity (New York: Cambridge University Press, 1993); Kevin J. Vanhoozer, ed., The Trinity in a Pluralistic Age: Theological Essays on Culture and Religion (Grand Rapids: Eerdmans, 1996).

9. For two especially helpful analyses of these proposals, see Veli-Matti Kärkkäinen, Trinity and Religious Pluralism: The Doctrine of the Trinity in Christian Theology of Religions (Aldersot, UK: Ashgate, 2004); Gerald R. McDermott and Harold A. Netland, A Trinitarian Theology of Religions: An Evangelical Proposal (New York: Oxford University Press, 2014).

10. This idea seems to have been first advanced by Erik Peterson, a German theologian in the 1930s. For an English translation of his key writings in this area, see "Monotheism as a Political Problem: A Contribution to the History of Political Theology in the Roman Empire," in Theological Tractates, ed. and trans. Michael J. Hollerich (Stanford, CA: Stanford University Press, 2011), 68–105.

11. Leonardo Boff, Trinity and Society (Maryknoll, NY: Orbis Books, 1988), 151. Boff builds on the foundation laid by Jürgen Moltmann in important ways. See esp. Jürgen Moltmann, The Trinity and the Kingdom: The Doctrine of God, trans. Margaret Kohl (Minneapolis: Fortress, 1993), 191–222.

12. Boff, Trinity and Society, 153–54.

potentially the most far-reaching and radical theological and political fruit of the doctrine of the Trinity," as it is in this view of God that we find a vision of "mutuality rooted in communion among persons."[13] As the perfect instantiation of persons in communion, the Trinity reveals—and through the Spirit, effects—a model of *koinōnia* (communion, fellowship) that "does not swallow up the individual, nor obscure his or her uniqueness and unique contribution."[14] Going further in the same direction, Miroslav Volf argues that the Trinity must be the basis of our social ordering, drawing a direct line between the perichoretic (mutually indwelling) interactions of Father, Son, and Spirit and the unity that humans can achieve in spite of their distinctive identities.[15]

Neither the "intellectual" application of the Trinity nor its "social" application can be dismissed entirely. The uniquely Christian confession of the triune God does hint at a solution to the longstanding problem of finding unity amid multiple perspectives and communities, and Christians are correct in seeking a kind of analogy between their behavior toward one another and the perfect love exhibited by God himself (Matt. 5:48; John 17:20–23; Eph. 5:1–2). Yet there are serious limitations and risks associated with both.

Regarding the social application of the Trinity, we should first question the premise that strict monotheism is destined to produce oppressive social structures. To the contrary, as Spanish theologian Antonio González highlights, the prophets of Israel appeal precisely to the "direct and exclusive rule" of God over Israel *as the basis for* social justice and concern for the poor. "Instead of signifying the legitimation of authoritarian forms of power on earth," he writes, monotheism was "the means by which those powers were critiqued."[16] That is, precisely because God alone is king of the universe, no one else may be permitted to rewrite the rules of justice. Moreover, the "good news" proclaimed by New Testament writers and early Christians is not the revelation that there is diversity in the Godhead, promoting egalitarian social

13. Catherine Mowry LaCugna, *God for Us: The Trinity and Christian Life* (San Francisco: HarperSanFrancisco, 1991), 399.

14. LaCugna, *God for Us*, 299.

15. Miroslav Volf, *After Our Likeness: The Church as the Image of the Trinity* (Grand Rapids: Eerdmans, 1998); Miroslav Volf, "'The Trinity Is Our Social Program': The Doctrine of the Trinity and the Shape of Social Engagement," *Modern Theology* 14, no. 3 (1998): 403–23.

16. Antonio González, "The Trinity as Gospel," in *Majority World Theology: Christian Doctrine in Global Context*, ed. Gene L. Green, Stephen T. Pardue, and K. K. Yeo (Downers Grove, IL: IVP Academic, 2020), 52.

structures; their understanding of the gospel is instead that the *singular God of creation* has come to dwell with and rescue his people through the life, death, and resurrection of Jesus. The New Testament church's "demand for equality and fraternity" is thus not rooted in "the communitarian images in the heavens," but in the radical claim that Jesus has inaugurated a new era of the one God's reign over the earth in which the first is last and the least the greatest.[17]

Perhaps equally important to the biblical critique raised by González, a wave of objectors have argued that "hard" social trinitarianism generally relies on a view of the Trinity that would have been rejected by most of classical Christianity, proposing an understanding of the trinitarian "persons" as independent cooperative beings.[18] In addition, it assumes an alliance between the Trinity and progressive politics that is unwarranted and historically naive. These critics rightly suggest instead that it is our *participation in* the life of the triune God—not the creation of societies that mirror the interrelations of the persons—that brings good news and liberation.

None of these arguments rule out a less direct and more disciplined connection between the doctrine of the triune God and social or ecclesial relations. But when one follows the discipline of attending to the details of the canonical witness and the historical commitments of the Christian church, what is "new" in the proposals of Boff, Volf, and others largely disappears, and we are left still needing better theological tools to address the problems of unity and diversity.

The intellectual application of the Trinity fares slightly better, as it generally does not rely on the questionable analogy between human persons and the "persons" of Father, Son, and Spirit. Yet, once again, the problem is that the doctrine of the Trinity as expressed in Scripture and as outlined in early Christian thought is simply not designed to map out a certain relationship of unity and diversity of creaturely realities. Thus, while early Christians recognized more than anyone the central importance of the doctrine of Trinity, they did not usually apply these insights to the plurality and unity

---

17. González, "Trinity as Gospel," 57.

18. Kathryn Tanner, *Christ the Key* (New York: Cambridge University Press, 2010), 207–46; Stephen R. Holmes, *The Holy Trinity: Understanding God's Life* (Milton Keynes, UK: Paternoster, 2012); Karen Kilby, "Trinity and Politics: An Apophatic Approach," in *Advancing Trinitarian Theology: Explorations in Constructive Dogmatics*, ed. Oliver D. Crisp and Fred Sanders (Grand Rapids: Zondervan, 2014), 75–93.

of human knowledge or religious pluralism.[19] Moreover, to the degree that we seek an analogy between the diversity and unity of the Trinity and the diversity and unity of human knowledge, cultures, and religions, great care must be taken to specify *what kind of analogy we are discovering*. For example, if there is a kind of "unity" to all religious traditions, what is the nature of that unity, and how is this similar to and different from the unity of the Father, Son, and Spirit as revealed in Scripture?[20] Again, we often find here that the way the doctrine of God can best exert influence on our conception of contextual theology is through the drama of salvation as narrated by the prophets and apostles—the triune God coming to the rescue of creation through the redemptive missions of the Son and Spirit, revealed especially in the incarnation and Pentecost—rather than through a direct line from the nature of the Trinity to the interactions of the church's diverse members.[21]

Incarnational Models of Contextual Theology

If we cannot rely on an analogy with the Trinity to frame our approach to the diversity and unity we seek in an evangelical contextual theology, then it makes sense to turn to the incarnation instead. The analogy between the incarnation and the mission of the church in bringing local expression to the universal and eternal truth of Christian faith is almost too obvious to need explanation. If one of the great insights of modern theology is that we must acknowledge that it is in Christ that we find the clearest revelation of God, then the God we discover in the incarnation is not some deity standing aloof and above all human contexts but instead a God who wills to participate in the deepest possible way with humanity in all its specificity, locality, and particularity. In Jesus, God speaks with a local accent, taking up a single culture while also demonstrating that such particularity is no barrier to communicating eternally and universally transformative good news.

19. It is good here to recall that Christians in antiquity lived before modern-day globalization, but still in a highly pluralistic environment. See, e.g., Bruce W. Winter, "In Public and in Private: Early Christians and Religious Pluralism," in *One God, One Lord: Christianity in a World of Religious Pluralism*, ed. Andrew D. Clarke and Bruce W. Winter (Grand Rapids: Baker, 1992), 125–48.

20. For an incisive analysis of this question and the others connected to it, see Keith E. Johnson, *Rethinking the Trinity & Religious Pluralism: An Augustinian Assessment* (Downers Grove, IL: IVP Academic, 2011).

21. For an excellent introduction to such an understanding of the Trinity, see Fred Sanders, *The Triune God* (Grand Rapids: Zondervan, 2016).

Examples of this argument in missions and theology literature abound, but a few key examples will suffice. Shoki Coe, who has exerted enormous influence since his coining of the term *contextualization* in the 1970s, explains the warrant for contextualization in part by direct appeal to this analogy: "I believe, in fact, that the incarnation is the divine form of contextualization, and if this is so, the way we receive this gift is also through our following his way. This is what I mean by contextualization."[22] Writing only a few years later, a group of evangelical theologians embraced this analogy as well, noting that the incarnation and birth of Jesus is "the most spectacular instance of cultural identification in the history of mankind, since by his Incarnation the Son became a first century Galilean Jew."[23] Citing Philippians 2:5–11 as a guiding text for missionary service, they argue that cross-cultural witness should model itself on the Son's commitment to self-sacrifice and servanthood, as well as his willingness to identify as fully as possible with those whom he seeks to reach: "The Incarnation teaches identification without loss of identity. We believe that true self-sacrifice leads to true self-discovery. In humble service there is abundant joy."[24]

In a book that has set the terms for developments in contextual theology, Stephen Bevans similarly contends that the incarnation is one of the most important internal factors spurring the church toward the calling of contextual theology. His argument is worth quoting at length:

> Incarnation is a process of becoming particular, and in and through the particular the divinity could become visible and in some way (not fully but in some way) become graspable and intelligible.
>
> It follows quite naturally that if that message, through our agency, is, to continue to touch people, we have somehow ourselves to continue the incarnation process. Through us God must become Asian or African, black or brown, poor or sophisticated. Christians must be able to speak to inhabitants of twenty-first-century secular suburban Lima, Peru, or to the Tondo slum dweller in Manila, or to the ill-gotten affluence of a Brazilian rancher. Christianity, if it is to be faithful

22. Shoki Coe, *Contextualization as the Way towards Reform*, 53–54, quoted in Po Ho Huang, "Revisiting the Methodology of Contextual Theology in the Era of Globalization," in *Wrestling with God in Context: Revisiting the Theology and Vision of Shoki Coe*, ed. M. P. Joseph, Po Ho Huang, and Victor Hsu (Minneapolis: Fortress, 2018), 23.

23. Lausanne Committee for World Evangelization, *The Willowbank Report on Gospel and Culture*, in *Making Christ Known: Historic Mission Documents from the Lausanne Movement 1974–1989*, ed. John Stott (Carlisle, UK: Paternoster, 1996), Section 6B.

24. Lausanne Committee, *Willowbank Report*, Section 6B.

to its deepest roots and to its most basic insight, must continue God's incarnation in Jesus by becoming contextual.[25]

Proponents of viewing the incarnation as a model for the church's witness and ministry in diverse cultures point to several New Testament texts that seem to gesture in exactly this direction. Most direct is Philippians 2, in which Paul instructs believers to "have this mind among yourselves, which is yours in Christ Jesus" (2:5), and highlights in particular the humility of the Son's incarnation and self-giving ministry. Similarly, in 1 Corinthians 9:19–23, Paul highlights the importance of giving up freedoms and prerogatives in order to "become all things to all people," removing as many potential barriers as possible to the reception of the gospel.[26] Finally, the passages in which the church is called the body of Christ (e.g., Rom. 12:3–9, 1 Cor. 12:12–31) have been taken by some to gesture at a notion of the church as, in some sense, a continuation of the incarnation.

There is some diversity in how the incarnation is deployed in each of these cases. But all share in common the conviction that the incarnation is not only a once-for-all revelation of God in time, place, and culture, but is also in some sense a model for the church to follow as it carries out its mission. Theologians are thus called to put local "flesh" onto the "bones" of Christian teaching, echoing the incarnation by making eternity accessible in space, time, and culture. But just as we should think twice about the degree to which the Trinity is a model for the social interactions of the church, we should stop again to ask: Is the incarnation, in fact, a paradigm for contextually sensitive ministry and theological reflection?

Hazards make this path less desirable than it first seems. Until the very recent appropriations of incarnation as a model for Christian life, Christians have fiercely guarded the uniqueness of the doctrine, recognizing in this historical event a singular divine act, the significance of which lies precisely in its unparalleled, eternal impact. Rather than a parable or paradigm,

25. Stephen B. Bevans, *Models of Contextual Theology*, rev. ed. (Maryknoll, NY: Orbis Books, 2002), 8. The first edition of this book was published in 1992. In addition to the incarnation, Bevans cites the "sacramental nature of reality," the interpersonal and contextual nature of revelation, the catholicity of the church, and the Trinity as internal factors that press theology toward attending to context as a major theological factor.

26. Though the incarnation is not mentioned here explicitly, many have noted the similarities between this passage and the description of Jesus's identification with humanity in Phil. 2:5–11. See, e.g., Sherwood G. Lingenfelter and Marvin K. Mayers, *Ministering Cross-Culturally: An Incarnational Model for Personal Relationships*, 2nd ed. (Grand Rapids: Baker Academic, 2003), 25.

classical Christian teaching regards the incarnation as the singular fulcrum on which all of salvation history hinges, an unrepeatable event in which God comes to dwell with his people once and for all. To transform it into a paradigm for ministry or theology risks not only the diminishment of its power and significance but also the improper exaltation of our own cross-cultural ministry and theologizing. As Todd Billings notes, "the close analogy between the incarnation as a culture-crossing action and our own culture-crossing action" is a recipe for messiah complexes among those doing cross-cultural work.[27] While Billings is focused on missionary service in particular, the same critique applies in the realm of theology—as we saw in chapter 1, when theologians assume they are working with a "God's-eye" view, outside of any culture, they are almost certainly elevating elements of their own culture in the process. In short, we must not equate a translation of the Christian faith into a new culture with the unique revelation of God in Christ.

What, then, are we to make of Paul's exhortation in Philippians 2? Many exegetes go so far as to deny that there is any kind of "imitation" called for in the passage, arguing instead that Paul is exhorting the Philippians to find a new identity in Jesus, rather than a model to be mimicked.[28] The great advantage of this reading is that it preserves the "fundamental asymmetry between Christ and his people, between the Head and the body, between Christ's redemptive work on the cross and the Christian's carrying of the cross, which does not redeem others."[29] Nevertheless, early Christians used language similar to Paul to explicitly exhort the imitation of Christ,[30] and a growing body of New Testament scholarship suggests that this is the most compelling way to understand the text.[31]

---

27. J. Todd Billings, *Union with Christ: Reframing Theology and Ministry for the Church* (Grand Rapids: Baker Academic, 2011), 135.

28. Billings offers a nice summary of arguments in this direction (*Union with Christ*, 138–43). For a more expansive introduction to this view, see Ralph P. Martin, *A Hymn of Christ: Philippians 2:5–11 in Recent Interpretation & in the Setting of Early Christian Worship* (Downers Grove, IL: InterVarsity, 1997).

29. Billings, *Union with Christ*, 148.

30. See, e.g., chap. 16 of the first letter of Clement to the Corinthians, one of the earliest surviving documents from the early church (Michael W. Holmes, ed. and trans., *The Apostolic Fathers in English*, 3rd ed. [Grand Rapids: Baker Academic, 2006], 49–51).

31. See, e.g., Stephen E. Fowl, *The Story of Christ in the Ethics of Paul: An Analysis of the Function of the Hymnic Material in the Pauline Corpus* (Sheffield, UK: Sheffield Academic, 1990); Michael J. Gorman, *Cruciformity: Paul's Narrative Spirituality of the Cross* (Grand Rapids: Eerdmans, 2001); John Ottuh, "The Concept of Κένωσις in Philippians 2:6–7 and Its Contextual Application in

Crucially, however, these readings do not suggest that it is the *incarnation* that Paul wishes Christians to imitate. Instead, Paul is training the Philippians' eyes on the self-giving humility and love that is revealed both in the incarnation of the Son and in the life, ministry, and death of Jesus. Thus, the disposition and posture of the Son in his "state of humiliation" is to be echoed by his followers, which makes way for genuine unity and fellowship (Phil. 2:1–2). This conformity to Christ is made possible only by the liberating, once-for-all work of the incarnation and the giving of the Spirit (Phil. 2:1). Thus, the power of the incarnation, life, and death of Christ is *primarily* its unique and objective accomplishment: the salvation of a people from every tribe, tongue, and nation. But this hardly exhausts its theological significance. As John Webster writes, "Because of their gracious participation in God through Christ, Christians are enabled to act in such a way that their acts correspond to the acts of the Saviour."[32]

If all of this is correct, then the incarnation has profound implications for the calling of contextual theology, though those implications are different than we might intuitively suppose. The church's embodiment of the gospel in its local environment is not best understood as an emulation of the incarnation, much less as a continuation of it. Rather, the incarnation provides the basis for contextual theology in two ways. First, it is the culmination of all of God's acts of revelation in and through human cultural resources, which lends dignity and warrant to the work of translating the good news and all of its implications. This also means that the work of human translators is derivative of, and not equal to, the work of God in revealing himself in human languages and cultures.

The second way in which the incarnation makes way for the possibility of contextual theology is that it functions as the fulcrum of salvation history, making possible what was previously inconceivable—the perfect dwelling of God with humanity and the creation of a new human community united by participation in Christ and his Spirit. As a creature formed by the Son and Spirit, the church is the place where people from every culture and subculture are enabled by divine grace to echo the humility and love of their servant king, thereby making way for a harmonious unity-in-diversity

---

Africa," *Verbum et Ecclesia* 41, no. 1 (2020); Eve-Marie Becker, *Paul on Humility*, trans. Wayne Coppins (Waco: Baylor University Press, 2020).

32. John Webster, "Christology, Imitability and Ethics," *Scottish Journal of Theology* 39, no. 3 (1986): 323.

impossible anywhere else in creation. It is to this creature—the church—and her calling into the theological enterprise, that we now must turn.

The Church as the Workshop of Contextual Theologies

It is not without merit that the ideas outlined above—globalization, the Trinity, and the incarnation—have been suggested as frameworks for understanding the task of contextual theology. Each speaks, in some way, to the realities at stake as Christians seek to identify the unifying threads in the Christian tapestry, preserving diversity in unity against both enforced uniformity and fragmented relativism. Yet each of these ideas is insufficient and incomplete in the absence of a fulsome understanding of the church as a distinctive creature of God's redeeming activity, designed to be the arena for the theological task. It is in the doctrine of the church more than any other that theology can find an orientation that suitably engages the diversity of human cultures while also attending to the once-for-all nature of revelation in Christ.

The New Testament uses a riot of images, metaphors, and analogies to describe the church. Consider the variety evident in just a few of the more than eighty images identified by Paul Minear: the church is a flock (e.g., Acts 20:28–30), an aroma (2 Cor. 2:14–17), a field (e.g., 1 Cor. 3:9), a household (e.g., Heb. 3:1–6), a temple (e.g., Eph. 2:18–22), a new humanity (e.g., Col. 3:10), a group of exiles (e.g., 1 Pet. 2:11), and "a chosen race, a royal priesthood, a holy nation, a people for [God's] own possession" (1 Pet. 2:9).[33] In general, it is worth noting here that evangelical Christians' meager ecclesiology would benefit from extended, close attention to this profusion of images and their dogmatic implications and interconnections.

But even a cursory examination of the descriptors the apostles showered on the church highlights the theme of diversity that builds into, rather than threatens, authentic unity. The church is the family or household of God (e.g., Heb. 3:1–6), suggesting an economy of diverse members, each contributing with their various gifts, callings, and personalities to the well-being of the clan.[34] In Ephesians 2, the household metaphor is deployed alongside

33. Paul S. Minear, *Images of the Church in the New Testament* (Louisville: Westminster John Knox, 2004).

34. This insight finds special emphasis in African treatments of ecclesiologies. See, e.g., A. E. Orobator, *The Church as Family: African Ecclesiology in Its Social Context* (Nairobi, Kenya: Paulines

temple imagery, not only to emphasize the church's identity as the defining locus of God's presence, but also and especially to highlight the new kind of unity God is achieving between Jews and Gentiles (2:19–22). In 1 Peter, the temple metaphor gets extended, with the motley group of "sojourners and exiles" (2:11) identified as individual stones who are being drawn together into a unified "spiritual house" (2:5). Further still, the passage describes the church as a newly constituted "race," "nation," and "people" (2:9–10), language that is then echoed in Revelation's description of the multitude who have acquired unity through the Lamb (Rev. 5:9–10; 7:9–10).

Perhaps the New Testament image that most clearly points in the direction of unity amid diversity is the body. In 1 Corinthians 12, Paul outlines the metaphor at length to compel believers in Corinth to embrace the genuine diversity in giftings and offices throughout the church. But in other applications of the imagery, the notion of unity amid diversity is applied more broadly. Ephesians 3:1–6, for example, applies the image directly to the membership of Jews and Gentiles in "the same body." The subsequent chapter deploys the image even more richly, finding in the body-of-Christ metaphor a basis not only for exhortations to use the church's diverse gifts in a unified manner (4:7, 11–12) but also for regulative guidelines that guard the holiness of Christ's body (4:25–32). Perhaps most importantly, the body image is applied here not merely statically but also developmentally, suggesting that, over time, the body of Christ is being built up, "until we all attain to the unity of the faith and of the knowledge of the Son of God, to mature manhood, to the measure of the stature of the fullness of Christ" (4:12–13). Andrew Walls has highlighted the remarkable implications of this metaphor, noting that, both in early Christianity and today, the Ephesian imagery calls the church to attend to its diverse composition as a necessary step for it to reach its full stature in Christ.[35] "Christ's completion," he writes, "comes from all humanity, from the translation of the life of Jesus into the lifeways of all the world's cultures and subcultures through history."[36]

Publications Africa, 2000); though note also the complications of this concept in the excellent study of Stephanie A. Lowery, *Identity and Ecclesiology: Their Relationship among Select African Theologians* (Eugene, OR: Pickwick, 2017), 148–49.

35. Andrew F. Walls, "The Ephesian Moment: At a Crossroads in Christian History," in *The Cross-Cultural Process in Christian History: Studies in the Transmission and Appropriation of Faith* (Maryknoll, NY: Orbis Books, 2002), 72–81.

36. Walls, "Ephesian Moment," 79.

In this way we finally arrive at a Christian doctrine that is explicitly designed for the problem we recognized at the start of the chapter: the balancing of theology's attention to the "once-for-all" aspects of the faith, in which we find perfect unity, and to the profound diversity that marks the church's existence across diverse contexts and times. Where globalization, the doctrine of the Trinity, and the doctrine of the incarnation ultimately fall short as guides for the task of contextual theology, the doctrine of the church holds more promise—it is here, after all, that the New Testament authors shine a light when they wish to define the nature of Christian unity in diversity.[37]

If this is right, then further specifying the nature of the church will allow us to develop and clarify our understanding of the calling of contextual theology. Based on what we have said so far, we can start with three assertions about the church that connect it to the concepts explored above. First, the church is a community in which cooperation across nations, cultures, and generations should emerge without exploitation or domination (in contrast to the excesses and distortions of globalization). Second, the church is the central locus of ongoing coordination between the triune God and his creatures; it is thus more an effect of, rather than a mirror to, the triune God, though it bears the divine fingerprint and invites all peoples into the perfect life of the Father, Son, and Spirit. Third, the church is the unique organism tying together the once-for-all work of Christ and the ever-evolving work of Son and Spirit in their missions to the world. As the offspring of the incarnate Lord, the church bears witness in the spirit of humility and service that animated Jesus of Nazareth, even if it could never claim to imitate the once-for-all work of the incarnation. With these three insights, we can begin to see the contours of a contextual theology anchored in a healthy ecclesiology.

Case Study: Ecclesiology and Contextual Theology in Asia

Simon Chan is a Singaporean theologian who taught for many years at Trinity Theological College in Singapore while also publishing a stream of

---

37. For a fascinating study bringing together close attention to Paul's exposition of the church in Ephesians and contemporary discussions of the African church and its relationship to pre-Christian African religions, see Fabrice S. Katembo, *The Mystery of the Church: Applying Paul's Ecclesiology in Africa* (Carlisle, UK: Langham, 2020).

important theological works. Chan's work is unusual in bringing together a deep appreciation of the church's historical tradition, a high view of the work of the Spirit, and an extensive grasp of theological trends in Asia as well as in the West. But what makes his work especially helpful for our purposes is that Chan reflects extensively on the formative shape of ecclesiology for the contextual theological task.

The Flawed Approach behind Dominant Approaches to Contextual Theology

Chan's interest in the doctrine of the church arises at least in part from a recognition that the contextual theologies advanced in Asia over the last several decades have failed to show significant development and have generally fallen far short of their calling to serve the church's mission. Chan argues that this is the result of a number of mistaken methodological commitments. For example, many Asian contextual theologies begin by highlighting the difference between "Western" and "Eastern" ways of thinking. Aside from the unhelpful generalizations that this approach requires from the start, this approach often requires that the project of building a contextual theology becomes primarily about finding ways to depart from the Western legacy.[38]

This generally leads to another fateful methodological choice: a tendency to focus the theological task almost exclusively on reflection upon the social, cultural, political, and economic dynamics at work in the local context and diminishing the role of Scripture and Christian tradition.[39] The theological project becomes focused primarily on discerning the redemptive activity of the Spirit *outside* of the pages of Scripture and the walls of the church. Yet this results in a lack of clarity, as various theologians come to different conclusions about where the Spirit is at work. "With no certainty of where or how to locate the Spirit," Chan laments, "there is little material left in the world to practice the theologian's craft. About the only situations where some confident pronouncements can still be made are those where the Spirit of God is *not* found," such as situations of cultural, political, or economic oppression.[40] This approach can quickly become

---

38. Simon Chan, *Grassroots Asian Theology: Thinking the Faith from the Ground Up* (Downers Grove, IL: IVP Academic, 2014), 9–10.
39. Chan, *Grassroots Asian Theology*, 25.
40. Chan, *Grassroots Asian Theology*, 26.

little more than social critique augmented by decorative theological language. Rather than learning from what God is doing among his people, such theology tends to reflect the personal interests and pet projects of elitist theologians.[41]

An Ecclesiological Corrective

Chan argues that the way to escape this dead end is for contextual theologies to shift their primary focus, prioritizing the Spirit's work *inside* rather than *outside* of the church. After all, it is in the Spirit's work in the New Testament church—at Pentecost and in the events described in the rest of the book of Acts—that the distinctive identity of the Spirit is ultimately revealed. Similarly, we come to understand the nature of the church especially as the unique locus of the Spirit's redemptive and transformative work. Thus, Chan observes, "the identities of the church and the Holy Spirit are so closely linked that they are mutually conditioning."[42] We cannot properly understand one without the other.

This is not to deny that the Spirit is at work outside of the household of God. Instead, it is to confess that "*whatever* the Spirit is doing in the world, he is working *ultimately* to draw people into communion, that is, to Christ and his church, the communion of saints."[43] This orientation is important because it reminds us that the Spirit's work in the wider world, including among participants of other religions, "is not to make the religions or social movements salvific in themselves but to prepare them to receive the knowledge of Christ."[44] It is surely good and proper to recognize these works of the Spirit in the wider world, especially in the context of mission, where the church seeks to sow seeds in soil that the Spirit has already been tilling.[45] Yet contextual theologies must not be reduced to mere reflection on this general work; theologians should instead make it their primary task to learn from and serve the household of God indwelt by the Spirit, since

41. Chan, *Grassroots Asian Theology*, 26–27.

42. Simon Chan, "Toward an Asian Evangelical Ecclesiology," in *Asian Christian Theology: Evangelical Perspectives*, ed. Timoteo D. Gener and Stephen T. Pardue (Carlisle, UK: Langham Global Library, 2019), 143.

43. Chan, *Grassroots Asian Theology*, 144, italics original.

44. Chan, *Grassroots Asian Theology*, 144.

45. See Lalsangkima Pachuau, *God at Work in the World: Theology and Mission in the Global Church* (Grand Rapids: Baker Academic, 2022).

this is where God is most clearly accomplishing his work of eschatological redemption.[46]

Putting it this way should alert us to the fact that the church is more than a mere social phenomenon. It is, instead, a theological reality, conceived by God before the foundation of the world as the vehicle by which he will renew all things in Christ (Eph. 1:3–10). Rather than being a merely human household, it is the household *of God*, and so shares in a way that no other creaturely reality does in the life, energy, and power of God himself.[47] This means that the church's work is "spiritual work, with spiritual effects"—not in the sense that it is "non-historical or non-material, . . . but in the sense that it is brought about by the work of the Spirit of God."[48]

If all of this is right, the task of theology is thrown into a new light. Rather than being "the result of the Church's work of reflecting upon its own religious experience" (an understanding likely to reduce theology "to anthropology and the Church to another social organization"), doctrine is "the result of divine action."[49] That is, "the Church's experience arises from the givenness of revelation."[50] In tradition, the church inherits the Spirit's work of ages past, though doctrine also undergoes development and growth over time, "since the Church is the on-going action of the Spirit."[51] Contextual theology is ultimately an eschatological work of the Spirit of God, "who anticipates the End, who reveals something of the end to us, and who guarantees the Church's fulfillment of its intended end."[52]

Ecclesiology from the Grassroots

Armed with a robust understanding of the church and the Spirit's cultivation of doctrinal development within it, Chan is able to offer a vision of contextual theology that corrects many of the flaws in other prominent

---

46. Chan's vision of the theologian as echoing and articulating what God is doing in the church is similar to the idea articulated by Ghanaian theologian John Pobee, who conceived the theologian as "an articulate individual in the womb of the community of faith" (quoted in Diane B. Stinton, *Jesus of Africa: Voices of Contemporary African Christology* [Maryknoll, NY: Orbis Books, 2004], 243).

47. Simon Chan, "The Church and the Development of Doctrine," *Journal of Pentecostal Theology* 13, no. 1 (2004): 63–64.

48. Chan, "Church and the Development of Doctrine," 64.

49. Chan, "Church and the Development of Doctrine," 64.

50. Chan, "Church and the Development of Doctrine," 64.

51. Chan, "Church and the Development of Doctrine," 72.

52. Chan, "Church and the Development of Doctrine," 72.

approaches. Central to his proposal is a call to focus on "the lived theology of the ordinary people of God"—what Chan calls "ecclesial experience"—to generate material theological insights.[53] Ecclesial experience "constitutes the primary theology (*theologia prima*) of the church" and represents a kind of "living tradition" resulting from the ongoing work of the triune God.[54] Ecclesial experience is certainly culturally inflected, since the Spirit aids the church in receiving divine revelation in distinctive ways in every time and place; but ecclesial experience is not the same as general "cultural experience," as it traces the transformative work of God primarily within his holy people.[55] "The task of the professional theologian," Chan argues, is "to listen carefully what the Spirit of truth who indwells the church is saying through the people of God" and to bring these insights into clarity and alignment with the legacy of the church catholic.[56]

This is exactly the method Chan seeks to carry out in his influential book *Grassroots Asian Theology*: treating traditional theological loci—God, humanity and sin, Christ and salvation, the Holy Spirit and spirituality, and the church—with special interest in the Asian church's contribution to our understanding of the doctrines. It is instructive to see how Chan's method works when he applies it to specific doctrines. In this case, we will consider his treatment of the doctrine of the church (which is itself informed by his ecclesiocentric method).

Chan observes that the most pressing ecclesiological issue for Christians in Asia is their relationship with the world's major faiths and understanding and articulating "the church's relation to these Asian religions." This struggle is complicated by the fact that "the primary locus of religious life is the home."[57] As a result, joining the Christian community often means severing or significantly harming biological family ties; to the degree that believers must withdraw from the religious practices of their previous faith, they must also withdraw from crucial aspects of familial life. Further, Christians often lose their place not only in their households but also within the broader social structure.

To make matters worse, the strand of evangelicalism that has largely helped birth the church in most Asian nations is oriented toward the individual, with

53. Chan, *Grassroots Asian Theology*, 28.
54. Chan, "Church and the Development of Doctrine," 16.
55. Chan, *Grassroots Asian Theology*, 18–27.
56. Chan, *Grassroots Asian Theology*, 30.
57. Chan, *Grassroots Asian Theology*, 162.

the church viewed "largely as a collectivity of individuals," with the corporate body essentially "ancillary to the faith of the individual." Thus, the church is "simply a way of organizing individuals to meet their spiritual needs and harness their collective resources to carry out the central task of evangelism and mission."[58] This anemic ecclesiology is not ideal for any context, but it is especially poorly suited to the Asian context, where Christians so palpably sense the need for a church structure that can help them recover what they have to give up in exchange for following Jesus.

This is exactly what Chan sees in the efforts of indigenous church movements throughout Asia. For example, the Ceylon Pentecostal Mission based in Sri Lanka embraces a unified dress code for ministers, designed to echo Buddhist ways of signaling clerical unity, and operates "faith homes" in which pastors and church workers hold their possessions in common and where "hospitality is extended to all, especially the destitute." In the group's mission efforts in India, they demonstrated remarkable readiness to integrate across caste, class, and social status, offering a unique and liberating vision of a new community.[59] Chan also highlights several other examples of church movements in Japan, India, and China that are instructive for the wider church, especially for churches in the West that are (or may soon be) grappling with their new status as a disfavored minority in their contexts.[60]

Chan's ecclesiological reflections push in a more doctrinal direction when he trains his sights on one of the thorniest challenges for Asian Christians: the matter of ancestral veneration. For centuries, Christians have been divided over how to handle the various expressions of ancestral veneration prevalent in the region (especially in East Asia and in East Asian diaspora communities). Beyond debates about which specific practices should be acceptable to Christians, Chan presses us to consider the metaphysical commitments that undergird the practices, as well as the theological implications of the practices for believers. In Asian cultures, ancestral veneration is a reminder that familial bonds are superlatively strong, such that even death cannot break them. This provides an unshakable sense of security and stability to both individuals and communities as they weather the storms of life and face the pain of death.

As he documents various Christian responses to ancestral veneration in the region, Chan highlights the doctrinal resources at the Christian's disposal

58. Chan, "Toward an Asian Evangelical Ecclesiology," 145.
59. Chan, Grassroots Asian Theology, 172.
60. Chan, Grassroots Asian Theology, 171–88.

that often go untapped.[61] Foremost among these is the Christian affirmation of the communion of the saints, which affirms that "in Christ, all the saints throughout the ages, in heaven and on earth, are united as one organic, living church by the power of the Holy Spirit."[62] This doctrine is powerful, fundamentally connecting Christology, pneumatology, and ecclesiology, as well as affirming that the triune God is directly bringing about a state of life-giving fellowship among his people that will eventually culminate in the marriage supper of the Lamb. Even if that divinely created fellowship remains imperfectly realized in the intermediate state, it is still real, binding together all Christians across space and time into a new family. This teaching should be a foundational element in both our theory and practice of the church, as Christians of the present age live with a consciousness of our full Christian family, living and dead.

Unfortunately, the doctrine is instead often downplayed and even viewed with suspicion in many modern cultures, where the notion of taking comfort in spiritual fellowship with the dead, let alone the honoring of their memory, may be viewed as superstition or paganism. Yet, as Chan demonstrates, Asian Christians can help us recover this doctrine's clear necessity and value for all Christians. We know that we need persistent fellowship with the living saints, and so we cultivate structures and practices to foster it, recognizing that our spiritual health will suffer otherwise (Heb. 10:25). Yet we also need practices and structures that will cultivate our awareness of the great cloud of witnesses with whom we presently share a common life (Heb. 12:1), which Asian Christians have shown can be achieved without violating the biblical prohibitions on seeking the spirits of the dead (Lev. 19:31; Isa. 8:19). Indeed, it is a great irony that Christians from North America and Europe, who often have such extensive legacies of Christian forebears, generally draw so little comfort and insight from the saints who have gone ahead of them, while Asian Christians make much more of their comparatively shorter family histories in the faith.

Conclusion

Hopefully it is becoming clearer how a robust ecclesiology provides crucial structure and direction for evangelical contextual theologies. While

---

61. Chan, *Grassroots Asian Theology*, 173–74, 189.
62. Chan, *Grassroots Asian Theology*, 189.

theologians are right to acknowledge the realities of globalization, and even to seek to make the most of them through fellowship across the globe, they must appeal to resources internal to the faith to underwrite intercultural theological cooperation, promoting genuine *koinōnia* in contrast to the often exploitative and homogenizing forces of economic globalization. Moreover, while the doctrines of the Trinity and incarnation surely provide important impetus for contextual theology—it is the triune God's redemptive work in the incarnation and Pentecost that confirm that local cultural resources are gifts of God—we must trace the line of redemption all the way to the one, holy, catholic, and apostolic church, the unique organism created and shaped by the gospel. Here, we find the creature whose special purpose is to coordinate the once-for-all work of God in Christ and the ever-new work of the Spirit among the nations. In the church we find a home for theological reflection that is big enough to foster unity and wholeness that is unthreatened by the diversity of the church's cultural gifts.

In this chapter, we have focused on the importance of the church's unique identity for addressing the tensions created by contemporary realities. As world Christianity becomes increasingly diverse and polycentric, and as globalization increasingly connects distant parts of the church, we need a framing for theological engagement with culture that can unify without cutting us off from the gifts of individual cultures.

In the next two chapters, we will get more specific about *how* ecclesiology shapes contextual theology, focusing especially on the church's catholicity. This aspect of the church's identity requires that contextual theologies attend to the fullness of the church in its present state, which is at once more possible than ever (because of globalization) and more difficult than ever. This will be the concern of chapter 5.

Yet, in addition to pursuing catholicity by attending to the full scope and breadth of the church's *present diversity*, seeking catholicity also means attending to *the church's witness to the gospel across the ages*. As we will see in chapter 6, it may be tempting to avoid difficult wrestling with the past by focusing only on finding unity and wholeness in the present age. Yet, rightly understood, the church's heritage—the accumulation of contextually situated theological judgments of the saints over time—provides substantive theological gains. It also offers important examples of how to do contextual theology well, alongside opportunities for corporate repentance. It is to a deeper understanding of the church, and especially its catholicity, that we now turn.

5

The Children of God Scattered Abroad

Contextual Theology in the Fellowship of the Worldwide Church

> He prophesied that Jesus would die for the nation, and not for the nation only,
> but also to gather into one the children of God who are scattered abroad.
>
> —John 11:51–52

Thus far, we have made three claims regarding the nature of evangelical contextual theologies. First, we argued that because of their concern to preserve the liberating good news revealed in Jesus and proclaimed in Scripture, *evangelical contextual theologies must look to Scripture as their magisterial authority, even as they increase their appreciation for the crucial ministerial role of culture for the theological task.* This high view of Scripture does not require us to downplay the contribution of culture to the theological process; to the contrary, it is only with a clear sense of our cultural context that we come to grasp the full impact of God's self-revelation in the biblical text.

Second, we made explicit that evangelical efforts at contextual theology are driven by the conviction that *culture is a material theological good, a gift from God designed for the benefit of the church.* Because God has revealed himself in and through (rather than above and beyond) human culture and language, the church is called to make the most of its local resources as it bears witness to, reflects upon, and worships the triune God. This is the glory of Pentecost—that surprising reversal of Babel in which a new people from every tribe and tongue is formed by the work of Jesus and empowered by the work of the Spirit.

Yet despite the Spirit's miraculous work in the church, we continue to face a challenge that echoes Babel: the more that each local church seeks to bring its own cultural resources to bear in the theological task, the more difficult it often becomes to recognize the ties that unite the church universal. Thus, as theology becomes more intentionally local, we are threatened by a church split into innumerable isolated tribes. To put it more concretely: the more we see the good news in terms of our own local cultures, the more we are in danger of obscuring its full reality, understanding and proclaiming the good news only on our own community's limited terms.

To begin to address this problem, the previous chapter made a third claim: that it is in the doctrine of the church that we find the tools needed to attend to the singular gospel while making the most of the many-splendored beauty of the faith refracted in the panoply of human cultures. Thus, we suggested that *evangelical contextual theologies should look to the Christian doctrine of the church in order to coordinate the once-for-all of the gospel and the remarkably diverse expressions of the faith that emerge in the real world.*

This chapter and the next will press further into the doctrine of the church, considering how the marks of the church outlined in the Nicene Creed—unity, holiness, apostolicity, and catholicity—help nurture a vision for evangelical contextual theologies that are faithful to the character and calling of God's people. In particular, we will find in the pairing of unity and catholicity a productive tension that addresses some of the most difficult questions evangelical theology faces in its engagement with cultural diversity.

You may recall from chapter 1 that theologians in the evangelical tradition have identified two significant risks posed by contextual theologies—namely, the twin challenges of cultural tribalism and historical discontinuity. By the former, we refer to the danger that emphasizing the cultural situatedness of theological claims may ultimately lead to the splintering of theological discourse into thousands of independent, even tribalistic, conversations, preventing genuine theological fellowship among Christians of diverse backgrounds. By the latter, we refer to the risk that the endless novelty involved in theological development as the church grows and expands into new cultures will threaten unity among the saints across time that Christians have historically fought to preserve.

The next two chapters will demonstrate that a sufficiently robust grasp of the church's catholicity is the best solution to these problems. In response to the problem of cultural relativism, we will contend that *evangelical contextual theologies should seek to discern the plenitude of the riches of Christ through the cultivation of authentic Christian witness in every culture while seeking the unity of the Spirit by rejecting local theologies that fail to engage the worldwide church.* The subsequent chapter will focus on the second problem—that of historical discontinuity—contending that, for the sake of genuine catholicity, *evangelical contextual theologies should engage the Great Tradition of the church, finding there a partner that helps prevent slavish obedience to all things present and that tempers theological novelty in favor of considered overtures toward unity.*

Four Marks

Before diving into the meaning and contemporary significance of catholicity, we should begin by noting the setting of this concept alongside the other traditional "marks" of the church. Since at least the fourth century, Christians have committed themselves to describing the church in terms of four characteristics distilled in the Nicene-Constantinopolitan Creed: the church is one, holy, catholic, and apostolic. The two marks that have the most relevance for the discussion at hand are *oneness* and *catholicity*—terms that provide signal clarity for contextual theology in the twenty-first century. But first, we will consider how the church's holiness and apostolicity should shape contemporary contextual theologies in important ways.

Holiness

The church's holiness is a basic implication of its association with the triune God, who draws creatures to himself and graciously sanctifies them to serve their rightful purposes.[1] Thus, the church is holy not because of its

---

1. John Webster, *Holiness* (Grand Rapids: Eerdmans, 2003), 53–76.

unique and meritorious distinction from other creaturely institutions—one need merely experience the foibles of any local congregation to be assured of this—but because of the electing, sanctifying, and perfecting work of God. Moreover, the holiness of the church bears the imprint of divine holiness, which means that it is not merely "set apart" from other creatures (though it is, at least in some sense), but it is also designed to be an instrument of *contagious holiness*. The church is thus called to engage the world in a mission of reconciliation, acting as a kingdom of priests that calls the whole creation into a life of genuine flourishing and authentic fellowship with the triune God.[2]

This missional and all-encompassing sense of holiness is critical for the task of contextual theologies, as it sanctions a vision for the theological calling as a process of redeeming and sanctifying the cultural material of every society, rather than demanding that Christians seek to stand out from the world by creating doctrine out of nothing. Further, the *telos* of the church's holiness is the renewal and well-being of the world, which comes to its most perfect expression in the honor and worship of the triune God; this is what is meant by the church's office as royal priest.[3] The church occupies this office by virtue of its participation in Christ, unfolding the implications of his once-for-all reconciling work.[4] All of this suggests a vision of holy theology pursued by a holy church, a theology that will be marked not by its quest for a pure, acultural account of God and the gospel but, rather, by a messy and humble engagement with the cultures in which it finds itself. Importantly, this vision of holy theology means that Christian doctrine does not become holier with further distance from the products of human culture; instead, it maintains its holiness through its ongoing participation in the promises

---

2. C. René Padilla and Tetsunao Yamamori, eds., *The Local Church, Agent of Transformation: An Ecclesiology for Integral Mission*, trans. Brian Cordingly (Buenos Aires, Argentina: Ediciones Kairós, 2004); Ruth Padilla DeBorst, "Church, Power, and Transformation in Latin America: A Different Citizenship Is Possible," in *Majority World Theology: Christian Doctrine in Global Context*, ed. Gene L. Green, Stephen T. Pardue, and K. K. Yeo (Downers Grove, IL: IVP Academic, 2020), 498–509; Carlos Sosa Siliezar, "Ecclesiology in Latin America: A Biblical Perspective," in *Majority World Theology: Christian Doctrine in Global Context*, ed. Gene L. Green, Stephen T. Pardue, and K. K. Yeo (Downers Grove, IL: IVP Academic, 2020), 537–50.

3. Tom Greggs, *Dogmatic Ecclesiology: The Priestly Catholicity of the Church*, vol. 1 (Grand Rapids: Baker Academic, 2019), 113–47.

4. Uche Anizor and Hank Voss, *Representing Christ: A Vision for the Priesthood of All Believers* (Downers Grove, IL: IVP Academic, 2016).

of Christ, expressed in obedient and worshipful speech of God carried out by the joyful appropriation of the cultural resources that are ready to hand.

Apostolicity

If the church's holiness points primarily to her unique relationship with the triune God, apostolicity reminds us that the church is also rooted in the accidents of history. It exists because God has willed the creation of a new people who owe their spiritual lineage to specific persons taken up by the divine purpose to initiate the foundation of the church in a particular place and time. As Acts 1:8 memorably puts it, the church's *telos* is universal ("the ends of the earth"), but its origin is far more modest: a specific city (Jerusalem), and even a handful of households. Thus, although the church is a holy people whose identity is rooted in the God above all people and cultures, it has not dropped out of heaven; it has a lineage rooted in the ordinary languages, cultures, and personalities of the apostles.

In addition to reminding the church of its humble, local origins, the apostolicity of the church speaks especially to what makes the church itself through the centuries. In some accounts, apostolicity references a specific lineage of persons leading back to the apostles. In the spirit of the Reformation, however, evangelicals regard apostolicity to be connected to the church's faithful teaching and living out of the biblical faith. That is, the rightful inheritors of the apostolic tradition are not those who can document their lineage to the handful of persons identified as apostles but, rather, those who bear a filial resemblance to the apostles of Christ by their persistence in and fidelity to the gospel the apostles received and proclaimed.

Contextual theologies committed to apostolicity must thus be firmly rooted in the divinely inspired teaching of the apostles and prophets; in other words, they must ensure that Scripture is always the "main course" at the theological table. This is no simple matter. For as long as there has been a church, and especially in the last century, debates about what it means for theology to be sufficiently "biblical" have multiplied.[5] Moreover, contextual

5. Indeed, the first theological debates of the church related to what it meant for the church to remain faithful to the teaching of the Law and the Prophets while responding rightly to God's new work among the Gentiles. For an insightful overview and response to more recent debates about what it means for theology to be "biblical," see Kevin J. Vanhoozer and Daniel J. Treier, *Theology and the Mirror of Scripture: A Mere Evangelical Account* (Downers Grove, IL: IVP Academic, 2015), esp. chap. 2.

theologians who take world Christianity seriously must also contend with the dynamic encounter between apostolic teaching and local cultures—noting that the gospel in its original form is culturally rooted and wrestling with the challenge of how to translate the biblical witness and its implications in ever-changing cultural contexts.

The church cannot utter a single sentence of the apostolic message in any given culture without facing perilous and difficult questions. Which titles for God in local culture should be adopted to describe the triune God? Which local analogies for Christ's saving work do it justice, and which ones fall short? How adaptable should the church be in carrying out new forms of apostolic traditions, or in integrating local rituals around birth, adolescence, marriage, and death?[6] While we must admit that there is no simple metric for whether a new church practice or novel theological expression carries the faith forward in the same way as the apostles, the complexity involved in summing up and assessing apostolicity is no reason to forsake it as a defining mark of Christ's body.[7] To the contrary, it may be correct to assert that the church most embodies apostolicity when it engages in the difficult work of translation and adaptation, given the degree to which the apostles themselves were fiercely committed to precisely these processes.[8]

Unity and Catholicity

So, the church is holy (set apart as a unique organism devoted to spreading the power and presence of God throughout the earth) and apostolic (committed to bringing the gospel into the fullness of life in every culture on earth). Within these traits lie the seeds of the other two marks of the church: unity and catholicity. After all, if the church is singularly fit to carry forward the mission of God, it cannot do so as a house divided, so it must

6. These are precisely the kinds of questions addressed in the collected essays in Gene L. Green, Stephen T. Pardue, and K. K. Yeo, eds., *Majority World Theology: Christian Doctrine in Global Context* (Downers Grove, IL: IVP Academic, 2020).

7. See the work of Lamin Sanneh, who treats the persistent translation of Christian Scripture into various tongues as a signal achievement of the faith but also acknowledges the complex and fraught nature of the process in both its ancient and contemporary iterations (Lamin Sanneh, *Translating the Message: The Missionary Impact on Culture*, 2nd ed. [Maryknoll, NY: Orbis Books, 2009]).

8. This is the contention of John Flett, who argues that the church's apostolicity consists precisely in its commitment to transmitting the faith across cultural contexts and then helping it take root in ever-new cultural environments (John G. Flett, *Apostolicity: The Ecumenical Question in World Christian Perspective* [Downers Grove, IL: IVP Academic, 2016]).

be one (1 Cor. 1:10–17). Likewise, if it seeks to express the apostolic gospel faithfully, even as it multiplies across cultures and contexts, the one church must be genuinely catholic—with its local expressions participating both in the fullness of the gospel and in fellowship with the whole church across cultures and across the ages. Here at last we arrive at the most important theological tools in the dogmatic toolbox for addressing the tension inherent in the calling of contextual theologies.

Consider first *unity*, or *oneness*. The church's unity is frequently addressed in the New Testament in quite concrete terms. Thus, Paul rebukes believers in Corinth for becoming divided over their allegiances to various teachers (1 Cor. 1:10–13), and he calls for two women in the Philippian church (Euodia and Syntyche) to find their way through a difficult disagreement (Phil. 4:1–3). This tangible unity is underwritten by an invisible theological reality: because the whole church is inhabited by the one Spirit, thereby participating in the one Christ and directing worship to the one triune God, it is impossible for the church to be anything but unified on some deep, ontological level. When this reality is discussed explicitly in the New Testament, such as in Jesus's high priestly prayer (John 17:11–23) and in the Letter to the Ephesians (Eph. 4:1–6), the church's unity is at once a description already true of the church and also an ideal to be struggled toward.[9]

Yet threats to the church's unity are not all of the same sort. While the New Testament warns against the persistent danger of personal conflicts and doctrinal differences—in which cases unity must be preserved through a gentle but firm rejection of anyone promoting needless division (Rom. 16:17–18)—it is also alert to a natural tension that requires a different kind of negotiation: the church, unlike Israel, is a fundamentally heterogenous group that must constantly reckon with its unparalleled diversity. In this case, the cause of division is not malice or personal conflict, but simply the radically different lifeways of the church's various cultures. While globalization adds new dimensions to this reality, it is not by any means a new problem. Because of the centrifugal vision of the faith from its earliest days (Jerusalem, Judea, the ends of the earth), Christians were pressed from the time of the apostles to articulate a standard of unity that was flexible enough to incorporate ever-increasing levels of diversity.

---

9. This tension is present with all four marks of the church, as each describes an "already" and "not yet" reality for the people of God.

To describe this second type of unity—understood not in contrast to divisiveness but in contrast to egocentrism, ethnocentrism, and parochialism—early Christians used the term *catholicity*. While this descriptor for the church is not used in the New Testament,[10] the concept of a type of unity that binds across diverse giftings and cultural identities is clearly a major canonical theme. For example, Pauline epistles wrestle consistently both with what it means to maintain unity in the midst of diversity of temperaments, gifts, and offices (e.g., Rom. 12:3–8; 1 Cor. 12) and also with how the church can be a new humanity that includes both Jews and Gentiles (see the main arguments of Romans and Galatians).

This latter point is one of the central dramas of the book of Acts, where the Jerusalem Council of Acts 15 can be highlighted as a prime example of properly catholic unity. There, the apostles confront head-on the deep tensions that come along with the church's expanding mission among the nations—namely, that given the way in which culture, ethics, and theology are all intertwined, the different and conflicting customs of the groups joining the church were sure to introduce explosive tension. By the guidance of the Spirit, the apostles find a way to unify the church that not only honors the diversity of the church's membership but also acknowledges the novelty of Christ's redeeming work while maintaining appropriate continuity with the Jewish tradition Christ fulfills. The council was a major turning point and set the terms for the ancient church's remarkable vision, expressed in Ephesians—namely, that the diverse ways of carrying on the faith are to be regarded not only as a burden to be managed but also as a critical element by which the church would reach "the stature of the fullness of Christ" (Eph. 4:13).[11]

This concept of *fullness* or *completeness* (*plērōma*) adds a new dimension to catholicity. Not only is the church catholic, or universal—meaning scattered throughout the whole earth and comprising those of every culture, class, and time (already, these are remarkable claims!)[12]—but the church is

---

10. Robert Schreiter notes that the term seems to have come into common usage by around AD 100 (*The New Catholicity: Theology between the Global and the Local* [Maryknoll, NY: Orbis Books, 1997], 121).

11. Andrew F. Walls, "The Ephesian Moment: At a Crossroads in Christian History," in *The Cross-Cultural Process in Christian History: Studies in the Transmission and Appropriation of Faith*, 72–81 (Maryknoll, NY: Orbis Books, 2002).

12. These are the three aspects of catholicity highlighted, e.g., by Thomas Aquinas in his commentary on the Apostles' Creed (see Avery Dulles, *The Catholicity of the Church* [Oxford: Clarendon, 1985], 181).

also God's designated instrument for filling out the depth and fullness of his redemptive work.[13] This can be interpreted in quite maximalist ways, such as when Cyril, a fourth-century bishop of Jerusalem, claims that the catholicity of the church means that it teaches "universally and completely all the doctrines which man should know," contains in it "every conceivable virtue," and "treats and heals universally every sort of sin."[14]

But even if one is not as convinced as Cyril of the church's superlative glories, it is correct to affirm, in line with Paul's argument in Ephesians 4 and the trajectory of the New Testament generally, that the church's vocation is to subject all things to their rightful end: the worship and glory of the triune God. More specifically, the church is God's designated instrument for bringing citizens of every tribe, tongue, and nation into a single family. And, as this potential is realized, the church's catholicity is not only made *more extensive* (which could be construed as a merely numerical addition—more people, more nations, and more cultures represented); it is also *deepened*.

It is crucial to understand how and why catholicity brings new depth to Christian faith. The claim here is not, for example, that growth in the church's diversity across cultures mechanistically triggers a corresponding grasp of the fullness of faith. Theological understanding does not magically follow from the church's growth among the nations, and the ethnic (or any other kind of) diversity of a church, denomination, or theological faculty is not automatically correlated with greater catholicity, and therefore a deeper grasp of the faith.

Instead, there is an organic process whereby the church is increasingly able to plumb "the depth of the riches and wisdom and knowledge of God" (Rom. 11:33) through its studious attention to God's self-revelation in Christ and in the Scriptures. It is the contribution of contextual theologies to highlight that this labor of exegetical reason is culturally situated, and that culture is a material theological good chosen by God for unfolding the fullness of the divine drama of redemption. To call contextual theologies to embrace catholicity is simply to add another key element—namely, that every local church must bring its cultural gifts to bear in understanding and communicating the gospel and also bring its unique insights into interaction with the worldwide Christian community.

13. The language of height, depth, length, and breadth is employed by Dulles, though with some differences to the analysis here (Dulles, *Catholicity of the Church*, 9–10).
14. Cyril of Jerusalem, *Catechesis* 18, quoted in Dulles, *Catholicity of the Church*, 181.

On this account, then, catholicity is desirable not as an end in itself but precisely because it assists the church in rightly hearing the voice of God and responding with the holy reason, worship, and proclamation that the good news deserves. This is why giving substantial attention to tradition as part of the theological enterprise is not, as it might at first seem, at odds with the Protestant commitment to *sola Scriptura*.[15] The church, in all of its incredible diversity across time, is the "school of Christ"—the institution created and appointed by the triune God to guide us through its accumulation of knowledge of the faith—so that attention to our forebears is a way of honoring the Spirit's work among them.[16] As G. C. Berkouwer puts it, the church's catholicity is thus nothing more than the concrete and ongoing expression of the *plērōma* of riches it receives in the person and work of Christ.[17]

The recovery of the church's tradition as a critical resource for evangelical theology is one of the most important recent developments for the evangelical theological project, supplying it with deeper resources for leading the church in the exposition and living out of the good news. Yet recent accounts of evangelical theology have also called for a recognition that this new appreciation for historical depth should stand alongside attention to the church's contemporary breadth. In a recent book outlining the prospects for evangelical theology, Uche Anizor, Rob Price, and Hank Voss highlight the import of these two directions of catholicity: "We are responsible to engage the global church in conversation for some of the same reasons we would engage the historical church: to correct our myopia, strengthen our reading of Scripture, and enrich our doctrinal understanding."[18]

Similarly, in their exposition of "mere evangelical theology," Kevin Vanhoozer and Daniel Treier observe that such a project must be "catholic by being tethered to tradition, but also by being committed to extending the gospel into new contexts, and not merely by repeating earlier formulas identically."[19] As Scripture is translated into new languages and the faith

---

15. Thus, see Kevin J. Vanhoozer, *Biblical Authority after Babel: Retrieving the Solas in the Spirit of Mere Protestant Christianity* (Grand Rapids: Brazos, 2016), 109–46.

16. Michael Allen and Scott R. Swain, *Reformed Catholicity: The Promise of Retrieval for Theology and Biblical Interpretation* (Grand Rapids: Baker Academic, 2015), 17–47.

17. G. C. Berkouwer, *The Church*, trans. James E. Davison (Grand Rapids: Eerdmans, 1976), 113–14.

18. Uche Anizor, Rob Price, and Hank Voss, *Evangelical Theology* (London: Bloomsbury T&T Clark, 2021), 227.

19. Vanhoozer and Treier, *Theology and the Mirror of Scripture*, 118.

is cultivated in new cultures, the faith is deepened, and we experience the miracle of "Pentecostal plurality," the miraculous work by which the church's diversity results not in cacophony but in the harmonious proclamation of the good news.[20] Yet just as engagement with the saints departed is complicated because of the diversity of the Christian tradition, so also the cultivation of "Pentecostal plurality" rather than mere "pluralism" in the contemporary church requires wisdom to follow the lead of the unifying Spirit.[21]

The Challenge of Contemporary Catholicity

As Vanhoozer and Treier acknowledge, actually putting "contemporary catholicity" to work for theological benefit is more challenging than merely describing it in lofty terms. A starting point here is the reality that the church in the present moment is more interconnected globally than ever before as a result of advances in communication and widened access to travel. Thus, while we noted in the previous chapter that globalization is not, in itself, an ideal model for the cooperation and coordination of the church across its diverse communities, it is nevertheless a critical element of the church's present reality. The forces of globalization present important challenges for the church's theological collaboration; in particular, it must seek mutuality and fellowship patterned after the example of Jesus rather than adopting the prevailing model in which the economically powerful treat economically weaker counterparts as a source to be exploited or as a market for their own theological products. At the same time, the remarkable levels of global interconnectedness of the twenty-first century clearly offer unprecedented opportunities for theological exchange and collaboration, a substantial gift that would have been the envy of previous generations of Christians.

A second fact of the present moment is that, aside from being more interconnected than ever before, the present church is also much larger and more diverse than any previous generation of believers. Though this fact is frequently noted, we often fail to grasp the scale and complexity of the church's present diversity. Church historian Mark Noll helps us appreciate this reality by noting that "with the exception of the very earliest years of church history," the church has experienced greater geographical

---

20. Vanhoozer and Treier, *Theology and the Mirror of Scripture*, 119–22.
21. Vanhoozer and Treier, *Theology and the Mirror of Scripture*, 122–27.

"redistribution" and more substantial diversification in the past fifty years "than in any comparable period in its history."[22]

How so? To begin, Noll points out that there are far more Christians now than there have ever been. In fact, "more than half of all Christian adherents in the whole history of the church have been alive in the last one hundred years. Close to half of Christian believers who have ever lived are alive right now."[23] Specifically, the church has dramatically expanded in Asia, Africa, and Latin America while declining in Europe and remaining somewhat stagnant in North America. In 2009, Noll observed, "This past Sunday it is possible that more Christian believers attended church in China than in all of so-called 'Christian Europe,'" even though "there were no legally functioning churches in all of China" only four decades earlier. Likewise, he notes that "this past Sunday more Anglicans attended church in each of Kenya, South Africa, Tanzania and Uganda" than did their counterparts in Britain, Canada, and the United States combined. Moreover, the Anglican church in Nigeria was several times as large as the Anglican churches in Kenya, South Africa, Tanzania, or Uganda. Presbyterians in Ghana outnumbered their counterparts in Scotland. And more attended churches in Brazil's Pentecostal Assemblies of God denomination than the total of those who attended churches in "the two largest U.S. Pentecostal denominations."[24] The changing face of Christianity is evident even in Europe and North America. For example, Noll observes that "about half of the churchgoers in London" on any given Sunday are "African or African-Caribbean" and that most of the over fifteen thousand foreign missionaries doing evangelistic work in Great Britain hail from Africa and Asia.[25]

Aside from these geographic and cultural changes, Noll explains that Christianity has experienced an almost equally "dramatic multiplication of the forms of Christian faith that are now found on the planet."[26] In the distant background of this proliferation of diversity lies the Protestant Reformation.

---

22. Mark A. Noll, *The New Shape of World Christianity: How American Experience Reflects Global Faith* (Downers Grove, IL: IVP Academic, 2009), 21.

23. Noll, *New Shape of World Christianity*, 21.

24. Noll, *New Shape of World Christianity*, 20.

25. Noll, *New Shape of World Christianity*, 21. For a fascinating case study of African Christianity in a US city, see Mark R. Gornik, *Word Made Global: Stories of African Christianity in New York City* (Grand Rapids: Eerdmans, 2011).

26. Noll, *New Shape of World Christianity*, 23.

While Christians have always had different ways of expressing their faith, it is certainly true that this set of movements in sixteenth-century Europe reshaped the landscape of world Christianity in a way that allowed for far more local independence and experimentation in the practice of the faith than ever before.[27]

Yet the last century has seen a profusion of plurality driven not only by denominational diversity but also by the acceleration of Christianity putting down roots in new cultures. This story starts with the modern missionary movement, which, perhaps more importantly than anything else, resulted in the translation of Christian Scripture into hundreds of new languages. As Gambian historian Lamin Sanneh has demonstrated, this led to the empowerment of local communities of Christians all over the world, unleashing a profusion of new ways of responding in obedience to the good news.[28] It is for good reason that Timothy Tennent argues that we can compare this era to the time of the Protestant Reformation; it is a time in which there are ample opportunities for the church to recognize new dimensions to the gospel that were previously neglected, even if we have to face some of the inevitable chaos that comes with living on a seam of history.[29]

Over time, this comparison may actually turn out to understate the significance of the present moment. After all, while various Reformation movements differed with the Roman church and with one another regarding substantial matters of doctrine and practice, they generally shared common language when they wanted to discuss these matters and inherited a relatively well-developed set of assumptions about what it means to follow Jesus. Today, the church exists in a bewildering diversity of forms: from humble underground house church movements in China to jaw-dropping megachurches in Nigeria; from flamboyant Pentecostal Christian leaders in Brazil to Indonesian church leaders committed to rigorous explorations of Reformed theology; from African Initiated Churches accustomed to powerful displays of divine healing to reserved, devout Japanese congregations where such displays may be viewed with suspicion. And this is to say nothing yet of the vast (and rapidly increasing) number of Christians who

---

27. Even if this was only the case for Protestant Christians for some time, Roman Catholicism eventually found itself in a similarly diversifying landscape, especially after Vatican II.

28. Sanneh, *Translating the Message*.

29. Timothy C. Tennent, *Theology in the Context of World Christianity: How the Global Church Is Influencing the Way We Think About and Discuss Theology* (Grand Rapids: Zondervan, 2007), 1–24.

participate in hybrid cultural identities, seeking to find faithful expressions of the gospel in their particular circumstances.[30]

The good news here is that if our previous assessment is correct—namely, that cultures are material theological goods, gifts from God designed for the benefit of the church in its reception of and reflection on revelation (thesis 2)—then the many cultural incarnations of the faith are fields ripe for theological harvest. Yet even an optimistic theologian could be forgiven for looking upon this situation with some trepidation. How are the disagreements within this motley body of Christians to be resolved? What are the boundaries of acceptable Christian behavior and practice, and how are we to account for the contextual nature of such judgments without resorting to gospel-denying relativism? These questions have too often gone unanswered in discussions of the contemporary church's growing diversity, which is frequently treated as a purely positive development with no serious drawbacks, setting up practitioners for a sense of failure when they find that the task of cross-cultural theological collaboration can be difficult and even painful.

The Deliverances of Contemporary Catholicity

How, then, can a recovery and renovation of the Christian doctrine of catholicity nurture a vision of contextual theology that makes the most of local theological labors while preserving a sense of "according to the whole"? In an insightful and prescient book written in the 1990s and focused on the diversifying contemporary church, Robert Schreiter wisely highlights the need to recall and reinvigorate two aspects of catholicity to maintain "the unity and integrity of the Church worldwide": wholeness and fullness.[31]

---

30. Consider, e.g., the church profiled by Oscar García-Johnson and William A. Dyrness in their book introducing global theologies: a local congregation in Japan operating in Japanese, Spanish, and Portuguese in order to serve a mixture of immigrant and local families (William A. Dyrness and Oscar García-Johnson, *Theology without Borders: An Introduction to Global Conversations* [Grand Rapids: Baker Academic, 2015], 121–23). Though this church may present an unusually stark case of cultural hybridity, it is also the case that most congregations around the globe, especially in urban centers, must negotiate multiple cultural identities as they seek to follow Jesus authentically in their settings.

31. Schreiter, *New Catholicity*, 127. In fact, Schreiter adds "exchange and communication" as a third element in his explanation of catholicity (*New Catholicity*, 132). This volume builds upon a widely used and quite useful handbook providing guidelines for local theologizing in the 1980s: Robert J. Schreiter, *Constructing Local Theologies* (Maryknoll, NY: Orbis Books, 1985).

Wholeness

First, we can start by recalling that the church's catholicity fundamentally refers to its "wholeness" in the sense that it is the unique organism designed by God to help the good news take root among every tribe, tongue, people, and nation. Revelation 5 reminds us that this is ultimately the accomplishment of the triune God. The creatures and elders confess to the Lamb "Worthy are you to take the scroll and to open its seals" precisely because "by your blood you ransomed people for God from every tribe and language and people and nation" (Rev. 5:9). But this divine work is carried out through the ministry of the church, God's people. Indeed, it is notable that the next verse in this passage emphasizes the church's agency. They are not only a people purchased (which in itself is a totally passive reality); they are also called and assigned to be "a kingdom and priests" (Rev. 5:10), representative actors in the divine drama of redeeming a unified people from every culture in the world.[32] Thus, whatever the hardships involved, theologians have a mandate to help the gospel find a genuine home in every cultural context.

Schreiter wisely notes that understanding wholeness in this way requires us to trust that there is a "commensurability of cultures, in the sense that all cultures may receive the Word of God and be able in some measure to communicate with one another, despite real and legitimate differences."[33] In other words, if the church is God's vineyard, we must press ahead with confidence that every cultural soil is fundamentally capable of nourishing the vine of Christian faith. Moreover, we must believe and expect that because this cultivation is carried out by the church by means of the unifying Spirit, communication and unity across cultural boundaries is possible, even if it is sometimes challenging.[34]

Notably, the commensurability of cultures does not require asserting that all cultures offer equally hospitable soil for the flourishing of the gospel. Indeed, while Jesus clearly intends the parable of the soils (Matt. 13:3–23) to describe various types of individuals, each responding to the gospel in

32. For more biblical and theological support for this idea, see Anizor and Voss, *Representing Christ*.

33. Schreiter, *New Catholicity*, 128.

34. Schreiter is aware of the reality that, especially in the contemporary world, cultural boundaries and cultures themselves are in a constant state of flux—a reality that makes the pursuit of "wholeness" at once more possible (since cultures are interacting with one another more than ever before) and more challenging (since the pace of cultural change is more rapid than it has ever been).

distinctive ways, the principle can reasonably be applied to groups of people, including diverse cultures in various seasons. An experienced church planter or missionary can bear witness to this reality firsthand: in God's providence, some fields are ripe for harvest, while others require substantial tilling of the soil to produce even minimal fruit. Similarly, the church has found at times that some cultures seem to have underlying concepts and structures surprisingly well-suited to grasping and expressing the faith, while others include seemingly insuperable barriers that make it difficult for the gospel to take root.

At the same time, we should be conscious of the danger lurking here: a persistent temptation to regard our own cultures as superior vessels for the Christian message and to be unduly suspicious of the suitability of other cultures for the flourishing of the faith. Recall that, in the early church, some ethnically Jewish believers regarded themselves as having a distinct advantage over their Gentile counterparts, given in part the way that their culture had been shaped by God's redeeming activity over previous millennia. While acknowledging their privileged status as the stewards of divine revelation (Rom. 3:2), Paul is at pains to highlight that this does not give them the advantages in understanding the good news of Jesus that they might expect (Rom. 3:9–20).

Christians living in contemporary Western contexts may need a similar reminder; while the Judeo-Christian heritage of Western cultures is a rich legacy with many elements deserving of honor, preservation, and recovery, it is not uniquely appointed or suitable for hosting the vine of Christian faith. Moreover, the post-Christian secularism that has enveloped European and North American cultures may turn out to be one of the most difficult environments for the cultivation of flourishing Christian faith.[35] It is, in part, for this reason that Ghanaian theologian Kwame Bediako has argued that Christianity may in many ways be better suited to African cultures than to contemporary Western ones.[36]

Contextual theologies seeking to foster catholicity in the sense of *wholeness* will take as their starting point the expectation that the triune God can and

35. For trenchant analysis of this problem, see Charles Taylor, *A Secular Age* (Cambridge, MA: Harvard University Press, 2007); for a more accessible but still excellent introduction to Taylor's argument, see James K. A. Smith, *How (Not) to Be Secular: Reading Charles Taylor* (Grand Rapids: Eerdmans, 2014).
36. See the detailed and careful arguments in Kwame Bediako, *Christianity in Africa: The Renewal of a Non-Western Religion* (Maryknoll, NY: Orbis Books, 1995).

will make good on the promise to draw to himself a people from every tribe, tongue, and nation and that he will therefore bolster the church's efforts to join in the divine mission of causing Christian faith to flourish among all peoples. Schreiter rightly notes that this will require a certain generosity of spirit that allows for the necessary experimentation and trial and error that are inevitably part of the contextualization process, even as theologians seek to preserve the integrity of the message and unity of the church.[37] Christians from cultures that enjoy greater dominance in the theological landscape will need to be especially judicious in imposing requirements for unity on others—emulating James, in the Jerusalem Council, calling for unity in the most essential matters (Acts 15:20–21) while also emphasizing that "we should not trouble those of the Gentiles who turn to God" (15:19). This warning applies most clearly to Christians from North America and Europe at the moment, but it also has important implications for Majority World Christians who must grapple with the challenge of leading diverse churches with remarkably varied social norms and expectations.

Fullness

In addition to *wholeness*, Schreiter suggests that we update our conception of *fullness* as we foster catholicity in the present era.[38] To extend the vineyard metaphor from earlier: if the church is the Lord's vineyard, its workers are commanded to cultivate the gospel in every cultural soil—not only getting vines to grow but also allowing each to produce wine that makes the most of its specific natural environment. Schreiter rightly warns that theologians committed to this aspect of catholicity must be prepared for a challenge. Translating the Christian message "fully" into all human cultures will require patience, persistence, and a constant focus on ensuring that the message is really getting through, even as we acknowledge the imperfect nature of all efforts to sum up the glory of the faith.[39]

Even with these caveats in mind, the value of pursuing genuine "fullness" of faith in the communion of the saints is worthwhile. Indeed, for evangelicals this calling to cultivate the fullness of the faith among every culture should be understood to be an element of Jesus's primary command

---

37. Schreiter, *New Catholicity*, 129.
38. Schreiter, *New Catholicity*, 131.
39. Schreiter, *New Catholicity*, 131.

in the Great Commission; making disciples is, after all, not a matter of simply translating tracts and making converts. The kingdom of God demands nothing less than the submission of all things in every culture to the lordship of the triune God.

As the church pursues the fullness of faith in this way, Vanhoozer and Treier helpfully note that cultivating "Pentecostal plurality" will require discernment and wisdom "to know the difference between courageously preserving the truths of the gospel that cannot change and charitably acknowledging the interpretive diversity of nonessential truths."[40] While they propose three "levels" of doctrine that might assist in this discernment—which help at least to clarify that not all differences are of the same caliber—they rightly point out that there is no simple method for resolving these differences. Instead, evangelical theologians are called to cultivate virtuous habits of heart and mind—wisdom, humility, courage, charity, generosity, contextual sensitivity—that will assist the church in growing to its full stature.[41] Moreover, as we learn from the Jerusalem Council of Acts 15, Scripture must be the decisive factor in such disputes if the church is to continue discharging its apostolic duty faithfully. While there will inevitably be interpretive disagreements, this commitment at least provides an important boundary and centering value for those operating within the evangelical tradition.

Concretely, a commitment to fullness should translate into robust support for the youngest elements of the church, whether in terms of finances, prayer, or other kinds of partnership. The principle of catholicity tells us that such assistance is not merely altruistic. It is an investment in the long-term health of the whole church and may ultimately be an instrument of salvation for churches in regions where the church is more established. In addition, a commitment to catholicity should be reflected in substantial support for and participation in organizations such as the World Evangelical Alliance, the Lausanne Movement, and transcontinental denominational bodies. Each of these is imperfect in various ways, but they do offer historically unprecedented opportunities for collaboration and the exchange of ideas. They are key arenas for theologians seeking to cultivate a "catholic sensibility," as well as being practical avenues for the discovery of the full riches available in Christ.

40. Vanhoozer and Treier, *Theology and the Mirror of Scripture*, 123.
41. Vanhoozer and Treier, *Theology and the Mirror of Scripture*, 124–27.

Even as we engage in this pursuit of the fullness of the faith, we should be mindful of two extremes, both of which are often evident in current discussions of the value of engaging the worldwide church. The first is to expect too much, too fast from our engagements with the global church. It is true that the growth of the church in the Majority World has been extraordinarily fast and has been accompanied by remarkable reminders of the gospel's transforming power. It is also correct to expect, based on the church's history as well as the witness of Scripture, that as the gospel makes its home in places it has never been (or from which it has been absent for a long season), new insights and fresh perspectives on the glory of the gospel will emerge. As Andrew Walls has noted, as the church in the Majority World grows, we should expect that "the theological workshop is likely to be busier than ever before, its workers more varied in language, culture, and outlook."[42]

But Christians exploring various ways to penetrate, renew, and transform the thought worlds and lifeways of their cultures takes time (in the past, often centuries). Moreover, history suggests that these insights will usually look more like a "fine-tuning" of the faith than radical revisions of Christian doctrine and practice. This does not make the fresh insights of the emerging Majority World churches unimportant by any means; incremental growth over time adds up to substantial insight and is an important element in maintaining the church's ongoing vitality. But as much as a catholic sensibility will look for new insight into the gospel as the church spreads, it also acts as a constraint, pulling the church toward unity with its peers around the globe. Theological innovation unconstrained by catholicity would be more exciting and perhaps more efficient, but it is not God's design for his people.

The other extreme is to expect far too little. Sometimes this is a simple matter of myopia—a result of not seeing the worldwide Christian community as an important interlocutor at all. However, it can also be a result of a tendency to exoticize the parts of the church that are culturally different from our own, regarding them not as equal partners in the discovery of the riches available in Christ but, rather, as curiosities to be discussed and analyzed. Unintentionally, such an approach often results in the further marginalization of cultural expressions of the faith that are different from our own, insulating ourselves from the challenging work of cultivating

42. Andrew Walls, "The Rise of Global Theologies," in *Global Theology in Evangelical Perspective: Exploring the Contextual Nature of Theology and Mission*, ed. Jeffrey P. Greenman and Gene L. Green (Downers Grove, IL: IVP Academic, 2012), 33.

catholicity and relegating our culturally "other" neighbors to the margins of our theological reflection. Kenyan theologian John Mbiti gives voice to this reality when he observes, "We have eaten theology with you; we have drunk theology with you; we have dreamed theology with you. . . . We know you theologically. The question is: Do you know us, theologically? Would you like to know us, theologically?"[43] Both we and our counterparts are bound to suffer as we fail to make good on the promise of Pentecostal plurality, and the redeeming power of the Spirit is muted and tamed rather than unleashed.

When we fall into either of these extremes in our theologizing, we should repent and then keep pressing ahead. It should be clear that a world in which Christians are fearful of cross-cultural interaction is not one in which catholicity can truly be fostered. Yet, as anyone who has worked cross-culturally for long knows, the fear of offending or accidentally violating our neighbor's expectations can be paralyzing. Indeed, this is probably the first enemy that must be vanquished when learning to speak a new language and live in a new culture. This fear is a relic of Babel that must be driven out of the catholic fellowship created by Pentecost, replaced instead by a mixture of humility and confidence rooted in the unifying power of the one Spirit.

We should note, also, that catholic *fullness* has at least one further aspect—namely, that as the gospel finds its home in new cultures, not only does the church gain access to the fullness of its riches in Christ but the Spirit also draws out the full potential of every human culture and even of every human individual. As God's grace gets hold of us, we do not become *less* ourselves, and *less* (for example) Filipino; instead, we—and our communities—become increasingly what we were designed to be, and the diverse goods of our cultures become perfected by the sanctifying Spirit. In an essay on Christian ethics, Herman Bavinck describes the uniqueness of the kingdom of God in this way: "Precisely by means of the single shared life of the organism, the individual members of the organism are maintained and preserved in their differentiation and uniqueness. Exactly for that reason the Kingdom of God is the highest, the most perfect community, because it guarantees to each one's personality the most completely well-rounded and richest development of its content. For the unity of an organism becomes the more

43. John S. Mbiti, "Theological Impotence and the Universality of the Church," in *Third World Theologies*, ed. Gerald R. Anderson and Thomas F. Stransky, Mission Trends 3 (Grand Rapids: Eerdmans, 1976), 16–17.

harmonious, the more rich, and the more glorious to the degree that the multitude of parts increases."[44]

Only a church established by God's perfecting grace can realize this vision—one in which the triune God fosters the plurality of Pentecost rather than the chaos of Babel or the anemia of cultural tribalism. And only contextual theology grounded in catholic judgment can guide the church toward this divinely appointed end.

Case Study: Christology in Latin American and Global Perspective

Perhaps no locus of Christian doctrine is more promising for developing catholic dialogue across the church's cultural centers than Christology. In Jesus, we meet a person for all peoples, one whose embodiment of the local and universal foreshadows the dual identity of the church that he calls into existence. The biblical canon itself, by offering four distinctive but complementary witnesses to the life of Jesus, beckons for Christological reflection that is diverse in its emphasis while still pointing faithfully to the one Son. And, in the early church, most of the ecumenical councils focused on offering unified judgments regarding the nature and person of Jesus. These were local, contextual judgments about Jesus that were nevertheless endorsed by the worldwide church and offered material gains for the church of all eras.

So it is fitting that Christology has also been a primary focus for contextual theological reflections in recent decades.[45] It is evident that, in addition to the affirmations about Jesus that all Christians hold in common, certain aspects of Christ's identity tend to stand out in some cultures and times more than others, so that documenting the faith of Christians in other contexts may have the favorable effect of highlighting aspects of Christ that

44. Herman Bavinck, "The Kingdom of God, The Highest Good," trans. Nelson D. Kloosterman, *The Bavinck Review* 2 (2011): 144. For an excellent treatment of how Bavinck's thinking provides a robust basis for contemporary calls to diversity in Christian organizations, see William E. Boyce, "A Doctrine for Diversity: Utilizing Herman Bavinck's Theology for Racial Reconciliation in the Church," *Journal of Markets and Morality* 23, no. 2 (2020): 319–36.

45. See, e.g., Leonardo Boff, *Jesus Christ Liberator: A Critical Christology for Our Time*, trans. Patrick Hughes (Maryknoll, NY: Orbis Books, 1978); Charles Nyamiti, *Christ as Our Ancestor: Christology from an African Perspective* (Gweru, Zimbabwe: Mambo, 1984); Michael Amaladoss, *The Asian Jesus* (Maryknoll, NY: Orbis Books, 2006).

are often overlooked in our own contexts.[46] A classic study of this sort is Diane Stinton's *Jesus of Africa*, which surveys formal African Christologies as well as popular expressions of faith (through interviews, analysis of hymns, etc.) to "explore how African Christians today respond to the fundamental question of Jesus Christ, 'Who do you say that I am?' (Mark 8:29)."[47] The African interpretations of Jesus that Stinton documents do not contravene classical expressions of Christology, but instead deepen them and cast them in a new light. For example, readers will come away from the study with a deeper sense of what it means for Jesus to be "the resurrection and the life" (John 11:25), given the extensive and nuanced perspective on "life" in African Christian thought.[48]

Other approaches to contextual Christology have been more constructive, proposing novel local categories and analogies to interpret Jesus, typically with the dual aim of serving local needs and enriching the global church's understanding of Christ.[49] In Africa, one prominent set of proposals has focused on the way Jesus fulfills the role played by ancestors in African traditional religions by offering guidance, protection, blessing, and insight to their community, but in a manner superior to merely human ancestors. Advocates of ancestor Christology propose that this image offers not only a connection between the biblical picture of Jesus and African culture but also new insight into the nature of Jesus's lordship. Notably, this view has been challenged by other African theologians, who have raised questions about the validity of the analogy and note substantial discontinuities between the role of ancestors and the mediating role of Jesus.[50] Similar dynamics are evident in Asia, where a slew of proposals have emerged in recent decades,

46. For a historical demonstration of this point, see Jaroslav Pelikan, *Jesus through the Centuries: His Place in the History of Culture* (New Haven: Yale University Press, 1985).

47. Diane B. Stinton, *Jesus of Africa: Voices of Contemporary African Christology* (Maryknoll, NY: Orbis Books, 2004), 21.

48. Stinton, *Jesus of Africa*, 54–108. See also Bénézet Bujo, *African Theology in Its Social Context*, trans. John O'Donohue (Maryknoll, NY: Orbis Books, 1992).

49. For a survey of such efforts, see Volker Küster, *The Many Faces of Jesus Christ: Intercultural Christology* (Maryknoll, NY: Orbis Books, 2001); Veli-Matti Kärkkäinen, *Christology: A Global Introduction*, 2nd ed. (Grand Rapids: Baker Academic, 2016), 143–74.

50. Among others, see Victor I. Ezigbo, *Re-imagining African Christologies: Conversing with the Interpretations and Appropriations of Jesus in Contemporary African Christianity* (Eugene, OR: Pickwick, 2010); Reuben Turbi Luka, *Jesus Christ as Ancestor: A Theological Study of Major African Ancestor Christologies in Conversation with the Patristic Christologies of Tertullian and Athanasius* (Carlisle, UK: Langham Monographs, 2019). For a very insightful survey of contextual Christological reflections currently emerging from African churches, see Rodney L. Reed and David K. Ngaruiya, eds., *Who Do You Say That I Am?: Christology in Africa* (Carlisle, UK: Langham Global Library, 2021).

with theologians in the region debating their validity and utility for under-standing the work of Christ.[51] These are cases in which all Christians can benefit from following the present discussion. Even when proposals turn out to be theological dead ends, we do well to recall that some of the richest theological insights emerged as the church wrestled with novel explanations of the gospel, rejecting some new expressions as departures from the *regula fidei* ("rule of faith") while recognizing others as faithful insights into the wonderful works of God.

Christology in Latin America

For the rest of this case study, however, we will focus on a deeper analysis of a specific Christological proposal from Puerto Rican theologian Jules Martinez-Olivieri. In an insightful recent work, Martinez-Olivieri presents a proposal for an approach to Christology that both builds upon and moves beyond previous developments in Latin American theology. He notes that, for several decades, first Catholics and then Protestants have labored to incorporate into Christology an emphasis on "God's dynamic action to rec-oncile the world in Christ," bringing about total transformation through "the reign of God in the body of Christ, the church."[52]

This focus on liberation, transformation, and Christian witness is an important contribution to the global church's understanding of the nature of Jesus's work. Yet Martinez-Olivieri notes a problematic lacuna: these proposals consistently fail to ground their descriptions of Christ and his liberating work in a robust doctrine of the Trinity. This is no minor quibble, for it is the triune God who accomplishes social transformation and libera-tion by the sending of the Son and Spirit, and it is only in the context of the Trinity that we can understand and appreciate the transformation Christ effects among his people.[53]

To address this gap, Martinez-Olivieri advances a proposal that makes the most of the insights that have emerged in the region regarding the transformative

---

51. For a survey, see Timoteo D. Gener, "Christologies in Asia: Trends and Reflections," in *Jesus without Borders: Christology in the Majority World*, ed. Gene L. Green, Stephen T. Pardue, and K. K. Yeo (Grand Rapids: Eerdmans, 2014), 59–79; Ivor Poobalan, "Christology in Asia: Rooted and Responsive," in *Asian Christian Theology: Evangelical Perspectives*, ed. Timoteo D. Gener and Stephen T. Pardue (Carlisle, UK: Langham Global Library, 2019), 83–100.

52. Jules A. Martinez-Olivieri, *A Visible Witness: Christology, Liberation, and Participation*, Emerging Scholars (Minneapolis: Fortress, 2016), 17.

53. Martinez-Olivieri, *Visible Witness*, 9–14.

power of Christ's atonement, while also situating this liberating work squarely within a classical trinitarian framework. The result is an excellent example of theology that is intentionally local—stating its confession of Christ "in light of concerns primal to the life of the Christian church in Latin America"—but also catholic in its engagement with the whole council of Scripture and the fullness of the Christian tradition, past and present.[54]

Martinez-Olivieri's account of Christology starts with a confession that "in the history of Jesus of Nazareth, humanity finds freedom from the bondage of sin, because Jesus comes from God, and in that commission he shares in particular ways the divine identity and prerogatives."[55] Martinez-Olivieri builds on the pattern of other Latin American Christologies by focusing on the kingdom (Greek, *basileia*) of God while also setting the concept in its broader canonical and doctrinal framework. This grand vision is not a utopian humanistic dream or a religious idealization; it is something far better: "a concrete historical reality that proleptically appears over a people that confesses to live for God" as foreshadowed in the Old Testament and fulfilled in Jesus.[56]

Martinez-Olivieri affirms that liberation Christologies are correct in emphasizing the radical, transformative power of Jesus's rule and reign, which is sometimes tamed or dulled in doctrinal treatments of Christology. But he notes that "the reality of the reign of God as a state of affairs implemented by God is crucially related to Jesus' identity and mission."[57] The Gospels clearly contend that the transformation, reconciliation, and freedom available in Jesus are available only because he is the divine Son, able to open the way for others to be "incorporated as friends of Jesus and adopted into the family of God."[58] As disciples of Jesus are incorporated into the divine life by means of their union with Christ, "they are brought to the Father and are given life by the Spirit" and thereby enabled to participate in the divine mission.[59]

The cross is thus more than a merely "quasi-heroic event" in which "Jesus reveals that God is with us in suffering and in pain."[60] To grasp the power of the salvation offered in the cross, we must first appreciate the depth and

---

54. Martinez-Olivieri, *Visible Witness*, 137.
55. Martinez-Olivieri, *Visible Witness*, 148.
56. Martinez-Olivieri, *Visible Witness*, 153.
57. Martinez-Olivieri, *Visible Witness*, 154.
58. Martinez-Olivieri, *Visible Witness*, 166.
59. Martinez-Olivieri, *Visible Witness*, 167–68.
60. Martinez-Olivieri, *Visible Witness*, 174.

breadth of sin as it is presented in the Old Testament. It is "a force that captivates human praxis," and in "its communal consolidation in social and political structures" it is also "an antikingdom . . . where the powers and principalities are arrayed against God and humanity."[61] Salvation is likewise expansive and multifaceted. It is a "definitive break from sin" that establishes "communion with God and communion with others and with creation" and effects liberation as people "are made free, righteous, and just, and are given the opportunity to live life in the present as a witness of Jesus' present reign of life."[62] The church thus becomes the "theater of liberation," called "by the Spirit's enablement to reproduce the Spirited praxis of Jesus in choosing the 'least of these'—the vulnerable, sick, and neglected—as a criterion of the presence of God's reigning activity."[63]

This is only a brief sketch of Martinez-Olivieri's work, which is full of interesting avenues for further reflection. His work is a primary example of theology done with an unswerving focus on the substantive contributions of local theology set alongside a commitment to bringing these insights into conversation with the concerns of the worldwide church. In the tension between the local and the catholic, there is productive energy to escape the dead ends and ruts of traditional theological debate and help us grasp the gospel with new depth and vitality.

Conclusion

In this chapter, we have argued that the marks of the church—and particularly its catholicity—point a productive way forward for evangelical contextual theologies. Approaches to the contextual theological task that are rooted in catholicity will have at least two advantages over alternatives. First and foremost, such approaches will use the judgments of the church across nations, peoples, and cultures to propel, assess, and temper novel local theological developments. As a prerequisite, this means cultivating awareness of and openness to the need for those developments, which in turn means admitting that the theological "status quo"—the dominant theological voices of the day, and even the utterances of our theological ancestors—is always limited and local in important ways. Even the earliest creeds, the most universally

---

61. Martinez-Olivieri, *Visible Witness*, 178, 176.
62. Martinez-Olivieri, *Visible Witness*, 179–80.
63. Martinez-Olivieri, *Visible Witness*, 193–94.

accepted summaries of the good news, must be recognized as contextual expressions of the faith, snapshots in a particular time and place rather than acultural descriptions of God and the gospel. A catholic contextual theology is therefore unafraid—and even recognizes a mandate—to try new things as it mines the riches of Christ with the tools of local culture and language.

The second advantage of catholic approaches to contextual theology is that such approaches will honor the unity of the Spirit by treating novel theological developments as participation in and expression of the full witness of Christ. This places important constraints upon those in the cultural majority, who must resist the temptation to consider the emerging theologies of the Majority World church (and of cultural minorities) as exotic samples or irrelevant exercises in "interest group" theologizing. Authentically catholic contextual theology requires, instead, viewing emerging local theologies as genuinely necessary partners in discovering and discerning the full riches of the faith and meeting the needs of the whole church. This process will require wisdom, discernment, and patience, as history demonstrates that the inculturation process takes time and often includes misses and dead ends. But, by the providence of God, it is the calling of his people to persist in continually cultivating our catholic sensibility.

At the start of the chapter, we noted that such a catholic approach to contextual theology must not attend solely to the diversity of the church in the present—which, indeed, is a unique opportunity—but must also include an appreciation for catholicity across time. Thus, while open, and even committed, to progressively understanding the fullness of the good news, contextual theologies rooted in the one, holy, catholic, and apostolic church will also have a necessarily "conservative" sensibility. In part this is because they seek to mirror the holiness and apostolicity of Christ's body, and so they always bear in mind their calling to bring all things into submission to the sanctifying Spirit (holiness) and the authoritative Word (apostolicity). In addition, they recognize that their obligations to the whole church complement and, in important ways, constrain their locality and novelty. Thus, although new theological developments are required as the church spreads into new cultural and national territory (and as cultures change over time), such doctrinal development must honor the hard-won insights into the faith from Christians throughout time and across the globe. This is precisely the tension that we will explore in more detail in the next chapter.

6

A Great Cloud of Witnesses

Contextual Theology in the Fellowship of the Saints

> Therefore, since we are surrounded by so great a cloud of witnesses, let us also lay aside every weight, and sin which clings so closely, and let us run with endurance the race that is set before us, looking to Jesus, the founder and perfecter of our faith, who for the joy that was set before him endured the cross, despising the shame, and is seated at the right hand of the throne of God.
>
> —Hebrews 12:1–2

In the previous chapter, we saw how contextual theologies committed to catholicity can avoid one of the dangers facing efforts to bring theological study into deep acquaintance with local cultures: the threat of cultural tribalism and fragmentation. Rightly understood, the calling to catholicity allows the church to bear unified witness to the fullness of the riches revealed in Christ, which is accomplished precisely *through* rather than *in spite of* the diversity of the church's cultures. As we observed, the practicalities of such work are daunting. Babel continues to exert its divisive effects, even among God's people. And while we have more opportunity to interact with one another across the globe than ever before, we are also a more diverse people than we have ever been, which brings genuine challenges to cultivating the

"Pentecostal plurality" to which we aspire. Despite these challenges, the divine calling is to keep laboring to make the gospel deeply rooted in our local cultures while never forgetting our belonging among all the people of God scattered abroad. This is how evangelical efforts at contextual theology must continue to proceed.

Yet catholic sensibility must push us not only further outward—into genuine interchange with our counterparts in other cultures and around the globe—but also backward, into constant conversation with our fathers and mothers in the faith. This aspect of catholicity is an extension of the logic of the divine economy of salvation: the gifts of God are distributed abroad among the church in all cultures and nations, but they are by no means given only to the church of the present age. So contextual theologies committed to the singular gospel must not only cultivate unity amid contemporary plurality but also be marked by catholic engagement with the saints of ages past. In so doing, they address the threat of fragmentation as well as that of historical discontinuity—the possibility that in the process of transmitting the gospel and making it at home in every place and among every people, the single story of redemption diverges into so many directions as to dissolve entirely. In addition, the present-day church can find crucial wisdom in its own engagement with culture as it learns from the successes and failures of contextual theological judgments of ages past. Thus, we come to thesis five: *evangelical contextual theologies should engage the Great Tradition of the church, finding there a rich treasury to support contemporary renewal as well as a community that helps prevent slavish obedience to the theological present.*

A Martian Walks into a Church

Like cultivating contemporary catholicity, pursuing genuine fellowship with the saints gone before is daunting because of the diversity of the Christian tradition. In an article first published in 1982, church historian Andrew Walls offers a fascinating thought experiment that can help us grasp the breadth and variance of Christian expressions of the good news over time. He asks us to imagine "a long-living, scholarly space visitor" who visits the Earth every few centuries and is interested in understanding Christianity.[1]

---

1. Andrew F. Walls, "The Gospel as Prisoner and Liberator of Culture," in *The Missionary Movement in Christian History: Studies in the Transmission of Faith* (Maryknoll, NY: Orbis Books, 1996), 3. The article was first published in *Faith and Thought* 108 (1982): 39–52.

He sets about seeking to observe "the practices, habits, and concerns of a representative sample of Christians" on each visit. On his first visit, a few years after Christ's ascension, he observes the original "Jerusalem Christians" and notes that they maintain most standard Jewish practices and are distinguished from other Jewish sects only in that they identify "the recent prophet-teacher Jesus of Nazareth" as having inaugurated the end of the current age. Our space visitor regards Christianity as essentially a denomination of Judaism, marked especially by a penchant for joyful obedience to God's law, tight-knit family lives, and the pursuit of personal holiness as the time for the Messiah's second coming draws near.[2]

Three hundred years later, the same visitor returns just in time to attend the Council of Nicaea. To his surprise, hardly any representatives at the council are Jewish; unlike their predecessors, they are "horrified at the thought of animal sacrifices," and none of them appear to be married or have children. They do not keep the Sabbath on the seventh day. They preserve the Jewish titles for Jesus, in Greek translation, but are especially focused on which obscure Greek term—*homoousios* or *homoiousios* ("same substance" or "like substance")—is better suited to describe the ontological relationship between the Father and the Son. On this visit, the space visitor concludes that a key characteristic of Christians may be that they are especially concerned "with metaphysics and theology," engaging in intensive attempts to clarify the precise meaning of theological terms. Yet he wonders whether this could have also been true of the Jewish Christians he visited three centuries prior.[3]

Three hundred years later still, he visits Ireland and finds a group of Christian monks gathered. Some are "standing in ice-cold water up to their necks, reciting the psalms. Some are standing immobile, praying—with their arms outstretched in the form of a cross. . . . Others are sitting quite alone in dark caves by the seashore, seeking no intercourse with men." He notices some continuity with the previous era: the monks "use the same formula that he heard being hammered out in Nicea." But he is surprised that "they do not in general seem very interested in theology or very good at metaphysics." Above all, he notes that these Christians are marked by "their desire for holiness and their heroic austerity in quest of it."[4]

2. Walls, "Gospel as Prisoner and Liberator of Culture," 3.
3. Walls, "Gospel as Prisoner and Liberator of Culture," 4.
4. Walls, "Gospel as Prisoner and Liberator of Culture," 4.

On his next visit, he lands over a millennium later, in 1840s London. Here he finds Christians gathered in an assembly discussing the promotion of Christianity in Africa, proposing that missionaries be sent thousands of miles away to spread Christianity and "civilization" to the far-flung continent. Our observer finds that most of the present group accept "without question the creed of Nicea" and that, "like the Irish, they also use the word 'holy' quite a lot; but they are aghast at the suggestion that holiness could be connected with standing in cold water, and utterly opposed to the idea of spending life praying in an isolated cave." Here, rather than being starved and isolated, he finds Christians to be relatively prosperous and highly engaged with the wider society, both locally and abroad.[5]

The final imagined visit is to Lagos, Nigeria, in 1980. Here, "a white-robed group is dancing and chanting through streets on their way to their church. They are informing the world at large that they are Cherubim and Seraphim; they are inviting people to come and experience the power of God in their services. They claim that God has messages for particular individuals and that his power can be demonstrated in healing." When asked, these Christians say that they "accept the creed of Nicea, but they display little interest in it: they appear somewhat vague about the relationship of the Divine Son and the Holy Spirit." They are not politically engaged, and while they sometimes fast like the Irish, it is only "on fixed occasions and for fixed purposes." What most characterizes this group of Christians? The space visitor concludes that it is "their concern with power, as revealed in preaching, healing, and personal vision."[6]

Now the space scholar is back on his planetary home, wondering how to correlate all his observations. He has managed to avoid some of the most strange and extreme versions of Christianity, which would have made for even more incoherence. Indeed, on each visit he has encountered an instance of Christianity somewhat representative of its place and time. He has been able to trace the major turning points of Christianity's growth and development—from a Jewish sect to a Hellenistic religion, to a faith driven largely by monastic concerns, to an activistic evangelicalism spreading across Europe, to a vibrant and large presence spreading across Africa. But he cannot help but observe that while all five groups claim to be Christians, they

---

5. Walls, "Gospel as Prisoner and Liberator of Culture," 5.
6. Walls, "Gospel as Prisoner and Liberator of Culture," 5.

seem to be concerned with remarkably different things, and "the concerns of one group appear suspect or even repellent to another."[7]

Nevertheless, Walls notes that if the space visitor is astute, he will recognize that there are at least two ways in which the groups are all connected. First, they share a common past; each generation of Christians owes its existence to the previous one in some sense. Aside from this, all five groups share significant continuity in their judgments about Jesus Christ, their reliance upon the same set of sacred writings (with the exception of the Jewish Christians, who did not yet have the New Testament), and their practice of special activities associated with bread and wine and water. Moreover, each group is conscious of its continuity with God's redeeming work in the ancient Near Eastern people of Israel. Yet the visitor must admit that "these continuities are cloaked with such heavy veils belonging to their environment that Christians of different times and places must often be unrecognizable to others, or indeed even to themselves, as manifestations of a single phenomenon."[8]

Walls uses this thought experiment to highlight the tension inherent within the Christian gospel. On the one hand, every culture can and must become a true home for the good news; on the other, the gospel also draws all of us out of our home cultures by "bringing into everyone's society some sort of outside reference."[9] Walls spent his career drawing out the implications of these two forces in Christian faith. As a historian of the church and particularly of its cross-cultural movement, one of his signal achievements was helping contemporary scholars to recognize the similarities between the rapid growth of the church in the twenty-first-century Global South and its expansion across cultural lines in the earliest centuries. More broadly, his work has helped generate an entirely new discipline, called "World Christianity," whose project it is to understand how the globalized faith of Christians today is not new but instead simply continues the (sometimes forgotten or minimized) history of the church as a people making the gospel at home in every nation.[10] In this way, perhaps more than anyone else, Walls has

---

7. Walls, "Gospel as Prisoner and Liberator of Culture," 5.

8. Walls, "Gospel as Prisoner and Liberator of Culture," 7.

9. Walls, "Gospel as Prisoner and Liberator of Culture," 9. Walls names these competing instincts the "indigenizing principle" and the "pilgrim principle." These tendencies sometimes pull in opposing directions, but Walls argues that they create a healthy tension for every Christian community to navigate.

10. William R. Burrows, Mark R. Gornik, and Janice A. McLean, eds., *Understanding World Christianity: The Vision and Work of Andrew F. Walls* (Maryknoll, NY: Orbis Books, 2011).

helped demonstrate that understanding how the church grappled with the gospel and culture in the past is the critical backdrop for understanding the interplay of these realities today.

Wrestling with the Great Tradition

Walls's proposal brings us into simultaneous contact with two live wires that evangelical theologians have been hesitant to handle for decades: culture and tradition. As we noted at the start of the book, evangelicals have had the intuition that giving too much attention to cultural context in constructing Christian doctrine will result in cultural idolatry. The concerns with tradition are similar—namely, that the evangel may be obscured or distorted by giving undue attention to the "tradition of the elders" (Mark 7:3). Jesus's warnings against "making void the word of God" by the application of tradition (Mark 7:13) and other New Testament warnings (e.g., Col. 2:8) are well-worn in Protestant and evangelical circles, and churches in the evangelical tradition (irony intended) are often marked by a conviction that the order of the day is recovering the Christianity of the earliest disciples of Jesus by leapfrogging over the intervening history, except to see where the institutional church has gone wrong.

Intriguingly, the instinct to distrust tradition is often amplified among those who have some interest in bringing the faith to bear in culturally relevant ways. Here, typical evangelical worries about tradition are compounded because tradition is viewed not only as a threat to the purity of the gospel but also as extra baggage weighing down missionary efforts to make the good news understandable and relevant to people from every tribe, tongue, and nation. Twentieth-century missiologists, aiming to correct the errors of previous, colonialist missionary endeavors, have often insisted that cross-cultural workers must divest themselves of their own (primarily) Western traditions if they want to initiate real outposts of the gospel, and not just embassies of Western culture.

In the introduction of his bestselling book, which describes his experience of evangelistic conversations in India, the influential American missionary E. Stanley Jones describes his evolution as a cross-cultural worker:

> When I first went to India I was trying to hold a very long line—a line that stretched clear from Genesis to Revelation, on to Western Civilization and to the Western

Christian Church. I found myself bobbing up and down that line fighting behind Moses and David and Jesus and Paul and Western Civilization and the Christian Church. . . . I found the battle almost invariably being pitched at one of these three places: the Old Testament, or Western Civilization, or the Christian Church. . . . Then I saw that I could, and should, shorten my line, that I could take my stand at Christ and before that non-Christian world refuse to know anything save Jesus Christ and him crucified. . . . I saw that the gospel lies in the person of Jesus, that he himself is the Good News, that my one task was to live and to present him. My task was simplified.[11]

As Jones expounds on this insight throughout the book, it becomes clear that his primary objection is to the association of Christianity with the racist attitudes and oppressive policies promoted by Westerners at the time. This insight was surely correct, as was Jones's intuition that a key step for the Christian church in India must be to disassociate itself from the West to some degree in the interest of offering Indians a genuine encounter with Jesus as the saving Son of God, rather than acting as ambassadors of Western culture. While this may seem obvious today, Jones deserves credit for helping a generation of missionaries reject colonialist and racist tendencies and genuinely appreciate the beauty and goodness in Indian culture.

Yet it is also notable that the expression of Christian faith favored by Jones and by many mission-minded evangelical thinkers tends to prioritize helping people experience Jesus in a personal and experiential manner. For this task, Christian doctrine and the history of the Christian church is viewed not only as superfluous but as a deterrent to the Christian calling. Jones argues at one point that "it is Christ who unites us; it is doctrines that divide."[12] Thus, while the body of doctrine developed by our Christian forebears is a legacy for which we can be grateful, the primary task of cross-cultural workers is to present the resurrected and living Christ, and even perhaps to hold back and lay to the side the body of Christian teaching that the church has generated over the centuries in order to make way for genuinely Indian Christianity to emerge.

---

11. E. Stanley Jones, *The Christ of the Indian Road* (New York: Abingdon, 1926), 7–8. On the next page, Jones clarifies that he still affirms the importance of the Old Testament as spiritual nourishment, even if he regards it as not the ideal starting point in evangelism. This text is available online at https://archive.org/details/in.ernet.dli.2015.122191/page/n1/mode/2up.

12. Jones, *Christ of the Indian Road*, 155.

In the 1970s, as theologians increasingly recognized that Majority World (or, in the language of the time, *Third World*) churches would develop theology distinct from their Western counterparts, proposals emerged that solidified this intuition into a hardened theological principle. In an influential article, Swiss theologian Daniel von Allmen argued that the calling of theologians today is to "take everything back to the very roots of the Christian faith" and to perform a similar act of contextualization to the first generation of Christians, who adapted an initially Jewish faith into a Hellenistic context.[13] Thus, theologians in Africa, Asia, or any setting must "start ever anew from the focal point of the faith" and build on it in a way "which is both faithful to the inner thrust of the Christian revelation and also in harmony with the mentality of the person who formulates it."[14]

This means that theologians today must start with "a kind of *tabula rasa*," rather than translating or migrating any pre-existing theological system. Even "biblical theologies" are unworthy starting points, for the goal must be to let the African church go "back beyond any already developed theology to the stage at which the theology of the New Testament was still being worked out," and to imitate the "dynamism" of the first generation of Christians contextualizing the faith.[15] In short, von Allmen proposes that Christians in the emerging churches of Africa and Asia—and even in Europe—not seek to "do theology" at all, but instead seek to worship and obey Jesus Christ while being fully themselves; this is what the earliest Christians did, he argues, and it should also be the manner for the development of theology today.[16]

What von Allmen proposed, evangelical missionaries and missiologists have often sought to put into practice. In a book widely used for training several generations of cross-cultural missionaries, Charles Kraft echoes and builds on von Allmen to propose a method of "dynamic-equivalence theologizing."[17] This process attempts to reproduce in today's cultural contexts "the theologizing process that Paul and the other scriptural authors exemplify."[18] Kraft is concerned with preventing theology from devolving

---

13. Daniel von Allmen, "The Birth of Theology," *International Review of Mission* 64, no. 253 (1975): 47.

14. Von Allmen, "Birth of Theology," 50.

15. Von Allmen, "Birth of Theology," 51.

16. Von Allmen, "Birth of Theology," 51–52.

17. Charles H. Kraft, *Christianity in Culture: A Study in Biblical Theologizing in Cross-Cultural Perspective*, rev. 25th anniversary ed. (Maryknoll, NY: Orbis Books, 2005), 228–46.

18. Kraft, *Christianity in Culture*, 228.

into mere "buying and selling" of previous theological products, and he is especially gimlet-eyed toward contemporary academic theology, which he considers unsuitably parochial. "Theology as we know it," Kraft asserts, "has been generated almost totally from within a single sociocultural context" and cultivated "almost totally within a single academic discipline," the practice of which has become disconnected from the life of most Christians even in the West, let alone those in emerging churches around the globe.[19]

To replace this theological monoculture, Kraft commends von Allmen's approach. To the extent that the history of the church is to be studied, it is primarily to reconsider the "cultural factors at work," and in particular to assess whether movements branded as "heresy" should actually be regarded as "valid contextualizations of scriptural truth." Kraft suggests it is "likely that most of the 'heresies' can validly be classed as cultural adaptations rather than as theological aberrations."[20] Though Kraft makes passing reference to learning from previous generations of Christians, his primary call is to stop focusing on "past products of the efforts of 'expert' theologians" and instead recapture the "dynamism of the early days of the Christian movement," generating novel theological insights in the same way that the early Christians did.[21]

Kraft's perspective is still prevalent today, especially among evangelicals engaged in cross-cultural missionary work. In a recent book, J. Paul Pennington picks up on Jones's insight that Christianity's history and cultural practices tend to be serious barriers to non-believers in India encountering Jesus.[22] To address this problem, Pennington commends an approach similar to von Allmen and Kraft: "Instead of starting with Western Christian and church traditions, I advocate for the more radical starting point. . . . Believers should be encouraged . . . to start with only Scripture, prayer to the Lord, the guidance of his Holy Spirit, and their knowledge of their culture."[23]

This instinct to construct local theologies by first rejecting the theological frameworks of previous generations is by no means peculiar to conservative evangelicals. The same intuition has often been expressed, though in different terms and for different reasons, in other Christian contexts as well. For

---

19. Kraft, *Christianity in Culture*, 229.
20. Kraft, *Christianity in Culture*, 233.
21. Kraft, *Christianity in Culture*, 232.
22. J. Paul Pennington, *Christian Barriers to Jesus: Conversations and Questions from the Indian Context*, rev. ed. (Littleton, CO: William Carey, 2022), xix.
23. Pennington, *Christian Barriers to Jesus*, 79.

example, in a key text introducing "Third World theologies" to readers in the West, John Parratt focuses primarily on such theologies' rejection of "the theological agendas which are set by the West."[24] The goal of the enterprise is precisely "to escape from the 'colonisation of the mind'" that came with Western Christianity and missionary efforts of decades past.[25] The fruit of these efforts began to emerge in the 1970s and 1980s, as theologians from Asia, Africa, and Latin America cast fresh vision for the theology rooted firmly in their contexts rather than in the soil of Western societies.[26] More recently, a loose alliance of thinkers connected in various ways to "post-colonialism" have highlighted the way in which Scripture and Christian doctrine have been used as instruments of political repression, and they seek to develop new approaches to the faith that expose and decenter this Western heritage to make way for more liberative expressions.[27]

Clearly, there are vast differences between these approaches and the missions-minded contextualization efforts noted earlier. While Kraft and other evangelicals encourage the development of new theology in dialogue with Scripture and local spiritual experience, liberation and postcolonialist thinkers look to a wider variety of tools for theological reconstruction. Yet they are united in a key methodological assumption—namely, that a necessary condition for the development of genuine contextual theology is a diminishment of the Christian past as a theological resource.

Recovering the Great Tradition

There is serious heft to these arguments, and they deserve a careful hearing. For centuries, the Christian faith was spread intentionally alongside

---

24. John Parratt, ed., *An Introduction to Third World Theologies* (New York: Cambridge University Press, 2004), 8.

25. Parratt, *Introduction to Third World Theologies*, 10.

26. See, e.g., José Míguez Bonino, *Doing Theology in a Revolutionary Situation* (Philadelphia: Fortress, 1975); Choan-Seng Song, *Third-Eye Theology: Theology in Formation in Asian Settings* (Maryknoll, NY: Orbis Books, 1979); Bénézet Bujo, *African Theology in Its Social Context*, trans. John O'Donohue (Maryknoll, NY: Orbis Books, 1992).

27. For a helpful introductory overview, see R. S. Sugirtharajah, "Postcolonial Biblical Interpretation," in *The Modern Theologians: An Introduction to Christian Theology Since 1918*, ed. David F. Ford with Rachel Muers, 3rd ed. (Malden, MA: Blackwell, 2005), 535–52. For examples of this process in action, see Pui-lan Kwok, *Postcolonial Imagination and Feminist Theology* (Louisville: Westminster John Knox, 2005); Emmanuel Yartekwei Amugi Lartey, *Postcolonializing God: New Perspectives on Pastoral and Practical Theology* (London: SCM, 2013).

Western culture, expanding by means that were often oppressive, racist, and extraordinarily destructive. After the colonial era ended, Christian missionaries' genuinely positive contributions (e.g., Bible translation, medical care, sacrificial efforts in church planting) were often mixed with other elements, such as a Western vision of the Christian faith and power structures that did not allow younger churches to flourish. Meanwhile, even when Western governments stopped exerting colonial control over nations in the Majority World, economic exploitation continued, sometimes yielding even crueler outcomes than the outright oppression of state-sponsored colonialism. More importantly for our discussion, the entire structure of Christian theology continued to be dominated by methods, theories, and products (books, articles, dictionaries, etc.) that rarely took into account the needs or the contributions of Majority World Christians, even as they became the most vibrant element of the church. This reality is starkly evident even today, as most theological writing and curriculum from mainstream presses and journals still proceeds as if the church is made up primarily of North Americans and Europeans, relegating engagements with the concerns of the Majority World church to the margins—if they are acknowledged at all. This history should stir within us a holy rage.

The inclination to start over is, therefore, understandable. Yet, like culture, tradition is an inescapable force. It is true that the Christian tradition has marred and obscured the gospel, yet it is also the case that we inevitably receive the good news and come to obey it in the presence of those who have run the race ahead of us (Heb. 12:1). In chapter 2, we saw that when theologians attempt to do theology that is "culture-free" they wind up reifying a culture anyway, while also missing a God-given resource for the theological task. The argument is similar here. Evangelical contextual theologies are best served if they can suppress the anti-tradition instinct in favor of an approach that embraces novel theological development among every people while also engaging the Christian tradition as a rich resource for that very project. Indeed, the pursuit of genuine catholicity will require no less.

Taking this approach will first require, especially for evangelicals, a renewed appreciation for the value and status of the church's tradition. This starts by recognizing the degree to which Scripture itself elevates tradition as a theological good, even as it warns against the risks of using it for improper ends. Thus, in Deuteronomy, the command of YHWH is that every household become a repository of Israel's tradition, declaring the saving work and holy will of God through rigorous daily and annual rhythms (Deut. 6:4–8). These practices are designed to foster holiness among God's people and are also a crucial step in God's design to draw all nations to himself. The mandate that each generation declare the wonderful works of God to the next (Ps. 145:4) is not merely about the handing down of history, or even of worship, though it certainly is not less than these tasks. Rather, it has an unmistakably missional force: tradition is passed down precisely "so that *all people* may know of your mighty acts and the glorious splendor of your kingdom" (145:12 NIV, italics added).[28] This insight helps us make sense of Jesus's and Paul's critiques of human traditions. Tradition turned against the purposes of God—for example, through the creation of clever loopholes to facilitate disobedience (Matt. 15:3–6; Mark 7:9–13) or through the imposition of requirements that diminish the accomplished work of Christ (Col. 2:8–15)—is a vicious tool of the enemies of the gospel.

Yet the gospel is not inherently anti-tradition. Jesus does not come "to abolish the Law or the Prophets . . . but to fulfill them" (Matt. 5:17). Even in his Matthew 5 refrain that might easily be construed as a rejection of what has gone before—"You have heard that it was said . . . . But I say to you . . ."—he offers not a repudiation of the Old Testament legal tradition but a heightened commitment to the divine intent behind it, reframed in light of the arrival of the kingdom.[29] Moreover, the epistles recognize that tradition, properly construed, is an essential element of the church's common life and calling. Paul affirms the centrality of tradition for understanding the gospel itself: "For I delivered to you as of first importance what I also received" (1 Cor. 15:3). Similarly, Timothy is exhorted to "guard the good deposit" (2 Tim. 1:14), and the Christian community is called to draw wisdom and strength from the great "cloud of witnesses" (Heb. 12:1) made up of saints gone ahead of them (Heb. 11:1–40). Thus the New Testament offers a vision of tradition as a central, life-giving force that acts not only to demarcate and

---

28. Similarly, observe how the extensive ceremony mandated in Deuteronomy 26, including the recital of a creedal statement that describes the history of Israel (vv. 5–10), ultimately culminates in an affirmation of Israel's purpose: to serve as a light to the nations (vv. 18–19). For further reflection on the missional force of Israel's history, see Christopher J. H. Wright, *The Mission of God: Unlocking the Bible's Grand Narrative* (Downers Grove, IL: IVP Academic, 2006), 467–74.

29. Ulrich Luz, *Matthew 1–7: A Commentary*, trans. James E. Crouch, rev. ed. (Minneapolis: Fortress, 2007), 210–32; Jonathan T. Pennington, *The Sermon on the Mount and Human Flourishing: A Theological Commentary* (Grand Rapids: Baker Academic, 2017), 179–81.

preserve doctrinal boundaries but also to spur the living saints on to a life of holy commitment to divine purposes.

This notion is not, as some Protestants might suppose, at odds with the spirit of the Reformation. The Reformers almost universally regarded tradition as a key resource for the renewal of the church and the right reading of Scripture. They differed from their Roman counterparts not by denying the relevance of church teaching altogether but by placing church teaching squarely in a ministerial (rather than magisterial) position—where it could gain binding authority only to the degree that it was connected to divine speech in Scripture.[30] Nor is tradition at odds with evangelical principles and habits of mind. Though individual theologians have certainly treated tradition with ambivalence at times, there is at present a robust consensus that tradition is a formative and informative source for doing theology that is motivated by and faithful to the good news.[31]

Advocates of theologies of retrieval contend that the church's tradition is not only a viable source for the theological calling but also a critical way of responding to the circumstances of our present age, especially the theological strictures ushered in by the Enlightenment. As John Webster puts it, theologies of retrieval hope, by means of "immersion in the texts and habits of thought of earlier (especially pre-modern) theology," to enable the practice of theology "unharassed by current anxieties."[32] In particular, Webster and other advocates of retrieval seek to recover a way of doing theology that is not hampered by the assumption that "intellectual inquiry in the 'modern' era" must generate a vision of the faith "without appeal to such contaminating notions as inspiration, illumination, providence, or church" and must focus instead on theories considered universally "rational."[33] Advocates of retrieval recognize that such a commitment to "critical reason" is a death sentence for theology, depriving it of the very conditions that allow for its survival

30. D. H. Williams, *Retrieving the Tradition and Renewing Evangelicalism: A Primer for Suspicious Protestants* (Grand Rapids: Eerdmans, 1999), 173–204; Kevin J. Vanhoozer, *Biblical Authority after Babel: Retrieving the Solas in the Spirit of Mere Protestant Christianity* (Grand Rapids: Brazos, 2016), 109–46.

31. See, e.g., Kevin J. Vanhoozer and Daniel J. Treier, *Theology and the Mirror of Scripture: A Mere Evangelical Account* (Downers Grove, IL: IVP Academic, 2015), 81–127; Gavin Ortlund, *Theological Retrieval for Evangelicals: Why We Need Our Past to Have a Future* (Wheaton: Crossway, 2019).

32. John Webster, "Theologies of Retrieval," in *The Oxford Handbook of Systematic Theology*, ed. John Webster, Kathryn Tanner, and Iain Torrance (New York: Oxford University Press, 2009), 584–85.

33. Webster, "Theologies of Retrieval," 585.

as genuine engagement with the lordship of the triune God. Instead, they propose engaging the pre-modern tradition to remind us that this modern method is not as universal or inevitable as it claims to be and to foster contemporary theological reflection that speaks of God and his works with confident joy in the good news, in accordance with the calling of the church.[34]

Since the middle of the twentieth century, and especially in the last three decades, theologians have increasingly acknowledged the prudence of retrieval as a strategy for responding to the dead ends of modern theology. Efforts toward renewal through attention to the past have taken hold in Roman Catholic, Orthodox, and Protestant circles alike.[35] The goal of these efforts is not to return to a golden, pre-critical past, nor is it to refuse the study of theological development after (for example) the year 1700. Instead, retrieval is a strategy that involves recovering the resources of the past in order to learn a different way of thinking than the one in which we are presently immersed; to situate modern assumptions in the long history of the church across the ages; and to engage, in particular, early Christian texts—which are especially insightful because of the generative theological work that occurred in these initial efforts to articulate and guard the gospel.[36]

Beyond being merely prudent responses to the impositions and challenges that modernity places upon our talk about God, the strategy of retrieval has clear theological warrant. As Michael Allen and Scott Swain put it, retrieval is a key strategy for the church of all ages precisely because "the anointing of Christ dwells within the church," making the church the "school of Christ" and the "seedbed of theology."[37] If this is so, then the teachings of the church

34. For further reflection from Webster on the path forward for theology in the contemporary moment, see John Webster, *The Culture of Theology*, ed. Ivor J. Davidson and Alden C. McCray (Grand Rapids: Baker Academic, 2019).

35. Webster, "Theologies of Retrieval," 585–97. Our discussion here focuses primarily on the dynamics in Protestant theology, but similar movements in Roman Catholic and Orthodox traditions preceded and helped feed this movement among Protestants. For helpful introductions, see Gabriel Flynn and Paul D. Murray, eds., *Ressourcement: A Movement for Renewal in Twentieth-Century Catholic Theology* (New York: Oxford University Press, 2011); Vladimir Lossky, *The Mystical Theology of the Eastern Church*, trans. members of the Fellowship of St. Alban and St. Sergius (Crestwood, NY: St. Vladimir's Seminary Press, 1976).

36. For further reflection here, see C. S. Lewis, "Introduction," in Athanasius, *On the Incarnation*, trans. a religious of C. S. M. V. (Crestwood, NY: St. Vladimir's Seminary Press, 1977), 3–10; Stephen R. Holmes, *Listening to the Past: The Place of Tradition in Theology* (Grand Rapids: Baker Academic, 2002); W. David Buschart and Kent D. Eliers, *Theology as Retrieval: Receiving the Past, Renewing the Church* (Downers Grove, IL: IVP Academic, 2015).

37. Michael Allen and Scott R. Swain, *Reformed Catholicity: The Promise of Retrieval for Theology and Biblical Interpretation* (Grand Rapids: Baker Academic, 2015), 18.

developed over time are not merely "human cultural activities and artifacts" but also "fruits of the Spirit" divinely appointed for the edification of the church throughout time.[38] The primacy of Scripture remains in place in this proposal; it is always God's spoken and inscripturated Word that stands above the church's teaching. Protestants affirm that in this Word lies sufficient riches to underwrite every theological claim, every utterance of true prayer and worship. Yet these riches must be mined, ordered, and allocated to their proper purposes, and tradition—which can be understood rightly as "the Spirit-enabled reception of Scripture"—is the means by which the triune God shepherds his flock throughout the globe and across the generations.[39] Tradition is, without question, fallible and prone to error of all kinds, and so its products must be accountable to the Word and the Spirit, by which they can be renewed and brought to new life.

Regaining Pentecost in the Presence of the Great Tradition

In a sense, theologians of retrieval and those advocating for a radical break with Christian tradition are in search of a solution to some shared problems. Both seek to help the church resist the imperious forces of Enlightenment rationality, which claim to be universal but in fact privilege the narrow perspectives of a particular place, time, and culture. This modern approach to theology is not as universal and rational as it claims to be, and it is also implicated in a harmfully ethnocentric view of modern Western culture's superiority over other cultural habits of heart and mind. In response, theologies of retrieval and contextual theologies seek, by different means, to free theology from its captivity to twentieth-century Western culture by critiquing the modern approach to theology and to liberate the church to proclaim the good news with confident joy.

Yet theology marked by catholic engagement with the gospel need not choose between a program of retrieval and a strategy of using local theological resources to apprehend and express the fullness of Christian faith. Rightly understood, these are complementary callings, designed to help the church access the gifts Christ has allocated for his people from every tribe, tongue, people, and nation. Many recent treatments of contextual

---

38. Allen and Swain, *Reformed Catholicity*, 25.
39. Allen and Swain, *Reformed Catholicity*, 36.

theologies have recognized the complementarity of attending to the church's diverse present and gaining what we can from churches of the past. William Dyrness and Oscar García-Johnson are honest about the deep shortcomings of the "Western theological heritage," but they ultimately argue that "it would be impossible, if not dangerous, for younger churches and theologies to disregard it entirely."[40] Instead, they call theologians from the West and the Majority World to "disarm themselves of unnecessary cynicism and recognize that Western culture is generative and nuanced (not monolithic) and hence useful for today's theologizing."[41] This "co-construction of theological discourse in globalized contexts not only is necessary and possible but also constitutes a communal act of worshiping the God of the global church as we learn to deal with our self-idolatrous tendencies."[42]

Similarly, Victor Ezigbo argues that contextual theologies are best served when they engage constructively with Christian tradition, finding there a "living memory that partly conditions its life and identity." When we engage our theological ancestors, Ezigbo notes, contemporary Christians find models, "raw materials," and guardrails to guide the theological task.[43] Similarly, Simon Chan calls for a vision of local theology rooted in the deposit of the faith: "Local cultures do shape the way the faith is received and expressed, but for a local theology to be authentically Christian, it must have substantial continuity with the larger Christian tradition."[44] Chan notes the temptation, especially in Asia—where Christianity wrestles with its legacy alongside major world religions with competing truth claims—to "create a new trajectory" that arises directly from Scripture and ignores the Christian past, sidestepping the offensive and problematic elements of Christian history, and making way for more fruitful dialogue with those of other faiths. Yet he argues that such efforts should be rightly regarded as sub-Christian, departing from the faith handed down from the apostles.[45]

---

40. William A. Dyrness and Oscar García-Johnson, *Theology without Borders: An Introduction to Global Conversations* (Grand Rapids: Baker Academic, 2015), 8.

41. Dyrness and García-Johnson, *Theology without Borders*, 8.

42. Dyrness and García-Johnson, *Theology without Borders*, 8.

43. Victor I. Ezigbo, *The Art of Contextual Theology: Doing Theology in the Era of World Christianity* (Eugene, OR: Cascade Books, 2021), 28.

44. Simon Chan, *Grassroots Asian Theology: Thinking Faith from the Ground Up* (Downers Grove, IL: IVP Academic, 2014), 11.

45. Chan, *Grassroots Asian Theology*, 14. Going further, Chan wisely notes that, in spite of the good intentions of such moves (especially to foster irenic dialogue with those of other faiths),

In short, these theologians contend that we must not be forced to choose between theology that is historically informed and theology that is contextually engaged. In light of the framework of catholicity that we have been developing, this is quite sensible because these movements are simply two different ways of honoring and making the most of the church's divinely designed plurality in unity. The church is clearly impoverished when her theology does not reflect the diversity of God's people and the gifts with which the Spirit has blessed them. We see now that a similar poverty is created by an approach to contextual theology that dismisses or overlooks the tradition of the church. While this might seem like an attractive corrective to the excesses of previous eras—which generally failed to question the theological "status quo" and diminished the contributions of emerging churches in the Majority World—it ultimately only trades one kind of theological poverty for another. Whether the motivation is to strip down the Christian faith to its most basic forms (as in the evangelical efforts at contextualized mission theology) or to strike a blow against the colonialist and racist theologies of previous eras, the result is that the church ultimately suffers, deprived of the fruit cultivated by the Spirit in saints of previous eras.[46]

In contrast, when contextual theologies engage tradition well, our vision of the faith is enriched and broadened in multiple directions. First, our study of the earliest generations of the church allows us to witness the birth of the church in a variety of new cultures, finding there both successful and ill-fated approaches to the inevitable fusion of Christian faith with its new host cultures.[47] These help us understand the dynamics of the cross-cultural transmission of the faith and alert us to patterns to expect as the church puts down roots in more and more cultures, and as the diverse churches that emerge in this process relate to one another in a manner faithful to the gospel.

Second, and relatedly, the study of tradition helps us put present-day controversies into proper perspective. The work of expressing Christian

genuine dialogue requires dealing honestly with the internal history and theology of each side rather than relying on a pretext designed to make the conversation more comfortable.

46. Ironically, while evangelical and postcolonial rejections of the Christian tradition stem from radically different motivations, they are both deeply shaped by the modern Enlightenment notion of humans as "self-originating, as free and creative in a radical sense," ungoverned by and unaccountable to the traditions of the past (Michael Allen Gillespie, *The Theological Origins of Modernity* [Chicago: University of Chicago Press, 2008], 2).

47. This is the primary claim of the collected essays published in Andrew F. Walls, *The Cross-Cultural Process in Christian History: Studies in the Transmission and Appropriation of Faith* (Maryknoll, NY: Orbis Books, 2002).

faith in a new cultural context is difficult and dangerous, and it is often hard to know, without the benefit of hindsight, which appropriations of local culture will help the faith be expressed more clearly and which will ultimately muddy the waters. Which words should we use for *God* when sharing the gospel in a new language? Should Christians take up traditions that honor ancestors, or reject them as idolatrous? Which local metaphors for salvation are sufficiently aligned with Scripture, and which will lead people astray? Armed with a deep knowledge of the church's previous contextual efforts, we are far better equipped to discern the difference between novel but faithful expressions of Christian doctrine and versions that depart in serious ways from "the faith that was once for all delivered to the saints" (Jude 3).

Third, contextual theologies engaging tradition are far more likely to avoid the excesses and fads of the present, being tempered by the long horizon of the church across the generations. By virtue of our status as finite creatures, we are all susceptible to misjudging the significance of the ideas and practices with which we are most familiar. In the case of fashion, getting too caught up in a current trend might mean some embarrassing pictures in a few years; but in the case of theology, the danger of making the church captive to the trends of the local and the present can be deadly serious, resulting in distortions of the gospel that make the church a collaborator in nationalistic or tribalistic ambitions.[48] While engagement with tradition is not a definitive protection against this risk, it does mitigate it substantially by reminding us that our local concerns are not ultimate and must not be elevated above our common identity as part of the church catholic.

Fourth, in at least some cases tradition acts not only as a tempering conversation partner but also as a boundary-marker, establishing what we mean when we speak of "Christian" faith, such that if a theology transgresses these boundaries it can be rightly described as something meaningfully distinct from Christianity. Protestants regard this to be true in cases where the tradition sums up the revelation of Scripture in such an important and powerful way that to depart from it would represent a departure from Christianity

48. In the most extreme examples of the twentieth century, we might cite the development of Christian justifications for Nazi ideology in pre–World War II Germany and the role of culturally inflected versions of Christianity in the horrific Rwandan genocide in the 1990s. See Richard Steigmann-Gall, *The Holy Reich: Nazi Conceptions of Christianity, 1919–1945* (New York: Cambridge University Press, 2003); Timothy Longman, *Christianity and Genocide in Rwanda* (New York: Cambridge University Press, 2009).

itself. Typically, this level of authority is associated with the earliest creedal formulations of the church, especially the Nicene Creed.[49]

To be sure, there is disagreement about which artifacts of early Christian tradition should be binding on "all Christians everywhere" and about the way in which these contextual expressions of faith should govern theological reasoning in other times and places. Thus, Kathryn Tanner rightly notes that what we mean by *tradition* is, in a sense, constructed by the decisions we make about whom and what to include in it each time we talk about and draw from it. Moreover, the Christian community across the ages is so vast and diverse that every attempt to describe which beliefs or practices give it continuity can be contested.[50] Ultimately, Tanner contends that continuity is to be found in a Christian *style* of engaging the world and the elements of our various cultures; it is a particular way of relating all things to the triune God, bringing them under the authority of the divine Word.[51] This allows us to reckon with the reality that a theological statement or a Christian practice that is out of bounds in one time and place may not be so in others. In a sense, then, engagement with the wild diversity of Christian tradition will make us more open to theological innovation; because we witness the radical plurality in the Christian family, we ought to have an open mind with regard to what the Spirit might be doing in diverse cultures today.

Yet this does not require that we dive higgledy-piggledy into the relativistic ether. Across the ages, Christians have consistently recognized that, in his Word and in Christ, God speaks, and he does so clearly enough that we can, empowered by the Spirit, honor Jesus as Lord in any time, place, or culture. Moreover, in affirmation of God's providential care over his people through the ages, we can recognize that while the church has often gotten it wrong, it has sometimes gotten the gospel spectacularly right, protecting against crucial errors that threaten the integrity of the Christian faith. And so, even if we are not bound by the exact language and concepts of previous eras, the theological judgments of the church catholic, especially as expressed in the earliest creeds, set boundaries for our creativity.[52] Like the space visitor

49. E.g., Vanhoozer and Treier, *Theology and the Mirror of Scripture*, 113–14.

50. Kathryn Tanner, *Theories of Culture: A New Agenda for Theology* (Minneapolis: Fortress, 1997), 128–32.

51. Tanner, *Theories of Culture*, 146–53.

52. Kevin J. Vanhoozer, "Christology in the West: Conversations in Europe and North America," in *Jesus without Borders: Christology in the Majority World*, ed. Gene L. Green, Stephen T. Pardue, and K. K. Yeo (Grand Rapids: Eerdmans, 2014), 11–36.

with whom we began our study, we recognize a family resemblance across the generations of the faithful and find in this cloud of witnesses both an exhortation to go on in the same way and the fruit of the Spirit accumulated through the ages and stored up for the benefit of God's people.

Case Study: African Theology and Second-Century Christians

Kwame Bediako was a Ghanaian theologian who founded the Akrofi-Christaller Institute for Theology, Mission and Culture and broke crucial ground in a series of works published in the 1990s and early 2000s, before his untimely death in 2008. Bediako grew up as a Presbyterian but experienced a loss of faith as he grew older and engaged contemporary existentialist philosophy. Despite achieving academic success and entering a rigorous postgraduate program in France, he felt a sense of emptiness and despair that led him to a radical personal conversion. In writing of his conversion years later, Bediako reflected on the cultural dynamics it involved:

> I wished to define myself as a Christian, as an African Christian. Not because a European has taught me so. Indeed, my exposure to Europe made me atheist. In becoming Christian, . . . I discovered I was becoming African again. I was recovering my sense of the spirituality of life. I was recovering my sense of the nearness of the living God. I was recovering my African sense of the wholeness of life. Indeed, I find, in becoming Christian, I am becoming more African than I think I was. I am being more who I am.[53]

The remainder of his life was devoted to investing his considerable intellectual gifts in casting a fresh vision for the interaction between the Christian gospel and African cultures. "From quite early in my Christian conversion experience," he writes, "I have felt the need to seek clarification for myself of how the abiding Gospel of Jesus Christ relates to the inescapable issues and questions which arise from the Christian's *cultural* existence in the world, and how this relationship is achieved without injury to the integrity of the Gospel."[54]

---

53. James Ault, *Kwame Bediako: His Life and Legacy* (James Ault Productions, 2020), https://vimeopro.com/jamesault/kwame-bediako-his-life-and-legacy-1/video/281714305.

54. Kwame Bediako, *Theology and Identity: The Impact of Culture upon Christian Thought in the Second Century and in Modern Africa* (Oxford: Regnum, 1992), xi, italics original.

Bediako quickly came to recognize exactly the dynamic we have observed in this chapter: "The usual approach to the question of Gospel and Culture," he writes, "was to seek the appropriate response solely from the Scriptures, particularly of the New Testament."[55] The problem with this approach was that it assumed that "the historical tradition of the Church has little value in interpreting the realities of our modern Christian existence."[56] Without diminishing the importance of using Scripture to judge the legitimacy of cultural expressions of Christian faith, Bediako recognized he needed an approach that could take "serious account of the developments and responses of Christians of other periods in the Christian story."[57]

In his first book, he considered this question through the study of second-century Christians, whose experience, he found, resonated helpfully with the realities of twentieth-century African Christianity. In Bediako's time, as in the second century, the church was growing explosively and seeking to make its home in new cultural contexts, many of which bore substantial similarities to the cultures that the second-century Christians had reckoned with. Bediako, following in the steps of Andrew Walls, argued that reading the history of the church with an eye on how to cultivate the future of African theology creates a number of benefits—first and foremost, it contributes fresh vision that can nourish a genuinely African Christian theology. At the same time, by drawing from the resources of the "organic tradition of Christianity as a whole," it empowers the African church to pursue genuine locality that deepens rather than diminishes its connection to the Christian faith.[58] Finally, this approach helps us to "read the Christian Fathers in their contexts with new eyes," allowing us to "ask fresh questions of the Christian tradition of the past, questions which can in turn illuminate the task of constructing local theologies."[59]

Through patient analysis of key second-century thinkers, Bediako helps us see how the early church became a laboratory of contextual theologies, with various thinkers each commending a distinctive vision for the interaction of faith and Greco-Roman culture. In engaging their cultures, thinkers like Tatian (AD 120–80) and Tertullian (AD 155–220) are primarily

55. Bediako, *Theology and Identity*, xi.
56. Bediako, *Theology and Identity*, xi.
57. Bediako, *Theology and Identity*, xi.
58. Bediako, *Theology and Identity*, xii.
59. Bediako, *Theology and Identity*, xiii.

"concerned to protect the truth from being adulterated by the world," rather than to "validate the relevance of the truth to the world."[60] Others, such as Justin Martyr (AD 100–165) and Clement of Alexandria (AD 150–215), saw the Christian faith as both a fulfillment and correction of the philosophical tradition of Greco-Roman culture, arguing that the truth found there was given by God, ultimately for the purpose of being a *preparatio evangelica*.[61]

Bediako then uses this detailed analysis of second-century Christian engagement with Greco-Roman culture to inform a nuanced and detailed analysis of the situation in twentieth-century Africa. He rightly notes that the African church's engagement with its local cultures has been substantially hampered by the theology of mission that Westerners brought along with them to the continent. In this worldview, the faith was closely aligned with Western "civilization" and identity (usually explicitly, though also implicitly); as a result, there was little doubt that local cultures must be replaced rather than renewed or redeemed as they received the good news. The early church benefited from the work of the apostle Paul, who "worked tirelessly to secure the conditions in which the Christian self-understanding of Gentiles could develop and flourish," an effort that ultimately "placed at the disposal of Christians of Graeco-Roman culture the basic tools for assessing their own heritage, for making their own contribution to Christian life and thought and also for testing the genuineness and Christian character of that contribution."[62] Tragically, for most of its history the African church had no equivalent figure.

Yet Bediako's hope in the gospel for a better mode of engagement with culture remains undeterred. He writes, "If African theological freedom was generally not facilitated by the Western missionary movement, the contemporary task of African theology is not thereby rendered impossible; African theologians also now share in the inheritance of the Gospel. Theological freedom is the freedom of the Gospel. This means that to adequately appreciate the concerns of African theologians in the post-missionary era, one must inquire into their understanding of the significance of the Gospel for the interpretation of African realities and for the meaning of African Chris-

---

60. Bediako, *Theology and Identity*, 124.
61. Bediako, *Theology and Identity*, 137–222. Bediako is careful to document the differences between these various thinkers, noting that Clement moves significantly beyond Justin in his positive engagement with the Greco-Roman tradition.
62. Bediako, *Theology and Identity*, 249.

tian identity."[63] This is precisely what Bediako attempts in the remainder of his book (and, in a sense, for the rest of his career). He highlights the work of giants in contemporary African theology, recognizing approaches to the gospel and culture that are complex but that bear similarities at points to those of second-century Christians. Thinkers like Byang Kato offer a contemporary analogue to Tertullian and Tatian, promoting a vision in which the gospel primarily brings critique and correction to the legacy of African cultures.[64] Meanwhile, thinkers like Bolaji Idowu and John Mbiti highlight the deep overlap between the African primal religions and the Christian faith, and like Justin and Clement, they present the Christian faith as a fulfillment of the deepest longings of Africans' hearts.[65]

Bediako refuses to make these correlations work too hard. He reads each thinker on their own terms and in their own context, and he clearly rejects the simplistic notion that "the solutions from the past . . . have a direct and unmediated relevance for the problems of the present."[66] Yet he brings African Christian theology to new vistas by drawing attention not only to the analogues of the past but also to the ways the Christian past has unavoidably shaped the present, as well as by showing that a positive response to this history is an essential precondition for any healthy contemporary contextual theology.

Bediako's theological project ultimately leads him to draw more specific conclusions about the ideal way forward for African theology. For example, he argues that the theological work of the church in the second century—when Christians were a religious minority contending with and taking in the work of many other faiths and worldviews—will likely prove more fruitful for African Christian theologians today than the work of later generations of Christians, after Christianity had become a state religion.[67]

Perhaps most importantly, Bediako argues that just as Clement, Justin, and other early Christian thinkers sought to make the gospel at home in the Greco-Roman context by highlighting the continuities between Christianity and the philosophical movements that their cultures had produced, African theologians today must likewise prioritize the task of "articulating the theological significance of the pre-Christian religious tradition."[68] In a sense, just

63. Bediako, *Theology and Identity*, 252.
64. Bediako, *Theology and Identity*, 386–425.
65. Bediako, *Theology and Identity*, 267–346.
66. Bediako, *Theology and Identity*, 427.
67. Bediako, *Theology and Identity*, 432–34.
68. Bediako, *Theology and Identity*, 437.

as philosophy was the "handmaiden of theology" in the Western tradition—a key dialogue partner for clarifying the faith and bringing it to expression in a manner that makes sense in local culture—so also the pre-Christian religious tradition in Africa should become a key tool for theological reflection.[69] When the African church can engage in such a process from a place of confidence, it will not only affirm the pre-Christian tradition but, like the early Fathers, it will also deliver judgments about the "blemishes of the religious past," judgments rooted in a rich, authentic vision of African Christian identity.[70]

This is precisely what Bediako spent the remainder of his life working toward, leaving a remarkable legacy.[71] In the African context, he offered a fresh vision for African theology that would allow it to be organically related to both the Christian tradition and the local pre-Christian past. As he did, he modeled an erudition and nuance that ensured historical and cultural realities were not merely treated in generalized terms or as props for contemporary arguments.

This work was not without critics, of course. Some observers have noted that, as a result of Bediako's approach of casting Christian faith as a fulfillment of the pre-Christian past, the Old Testament and Jesus's Jewishness are deemphasized.[72] Others have wondered whether Bediako overplays the significance of the particular context of Africa to the neglect of "the general human condition" as well as of "God Himself as he remains the same for ever."[73] And still others have raised questions about the workability of Bediako's Christological proposal in light of the African perspective on ancestors.[74] We might also wonder whether Bediako's theological project might have been even more fruitful if brought into engagement more deeply with thinkers beyond the second century.[75]

---

69. Bediako, *Theology and Identity*, 434–41.

70. Bediako, *Theology and Identity*, 436–37.

71. The most important work he later produced, which filled out this vision, was Kwame Bediako, *Jesus in Africa: The Christian Gospel in African History and Experience*, rev. ed. (Oxford: Regnum, 2020), which was first published in 1999.

72. Tim Hartman, *Theology after Colonization: Kwame Bediako, Karl Barth, and the Future of Theological Reflection* (Notre Dame, IN: University of Notre Dame Press, 2020), 121.

73. Benno van den Toren, "Kwame Bediako's Christology in Its African Evangelical Context," *Exchange* 26, no. 3 (1997): 230.

74. Victor I. Ezigbo, *Re-imagining African Christologies: Conversing with the Interpretations and Appropriations of Jesus in Contemporary African Christianity* (Eugene, OR: Pickwick, 2010).

75. Bediako was generally skeptical about theological reflection done after Christianity's elevation to the status of state religion under Constantine (Tim Hartman, *Kwame Bediako: African Theology for a World Christianity* [Carlisle, UK: Langham Global Library, 2021], 122).

Yet Bediako unquestionably offered a vision for contextual theologies that intentionally connected contemporary, local realities to the church's Great Tradition. In this way, he demonstrated that there need not be any contradiction between honoring the Christian past in our theology and giving due place to local cultural insight. Rather than starting fresh, or with the sparse vision of Christianity so common in some modes of contextual theologizing, Bediako revealed that the cross-cultural transmission of the faith is fundamentally a process of growth as we comprehend in new ways the riches made available to us in Christ, seeing new facets of the diamond of the gospel.[76]

Conclusion

Bediako's work is an impressive illustration of the complementary relationship between the Great Tradition and contextual theologies in the twenty-first century. Yet it also stands as a sobering example of how difficult it can be to do contemporary contextual theology in close dialogue with previous generations of Christian theology. Bediako's work succeeds in part because he understood just how different previous generations of Christians were from our own as well as from one another. Rather than generalizing about their work, he interacted with early Christian theologians in painstaking detail, documenting their distinctive aims and strategies on their own terms. In Bediako's work, we see that the burden of good theological retrieval is not so different from the calling of a cultural anthropologist: it requires immersing oneself in another culture to understand the internal logic of what will initially seem foreign and bizarre. Only in this way can one make sense of what earlier generations of Christians were up to well enough to learn from them.

In contrast, a program of retrieval pursued without a keen commitment to understanding past generations from within their own time leads us to read the Christian tradition as little more than a monolithic and idealized entity, useful only as a prop in our contemporary arguments. As Robert Letham

---

76. This is a metaphor frequently used by Bediako in his later years to describe the work of contextual theologies around the globe (Gillian Mary Bediako, Benhardt Y. Quarshie, and J. Kwabena Asamoah-Gyadu, "Editorial," in *Seeing New Facets of the Diamond: Christianity as a Universal Faith; Essays in Honour of Kwame Bediako*, ed. Gillian Mary Bediako, Benhardt Y. Quarshie, and J. Kwabena Asamoah-Gyadu [Oxford: Regnum, 2014], ix).

notes, this is precisely how so many contemporary contextual theologies fall into the trap of discarding all or most previous theological work as the products of "Western theologians," ignoring all the while that this tradition is the product of "Egyptians (Athanasius and Cyril), Turks (the Cappadocians, Maximus the Confessor), Tunisians (Tertullian, Cyprian, Augustine), and a Syrian (John of Damascus), to say nothing of the apostles (Middle-Eastern Jews)"—and that's naming only a few.[77]

Bediako was able to avoid these pitfalls in part because he lived in multiple cultures (moving ably between life in Ghana, France, and the UK) and had an unusually broad set of intellectual skills, being trained in historical, literary, and cultural analysis, while also being an able exegete, theologian, and pastor. Often, all of these skills will not all find their home in a single individual, and so following Bediako's example will frequently require collaboration between Christians of various cultures and callings.

Sobering though it may be, the importance of Bediako's work lies in its demonstration that contemporary contextual theologies must not hold back from serious engagement with the Christian past. Even when pursued with the best intentions, such ahistorical approaches serve ultimately to impoverish the contemporary global church, depriving it of its birthright as part of the church catholic. Conversely, theological approaches that attend both to contemporary cultural dynamics *and* to the legacy of earlier generations offer the church the opportunity to cultivate authentic Christian unity across the miles and across the ages.

---

77. Robert Letham, "Catholicity Global and Historical: Constantinople, Westminster, and the Church in the Twenty-First Century," *Westminster Theological Journal* 72, no. 1 (2010): 55.

Conclusion

In a bracing series of lectures delivered in New Zealand in 1998, British theologian John Webster addressed the matter of theology and culture. His concern was not primarily with what it means for theologians to take account of the cultural contexts in which they work. Instead, he was calling Christian theologians to recognize that their work belongs, in some sense, to a "Christian culture," by which he meant "the assembly of forms and practices which seeks somehow to inhabit the world which is brought into being by the staggering good news of Jesus Christ, the world of the new creation." This new "world" is brought about by the miracle of the gospel, the "comprehensive interruption of all things in Jesus Christ," in whom "all things are faced by the one who absolutely dislocates and no less absolutely reorders." Confronted by the declaration of the risen and ascended Christ—"Behold, I am making all things new" (Rev. 21:5)—Christian theology is a practice designed to help humans live into the astonishing redemptive work God is accomplishing among his people.[1]

Webster found this reminder necessary because Christian theology has increasingly struggled to flourish in the "inhospitable intellectual and institutional environment" generated by modern expectations of rationality and scholarship. In this world, the special claims of Christianity must be muted or transformed in order to conform to standardized and "universal" models of reason and inquiry that have little room for a revelatory, active

1. John Webster, *The Culture of Theology*, ed. Ivor J. Davidson and Alden C. McCray (Grand Rapids: Baker Academic, 2019), 43–44.

triune God.[2] As a result, theologians tend to shrink back from their primary task and instead pursue secondary ones. Rather than guiding people into the wonderful world created by the gospel, they tend to focus on adjacent territory, such as the history of religions or comparative religious studies.[3]

Ironically, one common method of distraction that Webster highlights is, in fact, the study of culture. Especially in the university context that developed out of eighteenth-century Germany, it became much more acceptable to analyze religious beliefs and practices *as social phenomena* than to make claims about God himself. As a result, "for much of the history of modern Protestant theology, talk of God and talk of the cultural realities of the Christian religion have been inversely proportional."[4]

Webster's primary concern here is the practice of theology in "mainstream academic institutions," which tends to discourage the study of claims that cannot be tested by data (e.g., "In Christ, God is making all things new") and incentivizes the investigation of questions with observable answers (e.g., "What difference does church-going make to standard measures of psychological health?"). Yet this is not only a problem for academics. In an urbanizing and globalizing world, more and more of our social space is occupied by the restrictive habits of mind dictated by Enlightenment rationality. As a result, the temptation to shrink back from the strong, particular claims of Christian revelation is ever-present and, in most contexts, growing.

In response, Webster does not call for the rejection of all study with measurable outputs. Nor does he commend keeping our heads in the sand and seeking to disengage from our local cultural context. On the contrary, he recognizes that leading the church in this season requires that a theologian "be a skilled inhabitant of a particular cultural world," someone who will "demonstrate skills in reaching judgments about circumstance, and skills in reading his or her situation well."[5] Yet, mindful of the prevailing headwinds, Webster calls Christian theologians to cultivate a laser focus on their primary vocation: the disciplined and patient response of the church to God's revealing and redeeming work.

2. Webster, *Culture of Theology*, 133.
3. To see how this change transformed the academic study of the Bible, ultimately impacting pastors and churches, see Michael C. Legaspi, *The Death of Scripture and the Rise of Biblical Studies* (New York: Oxford University Press, 2010).
4. Webster, *Culture of Theology*, 52.
5. Webster, *Culture of Theology*, 59.

Theology must therefore always remain an eschatological vocation, propelled by the "disruptive presence" of Jesus and his saving work and oriented toward helping the church inhabit the "strange cultural space in which the re-creative work of God is confessed."[6] Theologians aim to help the church dwell in this space, which Hebrews 12:22–23 calls "the city of the living God, the heavenly Jerusalem, . . . the assembly of the firstborn who are enrolled in heaven." This makes theology a peculiar discipline, inevitably different in many ways from the other intellectual pursuits with which it often competes or rubs shoulders. Properly conceived, Christian theology revolves around a radical claim: that God in Christ has broken into created reality and is restoring all things by the power of his Spirit working through his people. From start to finish, the theologian's task is to understand this truth and help the church live into its reality. Elsewhere, Webster would refer to this as a call for "theological theology"—that is, theology that insists on placing the triune God and his work in the world at the center of our reflection and teaching and stubbornly refuses to let other, adjacent types of reflection displace this task.[7]

Webster's word remains timely today, and all the more as we seek to do theology in light of the church's diverse cultural gifts. After all, as we observe what God is doing through his people, we are rightly awestruck at the way the church brings together those from every background, walk of life, and culture into a unified people. We marvel, as we ought, at this new creation—a church from every tribe and tongue, the vehicle through which new dimensions of the good news are made known in every culture of the world. As Andrew Walls puts it, the glory of living in the present moment is that "the theological workshop is likely to be busier than ever before, its workers more varied in language, culture and outlook."[8] Yet precisely because we live in such a moment, and because contextual theologies help us recognize the power of culture in shaping our theological witness, we are at special risk of being distracted from the work of the triune God. Inadvertently, contextual theologies can serve to narrow our field of vision to only the church and its cultural dynamics.

6. Webster, *Culture of Theology*, 53.

7. John Webster, "Theological Theology," in *Confessing God: Essays in Christian Dogmatics II* (New York: T&T Clark, 2005), 11–31.

8. Andrew Walls, "The Rise of Global Theologies," in *Global Theology in Evangelical Perspective: Exploring the Contextual Nature of Theology and Mission*, ed. Jeffrey P. Greenman and Gene L. Green (Downers Grove: IVP Academic, 2012), 33.

We must be clear-eyed here. The study of the culture, language, and customs of Christians (and all people) around the globe is surely a worthy endeavor. Further, because culture is a material theological good, the practices of cultural analysis are critical tools for unwrapping the gifts of God, and theologians must become wise in deploying these tools. But Webster is wise to warn against the temptation in modern intellectual life to focus on cultural questions in themselves, questions that fit neatly within the immanent frame of secular thought and do not require reckoning with the special summons of a triune God who is reconciling all things to himself by the blood of his cross (Col. 1:20).

The theses we have advanced in this book are an effort to preserve this delicate balance of doing theology with increased appreciation for the contributions of culture while also maintaining evangelical commitments. Because God has spoken in Scripture, we must make studious attention to the biblical text our primary theological task, even as we grow in appreciation for the crucial role of culture in understanding and obeying it (thesis 1). When we attend to Scripture and keep culture in mind, we learn that culture itself is a blessing rather than a burden, a means appointed by God as an instrument of redemption, not only in the present age but into the eschaton (thesis 2). The church's diversity is part of her God-given glory, for only there do we meet a creature designed by God to showcase the compatibility of the once-for-all redemptive work of Jesus and the remarkable diversity it creates and redeems (thesis 3). Moreover, because God designs his church to be one and catholic, theologians must serve the church with the local context in mind while also attending to the whole people of God scattered abroad (thesis 4), as well as to the witness of the saints who have gone ahead of us (thesis 5). Contextual theologies that fail to attend to either element of catholicity—that do not gain from rigorous exchange either with our cross-cultural neighbors in the present or with the generations of Christians past—ultimately shortchange the church and hold it back from its full destiny in God's design.

These theses are by no means a comprehensive or exclusive guide to the cultivation of theology that is mindful of the shaping power of culture while also preserving joyful, studious attention on God and all things in relation to him. Yet I hope they are a step in the direction of doing theology in light of the church's eschatological vocation to be a distinctive people in every generation and place. No biblical image better sums up this special calling of the church than the description in Revelation 7:9–17. In that "great multitude that no one could number," we see a vision of unity that only God can accomplish, in which those "from every nation, from all tribes and peoples and languages" (7:9), exalt the Lamb who was slain. Here, those of each culture offer praise in their own unique melody while also displaying a mysterious and divinely created unity. Yet as miraculous as this crowd surely is—the final reversal of Babel and ultimate fulfillment of Pentecost—it is nothing compared to the enthroned Lamb whom they worship. If contextual theology is to be also "theological theology," then it is to the praise and proclamation of this one that we must always and ever remain fixed.

Bibliography

Adeyemo, Tokunboh, ed. *Africa Bible Commentary*. Grand Rapids: Zondervan, 2006.

Allen, Michael, and Scott R. Swain. *Reformed Catholicity: The Promise of Retrieval for Theology and Biblical Interpretation*. Grand Rapids: Baker Academic, 2015.

Amaladoss, Michael. *The Asian Jesus*. Maryknoll, NY: Orbis Books, 2006.

Amalorpavadass, D. S., ed. *Research Seminar on Non-Biblical Scriptures*. Bangalore, India: National Biblical, Catechetical, and Liturgical Centre, 1974.

Anizor, Uche, Rob Price, and Hank Voss. *Evangelical Theology*. London: Bloomsbury T&T Clark, 2021.

Anizor, Uche, and Hank Voss. *Representing Christ: A Vision for the Priesthood of All Believers*. Downers Grove, IL: IVP Academic, 2016.

Ashford, Bruce Riley. *Every Square Inch: An Introduction to Cultural Engagement for Christians*. Bellingham, WA: Lexham, 2015.

Ashwin-Siejkowski, Piotr. *Clement of Alexandria: A Project of Christian Perfection*. New York: T&T Clark, 2008.

Augustine. *City of God*. In *A Select Library of Nicene and Post-Nicene Fathers of the Christian Church*, 1st series, edited by Philip Schaff, vol. 2, *St. Augustine's "City of God" and "Christian Doctrine."* Grand Rapids: Eerdmans, 1956.

Ault, James. *Kwame Bediako: His Life and Legacy*. James Ault Productions, 2020. https://vimeopro.com/jamesault/kwame-bediako-his-life-and-legacy-1/video/281714305.

Barth, Karl. *Church Dogmatics*. Study Edition. Edited by G. W. Bromiley and T. F. Torrance. 31 vols. New York: T&T Clark, 2009.

Bavinck, Herman. "The Kingdom of God, The Highest Good." Translated by Nelson D. Kloosterman. *The Bavinck Review* 2 (2011): 133–70.

———. *Reformed Ethics*. Edited by John Bolt. 2 vols. Grand Rapids: Baker Academic, 2019–21.

Bebbington, D. W. *Evangelicalism in Modern Britain: A History from the 1730s to the 1980s.* Boston: Unwin Hyman, 1989.

Becker, Eve-Marie. *Paul on Humility.* Translated by Wayne Coppins. Waco: Baylor University Press, 2020.

Bediako, Gillian Mary, Benhardt Y. Quarshie, and J. Kwabena Asamoah-Gyadu. "Editorial." In *Seeing New Facets of the Diamond: Christianity as a Universal Faith; Essays in Honour of Kwame Bediako,* edited by Gillian Mary Bediako, Benhardt Y. Quarshie, and J. Kwabena Asamoah-Gyadu, ix–xv. Oxford: Regnum, 2014.

Bediako, Kwame. *Christianity in Africa: The Renewal of a Non-Western Religion.* Maryknoll, NY: Orbis Books, 1995.

———. *Jesus in Africa: The Christian Gospel in African History and Experience.* Rev. ed. Oxford: Regnum, 2020.

———. *Theology and Identity: The Impact of Culture upon Christian Thought in the Second Century and in Modern Africa.* Oxford: Regnum, 1992.

Berkouwer, G. C. *The Church.* Translated by James E. Davison. Grand Rapids: Eerdmans, 1976.

Bevans, Stephen B. *Models of Contextual Theology.* Maryknoll, NY: Orbis Books, 1992.

———. *Models of Contextual Theology.* Rev. ed. Maryknoll, NY: Orbis Books, 2002.

Billings, J. Todd. *Union with Christ: Reframing Theology and Ministry for the Church.* Grand Rapids: Baker Academic, 2011.

———. *The Word of God for the People of God: An Entryway to the Theological Interpretation of Scripture.* Grand Rapids: Eerdmans, 2010.

Blocher, Henri. "Permanent Validity and Contextual Relativity of Doctrinal Statements." In *The Task of Dogmatics: Explorations in Theological Method,* edited by Oliver D. Crisp and Fred Sanders, 107–30. Grand Rapids: Zondervan, 2017.

Blomberg, Craig. "We Contextualize More Than We Realize." In *Local Theology for the Global Church: Principles for an Evangelical Approach to Contextualization,* edited by Matthew Cook, Rob Haskell, Ruth Julian, and Natee Tanchanpongs, 37–55. Pasadena, CA: World Evangelical Alliance Theological Commission, 2010.

Blum, Edward J., and Paul Harvey. *The Color of Christ: The Son of God and the Saga of Race in America.* Chapel Hill: University of North Carolina Press, 2012.

Boas, Franz. *The Mind of Primitive Man.* New York: Macmillan, 1922.

Boff, Leonardo. *Jesus Christ Liberator: A Critical Christology for Our Time.* Translated by Patrick Hughes. Maryknoll, NY: Orbis Books, 1978.

———. *Trinity and Society.* Maryknoll, NY: Orbis Books, 1988.

Bosch, David J. *Transforming Mission: Paradigm Shifts in Theology of Mission.* Maryknoll, NY: Orbis Books, 1991.

Botman, Russel. "The Church Partitioned or the Church Reconciled? South Africa's Theological and Historical Dilemma." In *Race and Reconciliation in South Africa: A*

Multicultural Dialogue in Comparative Perspective, edited by William E. Van Vugt and G. Daan Cloete, 105–19. Lanham, MD: Lexington Books, 2000.

Boyce, William E. "A Doctrine for Diversity: Utilizing Herman Bavinck's Theology for Racial Reconciliation in the Church." *Journal of Markets and Morality* 23, no. 2 (2020): 319–36.

Bujo, Bénézet. *African Theology in Its Social Context*. Translated by John O'Donohue. Maryknoll, NY: Orbis Books, 1992.

Burrows, William R., Mark R. Gornik, and Janice A. McLean, eds. *Understanding World Christianity: The Vision and Work of Andrew F. Walls*. Maryknoll, NY: Orbis Books, 2011.

Burton, Philip. *Language in the "Confessions" of Augustine*. New York: Oxford University Press, 2007.

Buschart, W. David, and Kent D. Eliers. *Theology as Retrieval: Receiving the Past, Renewing the Church*. Downers Grove, IL: IVP Academic, 2015.

Carson, D. A. *Christ and Culture Revisited*. Grand Rapids: Eerdmans, 2008.

———. "Church and Mission: Reflections on Contextualization and the Third Horizon." In *The Church in the Bible and the World: An International Study*, edited by D. A. Carson, 213–57. Grand Rapids: Baker, 1987.

Carter, Craig A. *Rethinking "Christ and Culture": A Post-Christendom Perspective*. Grand Rapids: Brazos, 2006.

Chafer, Lewis Sperry. *Systematic Theology*. Vol. 1. Dallas: Dallas Seminary Press, 1947.

Chan, Simon. "The Church and the Development of Doctrine." *Journal of Pentecostal Theology* 13, no. 1 (2004): 57–77.

———. *Grassroots Asian Theology: Thinking the Faith from the Ground Up*. Downers Grove, IL: IVP Academic, 2014.

———. "Toward an Asian Evangelical Ecclesiology." In *Asian Christian Theology: Evangelical Perspectives*, edited by Timoteo D. Gener and Stephen T. Pardue, 139–56. Carlisle, UK: Langham Global Library, 2019.

Clark, David K. *To Know and Love God: Method for Theology*. Wheaton: Crossway, 2003.

Cook, Matthew. "Contextual but Still Objective?" In *Local Theology for the Global Church: Principles for an Evangelical Approach to Contextualization*, edited by Matthew Cook, Rob Haskell, Ruth Julian, and Natee Tanchanpongs, 75–89. Pasadena, CA: World Evangelical Alliance Theological Commission, 2010.

Cook, Matthew, Rob Haskell, Ruth Julian, and Natee Tanchanpongs, eds. *Local Theology for the Global Church: Principles for an Evangelical Approach to Contextualization*. Pasadena, CA: World Evangelical Alliance Theological Commission, 2010.

Cortez, Marc. "Context and Concept: Contextual Theology and the Nature of Theological Discourse." *Westminster Theological Journal* 67 (2005): 85–102.

———. "Creation and Context: A Theological Framework for Contextual Theology." *Westminster Theological Journal* 67 (2005): 347–62.

Darnell, Regna. "The Anthropological Concept of Culture at the End of the Boasian Century." *Social Analysis* 41, no. 3 (1997): 42–54.

DeBorst, Ruth Padilla. In *Majority World Theology: Christian Doctrine in Global Context*, edited by Gene L. Green, Stephen T. Pardue, and K. K. Yeo, 498–509. Downers Grove, IL: IVP Academic, 2020.

DeCou, Jessica. "Barth and Culture." In *The Oxford Handbook of Karl Barth*, edited by Paul Dafydd Jones and Paul T. Nimmo, 609–21. New York: Oxford University Press, 2019.

de Mesa, José M., and Lode L. Wostyn. *Doing Theology: Basic Realities and Processes*. Manila: Claretian, 1990.

Dulles, Avery. *The Catholicity of the Church*. Oxford: Clarendon, 1985.

Dyrness, William A. *The Earth Is God's: A Theology of American Culture*. Maryknoll, NY: Orbis Books, 1997.

———. *Learning about Theology from the Third World*. Grand Rapids: Zondervan, 1990.

———. *Poetic Theology: God and the Poetics of Everyday Life*. Grand Rapids: Eerdmans, 2011.

———. *Visual Faith: Art, Theology, and Worship in Dialogue*. Grand Rapids: Baker Academic, 2001.

Dyrness, William A., and Oscar García-Johnson. *Theology without Borders: An Introduction to Global Conversations*. Grand Rapids: Baker Academic, 2015.

Erickson, Millard J. *Christian Theology*. 3rd ed. Grand Rapids: Baker Academic, 2013.

Ezigbo, Victor I. *The Art of Contextual Theology: Doing Theology in the Era of World Christianity*. Eugene, OR: Cascade Books, 2021.

———. "Contextual Theology: God in Human Context." In *Evangelical Theological Method: Five Views*, edited by Stanley E. Porter and Steven M. Studebaker, 93–115. Downers Grove, IL: IVP Academic, 2018.

———. *Re-imagining African Christologies: Conversing with the Interpretations and Appropriations of Jesus in Contemporary African Christianity*. Eugene, OR: Pickwick, 2010.

Flemming, Dean. *Contextualization in the New Testament: Patterns for Theology and Mission*. Downers Grove, IL: InterVarsity, 2005.

Flett, John G. *Apostolicity: The Ecumenical Question in World Christian Perspective*. Downers Grove, IL: IVP Academic, 2016.

Flynn, Gabriel, and Paul D. Murray, eds. *Ressourcement: A Movement for Renewal in Twentieth-Century Catholic Theology*. New York: Oxford University Press, 2011.

Fowl, Stephen E. *The Story of Christ in the Ethics of Paul: An Analysis of the Function of the Hymnic Material in the Pauline Corpus*. Sheffield, UK: Sheffield Academic, 1990.

Gaudium et Spes: Pastoral Constitution on the Church in the Modern World. Vatican II. December 7, 1965. Vatican Resource Library, https://www.vatican.va/archive/hist_councils/ii_vatican_council/documents/vat-ii_const_19651207_gaudium-et-spes_en.html.

Geertz, Clifford. *The Interpretation of Cultures*. 3rd ed. New York: Basic Books, 2017.

Gener, Timoteo D. "Christologies in Asia: Trends and Reflections." In *Jesus without Borders: Christology in the Majority World*, edited by Gene L. Green, Stephen T. Pardue, and K. K. Yeo, 59–79. Grand Rapids: Eerdmans, 2014.

———. "Divine Revelation and the Practice of Asian Theology." In *Asian Christian Theology: Evangelical Perspectives*, edited by Timoteo D. Gener and Stephen T. Pardue, 13–37. Carlisle, UK: Langham Global Library, 2019.

———. "Doing Contextual Systematic Theology in Asia: Challenges and Prospects." *Journal of Asian Evangelical Theology* 22, no. 1 (2018): 49–68.

———. "Fatalism." In *Global Dictionary of Theology: A Resource for the Worldwide Church*, edited by William A. Dyrness, Veli-Matti Kärkkäinen, Juan Francisco Martinez, and Simon Chan, 315–17. Downers Grove, IL: IVP Academic, 2008.

Gillespie, Michael Allen. *The Theological Origins of Modernity*. Chicago: University of Chicago Press, 2008.

González, Antonio. *God's Reign and the End of Empires*. Miami: Convivium, 2012.

———. *The Gospel of Faith and Justice*. Maryknoll, NY: Orbis Books, 2005.

———. "The Trinity as Gospel." In *Majority World Theology: Christian Doctrine in Global Context*, edited by Gene L. Green, Stephen T. Pardue, and K. K. Yeo, 48–59. Downers Grove, IL: IVP Academic, 2020.

González, Justo L. *Mañana: Christian Theology from a Hispanic Perspective*. Nashville: Abingdon, 1990.

González, Justo L., and Catherine G. González. "An Historical Survey." In *The Globalization of Theological Education*, edited by Alice Frazer Evans, Robert A. Evans, and David A. Roozen, 13–22. Maryknoll, NY: Orbis Books, 1993.

Gorman, Michael J. *Cruciformity: Paul's Narrative Spirituality of the Cross*. Grand Rapids: Eerdmans, 2001.

Gornik, Mark R. *Word Made Global: Stories of African Christianity in New York City*. Grand Rapids: Eerdmans, 2011.

Green, Gene L., Stephen T. Pardue, and K. K. Yeo, eds. *Majority World Theology: Christian Doctrine in Global Context*. Downers Grove, IL: IVP Academic, 2020.

Greenman, Jeffrey P., and Gene L. Green, eds. *Global Theology in Evangelical Perspective: Exploring the Contextual Nature of Theology and Mission*. Downers Grove, IL: IVP Academic, 2012.

Greggs, Tom. *Dogmatic Ecclesiology: The Priestly Catholicity of the Church*. Vol 1. Grand Rapids: Baker Academic, 2019.

Grudem, Wayne. *Systematic Theology: An Introduction to Biblical Doctrine*. Grand Rapids: Zondervan, 1994.

Gunton, Colin E. *The One, the Three, and the Many: God, Creation, and the Culture of Modernity*. New York: Cambridge University Press, 1993.

———. *The Promise of Trinitarian Theology*. Edinburgh: T&T Clark, 1991.

Gutiérrez, Gustavo. *A Theology of Liberation: History, Politics, and Salvation.* Rev. ed. Maryknoll, NY: Orbis Books, 1988.

Hamilton, Victor P. *The Book of Genesis: Chapters 1–17.* New International Commentary on the Old Testament 1. Grand Rapids: Eerdmans, 1990.

Harrison, Carol. *Beauty and Revelation in the Thought of Saint Augustine.* New York: Oxford University Press, 1992.

Hartman, Tim. *Kwame Bediako: African Theology for a World Christianity.* Carlisle, UK: Langham Global Library, 2021.

———. *Theology after Colonization: Kwame Bediako, Karl Barth, and the Future of Theological Reflection.* Notre Dame, IN: University of Notre Dame Press, 2020.

Hauerwas, Stanley, and William H. Willimon. *Resident Aliens: Life in the Christian Colony.* Nashville: Abingdon, 1989.

Hedlund, Roger E. "Indian Expressions of Indigenous Christianity." *Studies in World Christianity* 10, no. 2 (2004): 185–204.

Henry, Carl F. H. *God, Revelation, and Authority.* Vol. 1. Waco: Word Books, 1976.

Hesselgrave, David J., and Edward Rommen. *Contextualization: Meanings, Methods, and Models.* Grand Rapids: Baker, 1989.

Hiebert, Theodore. "The Tower of Babel and the Origin of the World's Cultures." *Journal of Biblical Literature* 126, no. 1 (2007): 29–58.

Hodge, Charles. *Systematic Theology.* Vol. 1. Grand Rapids: Eerdmans, 1986. First published 1872 by Charles Scribner (New York).

Holmes, Michael W., ed. and trans. *The Apostolic Fathers in English.* 3rd ed. Grand Rapids: Baker Academic, 2006.

Holmes, Stephen R. *The Holy Trinity: Understanding God's Life.* Milton Keynes, UK: Paternoster, 2012.

———. *Listening to the Past: The Place of Tradition in Theology.* Grand Rapids: Baker Academic, 2002.

Howell, Brian M., and Jenell Williams Paris. *Introducing Cultural Anthropology: A Christian Perspective.* 2nd ed. Grand Rapids: Baker Academic, 2011.

Huang, Po Ho. "Revisiting the Methodology of Contextual Theology in the Era of Globalization." In *Wrestling with God in Context: Revisiting the Theology and Vision of Shoki Coe,* edited by M. P. Joseph, Po Ho Huang, and Victor Hsu, 21–33. Minneapolis: Fortress, 2018.

Human Relations and the South African Scene in the Light of Scripture. Cape Town: Dutch Reformed Church, 1976.

Hunt, Robert A. *The Gospel among the Nations: A Documentary History of Inculturation.* American Society of Missiology Series, no. 46. Maryknoll, NY: Orbis Books, 2010.

Hunter, James Davison. *To Change the World: The Irony, Tragedy, and Possibility of Christianity in the Late Modern World.* New York: Oxford University Press, 2010.

Hwang, Jerry. *Contextualization and the Old Testament: Between Asian and Western Perspectives*. Carlisle, UK: Langham Global Library, 2022.

Jefford, Clayton N., ed. *The "Epistle to Diognetus" (with the "Fragment of Quadratus"): Introduction, Text, and Commentary*. New York: Oxford University Press, 2013.

Jenkins, Philip. *The New Faces of Christianity: Believing the Bible in the Global South*. New York: Oxford University Press, 2006.

———. *The Next Christendom: The Coming of Global Christianity*. 3rd ed. New York: Oxford University Press, 2011.

Johnson, Keith E. *Rethinking the Trinity & Religious Pluralism: An Augustinian Assessment*. Downers Grove, IL: IVP Academic, 2011.

Jones, E. Stanley. *The Christ of the Indian Road*. New York: Abingdon, 1925.

Kaiser, Walter C., Jr. "A Principlizing Model." In *Four Views on Moving beyond the Bible to Theology*, edited by Gary T. Meadors, 19–74. Grand Rapids: Zondervan, 2009.

———. *Toward an Exegetical Theology: Biblical Exegesis for Preaching and Teaching*. Grand Rapids: Baker, 1981.

Kärkkäinen, Veli-Matti. *Christology: A Global Introduction*. 2nd ed. Grand Rapids: Baker Academic, 2016.

———. *Trinity and Religious Pluralism: The Doctrine of the Trinity in Christian Theology of Religions*. Aldersot, UK: Ashgate, 2004.

Katembo, Fabrice S. *The Mystery of the Church: Applying Paul's Ecclesiology in Africa*. Carlisle, UK: Langham, 2020.

Keener, Craig. "Why Does Luke Use Tongues as a Sign of the Spirit's Empowerment?" *Journal of Pentecostal Theology* 15, no. 2 (2007): 177–84.

Kilby, Karen. "Trinity and Politics: An Apophatic Approach." In *Advancing Trinitarian Theology: Explorations in Constructive Dogmatics*, edited by Oliver D. Crisp and Fred Sanders, 75–93. Grand Rapids: Zondervan, 2014.

Kirkpatrick, David C. "C. René Padilla and the Origins of Integral Mission in Post-War Latin America." *Journal of Ecclesiastical History* 67, no. 2 (2016): 351–71.

———. *A Gospel for the Poor: Global Social Christianity and the Latin American Evangelical Left*. Philadelphia: University of Pennsylvania Press, 2019.

Koyama, Kosuke. *Waterbuffalo Theology*. Maryknoll, NY: Orbis Books, 1974.

Kraft, Charles H. *Christianity in Culture: A Study in Biblical Theologizing in Cross-Cultural Perspective*. Revised 25th anniversary ed. Maryknoll, NY: Orbis Books, 2005.

Kunhiyop, Samuel Waje. *African Christian Theology*. Grand Rapids: Zondervan, 2012.

Küster, Volker. *The Many Faces of Jesus Christ: Intercultural Christology*. Maryknoll, NY: Orbis Books, 2001.

Kuyper, Abraham. *Calvinism: Six Stone-Lectures*. Amsterdam: Höveker & Wormser, 1899.

———. "Sphere Sovereignty (1880)." In *Abraham Kuyper: A Centennial Reader*, edited by James D. Bratt, 461–90. Grand Rapids: Eerdmans, 1998.

Kwok, Pui-lan. *Postcolonial Imagination and Feminist Theology*. Louisville: Westminster John Knox, 2005.

Kwok, Pui-lan, Cecilia González-Andrieu, and Dwight N. Hopkins, eds. *Teaching Global Theologies: Power and Praxis*. Waco: Baylor University Press, 2015.

LaCugna, Catherine Mowry. *God for Us: The Trinity and Christian Life*. San Francisco: HarperSanFrancisco, 1991.

Larsen, Timothy. "Defining and Locating Evangelicalism." In *The Cambridge Companion to Evangelical Theology*, edited by Timothy Larsen and Daniel J. Treier, 1–14. New York: Cambridge University Press, 2007.

Lartey, Emmanuel Yartekwei Amugi. *Postcolonializing God: New Perspectives on Pastoral and Practical Theology*. London: SCM, 2013.

Lausanne Committee for World Evangelization. *The Willowbank Report on Gospel and Culture*. In *Making Christ Known: Historic Mission Documents from the Lausanne Movement 1974–1989*, edited by John Stott, 73–113. Carlisle, UK: Paternoster, 1996.

Lechner, Frank J., and John Boli. "General Introduction." In *The Globalization Reader*, edited by Frank J. Lechner and John Boli, 1–6. 6th ed. Hoboken, NJ: Wiley-Blackwell, 2019.

Legaspi, Michael C. *The Death of Scripture and the Rise of Biblical Studies*. New York: Oxford University Press, 2010.

Legrand, Lucien. *The Bible on Culture: Belonging or Dissenting*. Maryknoll, NY: Orbis Books, 2000.

Letham, Robert. "Catholicity Global and Historical: Constantinople, Westminster, and the Church in the Twenty-First Century." *Westminster Theological Journal* 72, no. 1 (2010): 43–57.

Lewis, C. S. "Introduction." In Athanasius, *On the Incarnation*, translated by a religious of C. S. M. V., 3–10. Crestwood, NY: St. Vladimir's Seminary Press, 1977.

Lingenfelter, Sherwood G., and Marvin K. Mayers. *Ministering Cross-Culturally: An Incarnational Model for Personal Relationships*. 2nd ed. Grand Rapids: Baker Academic, 2003.

Long, D. Stephen. *Theology and Culture: A Guide to the Discussion*. Cambridge: James Clarke, 2010.

Longman, Timothy. *Christianity and Genocide in Rwanda*. New York: Cambridge University Press, 2009.

Lossky, Vladimir. *The Mystical Theology of the Eastern Church*. Translated by members of the Fellowship of St. Alban and St. Sergius. Crestwood, NY: St. Vladimir's Seminary Press, 1976.

Lowery, Stephanie A. *Identity and Ecclesiology: Their Relationship among Select African Theologians*. Eugene, OR: Pickwick, 2017.

Luka, Reuben Turbi. *Jesus Christ as Ancestor: A Theological Study of Major African Ancestor Christologies in Conversation with the Patristic Christologies of Tertullian and Athanasius.* Carlisle, UK: Langham Monographs, 2019.

Lumen Gentium: Dogmatic Constitution on the Church. Vatican II. November 21, 1964. Vatican Resource Library, https://www.vatican.va/archive/hist_councils/ii_vatican _council/documents/vat-ii_const_19641121_lumen-gentium_en.html.

Luz, Ulrich. *Matthew 1–7: A Commentary.* Translated by James E. Crouch. Rev. ed. Minneapolis: Fortress, 2007.

MacArthur, John. "'Contextualization' and the Corruption of the Church." *Grace to You* (blog). Grace to You, September 22, 2011. https://www.gty.org/library/blog /B110922/.

Major, Tristan. *Undoing Babel: The Tower of Babel in Anglo-Saxon Literature.* Toronto: University of Toronto Press, 2018.

Martin, Ralph P. *A Hymn of Christ: Philippians 2:5–11 in Recent Interpretation & in the Setting of Early Christian Worship.* Downers Grove, IL: InterVarsity, 1997.

Martinez-Olivieri, Jules A. *A Visible Witness: Christology, Liberation, and Participation.* Emerging Scholars. Minneapolis: Fortress, 2016.

Mbiti, John S. *New Testament Eschatology in an African Background: A Study of the Encounter between New Testament Theology and African Traditional Concepts.* New York: Oxford University Press, 1971.

———. "Theological Impotence and the Universality of the Church." In *Third World Theologies,* edited by Gerald R. Anderson and Thomas F. Stransky, Mission Trends 3, 6–18. Grand Rapids: Eerdmans, 1976.

McDermott, Gerald R., and Harold A. Netland. *A Trinitarian Theology of Religions: An Evangelical Proposal.* New York: Oxford University Press, 2014.

Medina, Néstor. *Christianity, Empire and the Spirit: (Re)Configuring Faith and the Cultural.* Boston: Brill, 2018.

Míguez Bonino, José. *Doing Theology in a Revolutionary Situation.* Philadelphia: Fortress, 1975.

Miller, Donald E., and Tetsunao Yamamori. *Global Pentecostalism: The New Face of Christian Social Engagement.* Berkeley: University of California Press, 2007.

Minear, Paul S. *Images of the Church in the New Testament.* Louisville: Westminster John Knox, 2004.

Moltmann, Jürgen. *The Trinity and the Kingdom: The Doctrine of God.* Translated by Margaret Kohl. Minneapolis: Fortress, 1993.

Monaghan, John, and Peter Just. *Social and Cultural Anthropology: A Very Short Introduction.* New York: Oxford University Press, 2000.

Moreau, A. Scott. *Contextualization in World Missions: Mapping and Assessing Evangelical Models.* Grand Rapids: Kregel, 2012.

———. "Syncretism." In *Evangelical Dictionary of Theology*, edited by Daniel J. Treier and Walter A. Elwell, 850–52. 3rd ed. Grand Rapids: Baker Academic, 2017.

Mouw, Richard J. *Abraham Kuyper: A Short and Personal Introduction*. Grand Rapids: Eerdmans, 2011.

Newbigin, Lesslie. *The Gospel in a Pluralist Society*. Grand Rapids: Eerdmans, 1989.

Nicholls, Bruce J. *Contextualization: A Theology of Gospel and Culture*. Downers Grove, IL: InterVarsity, 1979.

Niebuhr, H. Richard. *Christ and Culture*. New York: Harper & Row, 1951.

Noll, Mark A. *From Every Tribe and Nation: A Historian's Discovery of the Global Christian Story*. Grand Rapids: Baker Academic, 2014.

———. *The New Shape of World Christianity: How American Experience Reflects Global Faith*. Downers Grove, IL: IVP Academic, 2009.

Nyamiti, Charles. *Christ as Our Ancestor: Christology from an African Perspective*. Gweru, Zimbabwe: Mambo, 1984.

Orobator, A. E. *The Church as Family: African Ecclesiology in Its Social Context*. Nairobi, Kenya: Paulines Publications Africa, 2000.

———. *Theology Brewed in an African Pot: An Introduction to Christian Doctrine from an African Perspective*. Nairobi, Kenya: Paulines Publications Africa, 2008.

Ortlund, Gavin. *Theological Retrieval for Evangelicals: Why We Need Our Past to Have a Future*. Wheaton: Crossway, 2019.

Osborne, Grant R. *The Hermeneutical Spiral: A Comprehensive Introduction to Biblical Interpretation*. 2nd ed. Downers Grove, IL: IVP Academic, 2006.

Ott, Craig, and Harold A. Netland, eds. *Globalizing Theology: Belief and Practice in an Era of World Christianity*. Grand Rapids: Baker Academic, 2006.

Ottuh, John. "The Concept of Κένωσις in Philippians 2:6–7 and Its Contextual Application in Africa." *Verbum et Ecclesia* 41, no. 1 (2020): 1–13.

Pachuau, Lalsangkima. *God at Work in the World: Theology and Mission in the Global Church*. Grand Rapids: Baker Academic, 2022.

Padilla, C. René. "Liberation Theology: An Appraisal." In *Freedom and Discipleship: Liberation Theology in an Anabaptist Perspective*, edited by Daniel S. Schipani, 34–50. Maryknoll, NY: Orbis Books, 1989.

———. *Mission between the Times: Essays on the Kingdom*. Rev. ed. Carlisle, UK: Langham Monographs, 2010.

Padilla, C. René, and Tetsunao Yamamori, eds. *The Local Church, Agent of Transformation: An Ecclesiology for Integral Mission*. Translated by Brian Cordingly. Buenos Aires, Argentina: Kairós, 2004.

Panikkar, Raimon. *The Unknown Christ of Hinduism: Towards an Ecumenical Christophany*. Rev. ed. Maryknoll, NY: Orbis Books, 1981.

Pardue, Stephen T. "Athens and Jerusalem Once More: What the Turn to Virtue Means for Theological Exegesis." *Journal of Theological Interpretation* 4, no. 2 (2010): 295–308.

———"What Hath Wheaton to Do with Nairobi? Toward Catholic and Evangelical Theology." *Journal of the Evangelical Theological Society* 58, no. 4 (2015): 757–70.

Parratt, John, ed. *An Introduction to Third World Theologies*. New York: Cambridge University Press, 2004.

Pelikan, Jaroslav. *Jesus through the Centuries: His Place in the History of Culture*. New Haven: Yale University Press, 1985.

Pennington, J. Paul. *Christian Barriers to Jesus: Conversations and Questions from the Indian Context*. Rev ed. Littleton, CO: William Carey, 2022.

Pennington, Jonathan T. *The Sermon on the Mount and Human Flourishing: A Theological Commentary*. Grand Rapids: Baker Academic, 2017.

Peterson, Erik. "Monotheism as a Political Problem: A Contribution to the History of Political Theology in the Roman Empire." In *Theological Tractates*, edited and translated by Michael J. Hollerich, 68–105. Stanford, CA: Stanford University Press, 2011.

Polanyi, Michael. *Personal Knowledge: Towards a Post-Critical Philosophy*. Chicago: University of Chicago Press, 1962.

Poobalan, Ivor. "Christology in Asia: Rooted and Responsive." In *Asian Christian Theology: Evangelical Perspectives*, edited by Timoteo D. Gener and Stephen T. Pardue, 83–100. Carlisle, UK: Langham Global Library, 2019.

Prince, Andrew J. *Contextualization of the Gospel: Towards an Evangelical Approach in the Light of Scripture and the Church Fathers*. Eugene, OR: Wipf & Stock, 2017.

Read, Leonard E. "I, Pencil." *The Freeman*, December 1958.

Reed, Rodney L., and David K. Ngaruiya, eds. *Who Do You Say That I Am?: Christology in Africa*. Carlisle, UK: Langham Global Library, 2021.

Re Manning, Russell, ed. *The Cambridge Companion to Paul Tillich*. Cambridge: Cambridge University Press, 2009.

Rieger, Joerg. *Globalization and Theology*. Nashville: Abingdon, 2010.

Ringma, Charles R., Karen Hollenbeck-Wuest, and Athena O. Gorospe, eds. *God at the Borders: Globalization, Migration and Diaspora*. Mandaluyong, Philippines: OMF Literature, 2015.

Ro, Bong Rin, and Ruth Eshenaur, eds. *The Bible and Theology in Asian Contexts: An Evangelical Perspective on Asian Theology*. Taiwan: Asia Theological Association, 1984.

Rodríguez, Rubén Rosario. *Dogmatics after Babel: Beyond the Theologies of Word and Culture*. Louisville: Westminster John Knox, 2018.

Romero, Robert Chao. *Brown Church: Five Centuries of Latina/o Social Justice, Theology, and Identity*. Downers Grove, IL: IVP Academic, 2020.

Rowland, Christopher, ed. *The Cambridge Companion to Liberation Theology*. New York: Cambridge University Press, 1999.

———. "Liberation Theology." In *The Oxford Handbook of Systematic Theology*, edited by John Webster, Kathryn Tanner, and Iain Torrance, 634–52. New York: Oxford University Press, 2007.

Rowland, Tracey. *Culture and the Thomist Tradition: After Vatican II*. New York: Routledge, 2003.

Saldanha, Julian. "Vatican II and the Principle of Inculturation." In *Vatican II: A Gift and a Task*, edited by Jacob Kavunkal, Errol D'Lima, and Evelyn Monteiro, 195–211. Mumbai: Bombay Saint Paul Society, 2006.

Salinas, Daniel. *Latin American Evangelical Theology in the 1970's: The Golden Decade*. Boston: Brill, 2009.

Salinas, J. Daniel. *Taking Up the Mantle: Latin American Evangelical Theology in the 20th Century*. Carlisle, UK: Langham Global Library, 2017.

Sanders, Fred. *The Triune God*. Grand Rapids: Zondervan, 2016.

Sanneh, Lamin. *Translating the Message: The Missionary Impact on Culture*. 2nd ed. Maryknoll, NY: Orbis Books, 2009.

———. *Whose Religion Is Christianity? The Gospel beyond the West*. Grand Rapids: Eerdmans, 2003.

Schleiermacher, Friedrich. *Brief Outline of Theology as a Field of Study*, 3rd ed., *Revised Translation of the 1811 and 1830 Editions*. Translated by Terrence N. Tice. Louisville: Westminster John Knox, 2011.

Schreiter, Robert J. *Constructing Local Theologies*. Maryknoll, NY: Orbis Books, 1985.

———. Foreword to *Models of Contextual Theology*, by Stephen B. Bevans, ix–xi. Maryknoll, NY: Orbis Books, 1992.

———. *The New Catholicity: Theology between the Global and the Local*. Maryknoll, NY: Orbis Books, 1997.

Selvanayagam, Israel. "Waters of Life and Indian Cups: Protestant Attempts at Theologizing in India." In *Christian Theology in Asia*, edited by Sebastian C. H. Kim, 41–67. New York: Cambridge University Press, 2008.

Siliezar, Carlos Sosa. "Ecclesiology in Latin America: A Biblical Perspective." In *Majority World Theology: Christian Doctrine in Global Context*, edited by Gene L. Green, Stephen T. Pardue, and K. K. Yeo, 537–50. Downers Grove, IL: IVP Academic, 2020.

Silva, Moisés. *God, Language, and Scripture: Reading the Bible in the Light of General Linguistics*. Grand Rapids: Zondervan, 1990.

Smith, James K. A. *How (Not) to Be Secular: Reading Charles Taylor*. Grand Rapids: Eerdmans, 2014.

Sobrino, Jon. *Spirituality of Liberation: Toward Political Holiness*. Translated by Robert R. Barr. Maryknoll, NY: Orbis Books, 1988.

Song, Choan-Seng. "New China and Salvation History: A Methodological Enquiry." *Southeast Asia Journal of Theology* 15, no. 2 (1974): 52–67.

———. *Third-Eye Theology: Theology in Formation in Asian Settings*. Maryknoll, NY: Orbis Books, 1979.

Stackhouse, John G., Jr. *Making the Best of It: Following Christ in the Real World*. New York: Oxford University Press, 2008.

Steigmann-Gall, Richard. *The Holy Reich: Nazi Conceptions of Christianity, 1919–1945.* New York: Cambridge University Press, 2003.

Stinton, Diane B. *Jesus of Africa: Voices of Contemporary African Christology.* Maryknoll, NY: Orbis Books, 2004.

Stott, John. *Evangelical Truth: A Personal Plea for Unity, Integrity and Faithfulness.* Rev. ed. Carlisle, UK: Langham Global Library, 2013.

Sugirtharajah, R. S. "Postcolonial Biblical Interpretation." In *The Modern Theologians: An Introduction to Christian Theology Since 1918,* edited by David F. Ford with Rachel Muers, 535–52. 3rd ed. Malden, MA: Blackwell, 2005.

Sunquist, Scott W. *The Unexpected Christian Century: The Reversal and Transformation of Global Christianity, 1900–2000.* Grand Rapids: Baker Academic, 2015.

Tamez, Elsa. *The Amnesty of Grace: Justification by Faith from a Latin American Perspective.* Translated by Sharon H. Ringe. Nashville: Abingdon, 1993.

Tan, Jonathan Y., and Anh Q. Tran, SJ, eds. *World Christianity: Perspectives and Insights; Essays in Honor of Peter C. Phan.* Maryknoll, NY: Orbis Books, 2016.

Tanner, Kathryn. *Christ the Key.* New York: Cambridge University Press, 2010.

———. *Theories of Culture: A New Agenda for Theology.* Minneapolis: Fortress, 1997.

Taylor, Charles. *A Secular Age.* Cambridge, MA: Harvard University Press, 2007.

Taylor, Joan E. *What Did Jesus Look Like?* New York: Bloomsbury, 2018.

Tennent, Timothy C. *Theology in the Context of World Christianity: How the Global Church Is Influencing the Way We Think About and Discuss Theology.* Grand Rapids: Zondervan, 2007.

Theological Education Fund. *Ministry in Context: The Third Mandate Programme of the Theological Education Fund (1970–77).* London: Theological Education Fund, 1972.

Third Lausanne Congress. *The Cape Town Commitment: A Confession of Faith and a Call to Action.* Cape Town: Lausanne Movement, 2011. https://lausanne.org/content/ctc/ctcommitment.

Tillich, Paul. *Systematic Theology.* Vol. 1. Chicago: University of Chicago Press, 1973.

———. *Theology of Culture.* Edited by Robert C. Kimball. New York: Oxford University Press, 1959.

Tombs, David. *Latin American Liberation Theology.* Boston: Brill, 2002.

Torrance, T. F. *Christian Theology and Scientific Culture.* New York: Oxford University Press, 1981.

———. *Theology in Reconstruction.* Grand Rapids: Eerdmans, 1966.

Treier, Daniel J. *Introducing Theological Interpretation of Scripture: Recovering a Christian Practice.* Grand Rapids: Baker Academic, 2008.

van den Toren, Benno. "Kwame Bediako's Christology in Its African Evangelical Context." *Exchange* 26, no. 3 (1997): 218–32.

van der Kooi, Cornelis. "The Concept of Culture in Abraham Kuyper, Herman Bavinck, and Karl Barth." In *Crossroad Discourses between Christianity and Culture*, edited by Jerald D. Gort, Henry Jansen, and Wessel Stoker, 37–52. New York: Rodopi, 2010.

Vanhoozer, Kevin J. *Biblical Authority after Babel: Retrieving the Solas in the Spirit of Mere Protestant Christianity*. Grand Rapids: Brazos, 2016.

———. "Christology in the West: Conversations in Europe and North America." In *Jesus without Borders: Christology in the Majority World*, edited by Gene L. Green, Stephen T. Pardue, and K. K. Yeo, 11–36. Grand Rapids: Eerdmans, 2014.

———. *The Drama of Doctrine: A Canonical-Linguistic Approach to Christian Theology*. Louisville: Westminster John Knox, 2005.

———. *Is There a Meaning in This Text? The Bible, the Reader, and the Morality of Literary Knowledge*. Grand Rapids: Zondervan, 1998.

———. "On the Very Idea of a Theological System: An Essay in Aid of Triangulating Scripture, Church and World." In *Always Reforming: Explorations in Systematic Theology*, edited by A. T. B. McGowan, 125–82. Downers Grove, IL: IVP Academic, 2007.

———. "'One Rule to Rule Them All?' Theological Method in the Era of World Christianity." In *Globalizing Theology: Belief and Practice in an Era of World Christianity*, edited by Craig Ott and Harold A. Netland, 85–126. Grand Rapids: Baker Academic, 2006.

———, ed. *The Trinity in a Pluralistic Age: Theological Essays on Culture and Religion*. Grand Rapids: Eerdmans, 1996.

Vanhoozer, Kevin J., and Daniel J. Treier. *Theology and the Mirror of Scripture: A Mere Evangelical Account*. Downers Grove, IL: IVP Academic, 2015.

Volf, Miroslav. *After Our Likeness: The Church as the Image of the Trinity*. Grand Rapids: Eerdmans, 1998.

———. "'The Trinity Is Our Social Program': The Doctrine of the Trinity and the Shape of Social Engagement." *Modern Theology* 14, no. 3 (1998): 403–23.

von Allmen, Daniel. "The Birth of Theology." *International Review of Mission* 64, no. 253 (1975): 37–55.

von Harnack, Adolf. *Outlines of the History of Dogma*. Translated by Edwin Knox Mitchell. New York: Funk and Wagnalls, 1893.

Walls, Andrew F. *The Cross-Cultural Process in Christian History: Studies in the Transmission and Appropriation of Faith*. Maryknoll, NY: Orbis Books, 2002.

———. "The Ephesian Moment: At a Crossroads in Christian History." In *The Cross-Cultural Process in Christian History: Studies in the Transmission and Appropriation of Faith*, 72–81. Maryknoll, NY: Orbis Books, 2002.

———. "The Gospel as Prisoner and Liberator of Culture." In *The Missionary Movement in Christian History: Studies in the Transmission of Faith*, 3–15. Maryknoll, NY: Orbis Books, 1996.

———. *The Missionary Movement in Christian History: Studies in the Transmission of Faith.* Maryknoll, NY: Orbis Books, 1996.

———. "The Rise of Global Theologies." In *Global Theology in Evangelical Perspective: Exploring the Contextual Nature of Theology and Mission,* edited by Jeffrey P. Greenman and Gene L. Green, 19–34. Downers Grove, IL: IVP Academic, 2012.

Walton, John H. *Ancient Near Eastern Thought and the Old Testament: Introducing the Conceptual World of the Hebrew Bible.* 2nd ed. Grand Rapids: Baker Academic, 2018.

Webster, John. "Christology, Imitability and Ethics." *Scottish Journal of Theology* 39, no. 3 (1986): 309–26.

———. *The Culture of Theology.* Edited by Ivor J. Davidson and Alden C. McCray. Grand Rapids: Baker Academic, 2019.

———. *Holiness.* Grand Rapids: Eerdmans, 2003.

———. "Theological Theology." In *Confessing God: Essays in Christian Dogmatics II,* 11–31. New York: T&T Clark, 2005.

———. "Theologies of Retrieval." In *The Oxford Handbook of Systematic Theology,* edited by John Webster, Kathryn Tanner, and Iain Torrance, 583–99. New York: Oxford University Press, 2009.

Wilken, Robert Louis. *The Spirit of Early Christian Thought: Seeking the Face of God.* New Haven: Yale University Press, 2003.

Williams, D. H. *Retrieving the Tradition and Renewing Evangelicalism: A Primer for Suspicious Protestants.* Grand Rapids: Eerdmans, 1999.

Winter, Bruce W. "In Public and in Private: Early Christians and Religious Pluralism." In *One God, One Lord: Christianity in a World of Religious Pluralism,* edited by Andrew D. Clarke and Bruce W. Winter, 125–48. Grand Rapids: Baker, 1992.

Wintle, Brian C., ed. *South Asia Bible Commentary: A One-Volume Commentary on the Whole Bible.* Grand Rapids: Zondervan, 2015.

Wright, Christopher J. H. *The Mission of God: Unlocking the Bible's Grand Narrative.* Downers Grove, IL: IVP Academic, 2006.

Wrogemann, Henning. *Intercultural Theology.* Translated by Karl E. Böhmer. Vol. 1, *Intercultural Hermeneutics.* Downers Grove, IL: IVP Academic, 2016.

Yeh, Allen. *Polycentric Missiology: Twenty-First Century Mission from Everyone to Everywhere.* Downers Grove, IL: IVP Academic, 2016.

Yeh, Allen, and Tite Tiénou, eds. *Majority World Theologies: Theologizing from Africa, Asia, Latin America, and the Ends of the Earth.* Littleton, CO: William Carey, 2018.

Yong, Amos. *Beyond the Impasse: Toward a Pneumatological Theology of Religions.* Grand Rapids: Baker Academic, 2003.

———. *The Future of Evangelical Theology: Soundings from the Asian American Diaspora.* Downers Grove, IL: IVP Academic, 2014.

———. *Hospitality and the Other: Pentecost, Christian Practices, and the Neighbor.* Maryknoll, NY: Orbis Books, 2008.

———. "Preface to the 2018 Reprint Edition." In *Discerning the Spirit(s): A Pentecostal-Charismatic Contribution to Christian Theology of Religions*, 1–4. Eugene, OR: Wipf & Stock, 2018. First published 2000 by Sheffield Academic.

———. *Renewing Christian Theology: Systematics for a Global Christianity*. Waco: Baylor University Press, 2014.

Yu, Carver T. "The Bible and Culture in the Shaping of Asian Theology." *Transformation* 15, no. 3 (July 1998): 16–20.

———. "Culture from an Evangelical Perspective." *Transformation* 17, no. 3 (2000): 82–85.

———. "Theology in a Context of Radical Cultural Shift: A Chinese Reflection." In *Asian Christian Theology: Evangelical Perspectives*, edited by Timoteo D. Gener and Stephen T. Pardue, 297–314. Carlisle, UK: Langham Global Library, 2019.

Yung, Hwa. *Mangoes or Bananas? The Quest for an Authentic Asian Christian Theology*. 2nd ed. Maryknoll, NY: Orbis Books, 2014.

Index